The Story of the Shadows

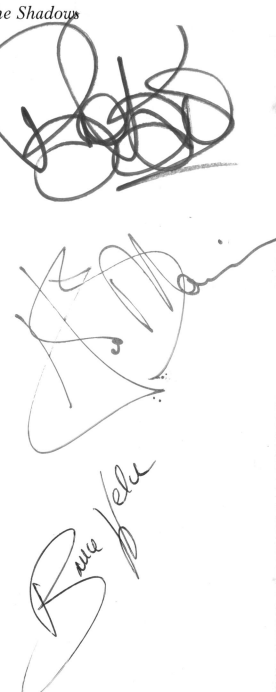

 The **SHADOWS**

The Story of the SHADOWS

An Autobiography with Mike Read

ELM TREE BOOKS
London

First published in Great Britain 1983
by Elm Tree Books/Hamish Hamilton Ltd
Garden House 57-59 Long Acre London WC2E 9JZ

Copyright © 1983 by Mike Read, Hank Marvin, Bruce
Welch, Brian Bennett

British Library Cataloguing in Publication Data

The Story of the Shadows.
   1. Shadows—History
   I. Read, Mike
   784.5'0092'2   ML421.S/
   ISBN 0-241-10861-6
   ISBN 0-241-10887-X Pbk

Filmset by Pioneer
Printed and bound in Great Britain by
R. J. Acford, Chichester, West Sussex

Contents

Foreword

When you're young, everything seems to be exciting, and my memories of bygone days are of better summers, longer days, with lots to do in them. The fact is of course that the summers weren't any better really; certainly the days were no longer — and I most definitely have more to do in them now I'm in my forties!

But some memories of the past remain true to what they were. Those, for instance, of the Shadows and myself starting out on what turned out to be historic, as far as the British pop/rock scene was concerned.

Tim Rice once said to me that there was no-one before us in Europe — lead singer, two guitars, bass and drums — and, looking back, it would seem to be true. And now, when I'm touring with my new band, Thunder, I'm aware that my name will forever be linked with the Shadows. Wherever I go in the world, I'm asked, 'How are the Shads?' or 'Where are the Shads?', and I must admit that I feel proud to have had something to do with one of the greatest bands ever.

My memories are intact — the Bedford, for instance, that carried us from town to town, the race for the cheapest digs, the raw excitement of going on stage and not really understanding why, night after night, kids screamed and shouted, 'More!' If it hadn't lasted, it would have been worth it, but it did last, and we're still doing the rounds and loving it.

I shall always be grateful to Hank, Bruce and Brian — as well as to Jet, Tony, Licorice and John of course — for creating sounds that cushioned me into my current career.

There's no band like the Shadows. Long may they reign!

A Note from Mike Read

I'd like to thank a lot of people who have helped me put this book together: Roger Houghton, then of Elm Tree Books, for his belief in the book, and Caroline Taggart who got lumbered with me when Roger couldn't take any more; Brian Goode for his constant help, for running up enormous telephone bills trying to get everyone together, for bullying and trying to keep us off the tennis court; Cliff for taking time off between sets to write the Foreword; Pete Townshend, Shakin' Stevens, Tim Rice, Eric Clapton, Steve Gray, Bert Weedon, Roger Taylor and Brian May for acknowledging their roots with such affection and pride in the tributes at the end of the book — and the hundreds of others whom we simply couldn't fit in. Thanks also to Carole Marvin, Lynne Welch and Margaret Bennett for occasional five star board and lodging; to Amanda Oke, Julie Allen and Mandy Trice for deciphering my appalling scrawl and for not getting too shirty with me whilst tackling the bulk of the typing; John Friesen who is now running the worldwide Cliff and the Shadows mail order service from 56 Stanwell Road, Ashford.

I'd also like to acknowledge the thousands of guitarists and drummers who were influenced by the Shadows but never actually made it past the local church hall, and those who didn't make it as far as playing the guitar but, like me, lived out their fantasies by drawing Hank's Fender Stratocaster on any scrap of paper they could lay their hands on.

And finally, thanks most of all to the Shadows and Drifters past and present, from all the fans who've followed them for the last twenty-five years.

Acknowledgements

The authors and publishers would like to thank everyone who gave permission for their photographs to be used in this book, particularly Thorn EMI Elstree Studios for stills from *The Young Ones, Summer Holiday, Wonderful Life* and *Rhythm and Greens*. Other photographs are by Rick Hardy, then known as Rick Richards (pp. 35, 37, 47, 51, 61 and 212 — photo of Ian Samwell); Rex Features Ltd (pp. 147 bottom picture, 165, 201, 205, 213 — photos by Dezo Hoffmann — and p. 227 bottom picture — photo by Richard Young; ABC TV (p. 81 bottom picture); Monty Fresco (p. 129 bottom picture); PIC Photos Ltd (p. 72 top picture); Capital Radio (p. 227 top picture — photo by David Clancy); Hanne Jordan (p. 212 — photo of Jack Good and John Foster); Mark Bourdillon (p. 229 bottom picture); John Woodward (p. 225 — photo of Alan Jones); Margaret Wells (pp. 221, 225 — photo of Cliff Hall); Steve Rapport (p. 233). The performance photos in the colour section are by Gerard Métrot and the photo of Paul McCartney by Linda McCartney.

Thanks also to Pete Frame for the family tree — his two books of rock family trees are published by Omnibus Press; to Guinness Superlatives Ltd and Grrr Books for the statistics quoted at the end of the book; and to *New Musical Express* and *Melody Maker* for permission to use material from these magazines.

Permission to use *Teenage Idol* by Jack Lewis from Belwin-Mills Music Ltd, 250 Purley Way, Croydon, Surrey. © 1962 Mills Music Limited for the World excluding USA and Canada. Canadian rights courtesy of Mrs Patricia Fern Lewis and the estate of Jack Lewis.

Every effort has been made to trace the copyright holders of photographs used in this book. Should any omission have been made, we apologise and will be pleased to make appropriate acknowledgement in any future editions.

1 / Hank's Story

(1941 — Spring 1958)

From the end of 1941, I'm sure our neighbours must have thought that 138 Stanhope Street in Newcastle was haunted — it certainly sounded it. Every evening the air was full of the most unearthly screams and wails.

There was only one solution guaranteed temporarily to silence the wailing banshee of Stanhope Street — stick a bar of soap in his mouth!

I hated baths basically, and every time the little pink lump, unaware that he was Brian Robson Rankin, was planted in the tub, it was squealing and squeaking time. But I *was* cute and lovable! And contrary to popular belief I didn't wear black horn-rimmed glasses at fifteen months!

As soon as I could stagger and lurch around a bit I began exploring the big wide wonderful world that my Mum and Dad called 'the flat' — heaven knows why, there were certain bits of it that were positively lumpy, like that bit of lino where I'd wedged a couple of marbles. There were two bedrooms, one which I wasn't really allowed in, and the other that I was supposed to keep tidy and which was mine all mine for the first exciting three years and eleven months of my life. Finally there was the scullery (which is basically a good old nitty gritty northern word for kitchen).

The scullery was pretty exciting to me, there always seemed to be things going on there. I was never quite sure what things, but I think when you're that age, there's something about a scullery that draws you to it like a magnet. Maybe it was the smell of food and the presence of my mum — anyway it was a lot busier than the sitting room, where you had to sit down and behave. There was the wireless in the sitting room, though — that was always interesting, although at that age I didn't really understand the odd sounds that came out of it. Like most little kids with old radios I think the most fascinating aspect of it was when you twiddled the dial and got whooshing and whistling sounds; I actually thought for years that an orchestra was something in the radio. You see, I was an intellectual from an early age! I also have a certain empathy for various articles of clothing — shirts, pants, socks and the like — having spent a substantial part of my life with them during the first half of the 40s, not just on my wiry Geordie frame but as friends and close comrades. I spent a lot of time getting acquainted with pullovers that smelt of mothballs, nests of ties and the odd collar stud. It was basically Hitler's fault — I blame him. Every time there was an air raid my mum would bung me in a drawer with the clothes! I think I'd rather have taken my chance avoiding doodlebugs than get a face full of socks every time the Germans fancied a bash at Newcastle. At least they thought I was worth hanging on to for a while, to see how I turned out! I must have been wonderful — Joseph and Margaret decided to have another baby Rankin. The day he arrived — goodness knows how — everyone was in my parents' bedroom, and I think my mother must have been overcome with the emotion of the spectacle — she was lying down on the bed. The midwife arrived, Auntie Doris who lived in the flat above at 140 came down and there was general excitement in the air. Now if something was going on, *I* wasn't going to be left out. After all he was going to be *my* brother and I ought to get a good look at him to decide whether he'd fit in with my life style! I only realised I had no part to play in his arrival when I was firmly ushered outside. Amazing isn't it, your own brother turns up for the first time and you're not even allowed to hang around and say, 'Hello', 'Good to have you along' or 'Listen, mate, *my* bed's the one by the window, see, I was here first.' Feeling it was a little unjust I feigned a twisted ankle so they'd have to let me stay, but as I had never genuinely twisted one before, my Laurence Olivier bit was rumbled and I was turfed out. Of course as soon as I'd gone out, Joe arrived — all ten and a half pounds of him. Pretty big eh?

My world gradually grew larger as I explored the back lanes near the flat, which seemed to teem with kids of a similar sort of age finding their feet in life and weighing up their potential friends, enemies or unknown quantities from the next street. And of course the law of the jungle prevailed — you steered clear of the big kids, unless you were fortunate enough to have one as an ally; you lorded it over the weeds, and you respected the guys who could dribble a ball like Newcastle United's Jackie Milburn. Jackie was one of the major local heroes, having joined the Magpies in 1946 and immediately helped them to an explosive Guy Fawkes night 13-0 thrashing of Newport County, which is talked about and exaggerated even to this day, and which still stands as the club's record victory.

In the back alleys, a far cry and many schoolboy dreams away from St James Park, the rule usually was 'if it's your ball — *you* can be Jackie Milburn!' You always had to *be* somebody and it was best to get in quick and 'bags' the most famous players, otherwise you got lumbered with being someone not quite so well-known. This of course affected your game tremendously. If you got to be Stanley Matthews or Tom Finney you immediately assumed enough talent and skill to be able to hit a milk bottle with a tennis ball at twenty paces. Cricket was a really popular game in our alley, where we had the wicket painted on a dustbin, which we thought was a cut above the other streets who just had the usual old three vertical lines chalked on a wall. At the ages of six, seven and eight we obviously weren't as well-acquainted with the rules of the game as we thought, and most matches ended in arguments about what you were or weren't allowed to do. It was always best to try and avoid any head-on clashes with the lad who owned the piece of wood that most resembled a bat — if *he* went home we were all stumped!

One aspect of our England v Australia test matches in the yard that we were *all* agreed on was the scoring. If you hit the ball over a roof it was a six, if it hit a house you scored four and if it smashed a window you scarpered! A couple of guys who used to play with me a lot were Harold Dodds and Walter Sales. Now even though Walter was my mate, I could have bashed him sometimes as he was always spotlessly clean, and was always held up as a (literally) shining example to me. I often wondered if the *Beano* based Dennis the Menace's arch-rival Walter the goody-goody on my pal Sales! He could even stay clean after being involved in a scrap, and there were plenty of those! Violent fights between our back lane, which had a big youthful population, and an alliance of the other neighbouring back lanes was a major feature in my life for a while, until I realised that I had a strange yearning to go through life intact, not with bits missing or half an ear chewed off.

It's peculiar how small boys often show no mercy and invariably have no fear, as we'd fight with stones, half-bricks, broom-handles or whatever came to hand, until the fracas was broken up by somebody's dad tearing out and scattering both sides to the four winds. I don't think we were naturally violent, it just seemed like fun, and because we'd seen other local gangs having a go at each other we assumed that that's how life was meant to be some of the time — I ended up in Newcastle Infirmary at eight years old having had half a brick bashed on my head. My days fighting for our gang came to an end one day when I rushed out to join my mates who were in the midst of a pitched battle with some local nasties. It was quite bizarre, as there were so many potatoes and vegetables being thrown that at first glance you would have thought it was two rival gangs of greengrocers having a go at each other! Eager to get involved I bent down to pick up what I thought was a piece of old cabbage. Wrong! As the blokes around me dived for cover and I nearly threw up on the spot, I realised what I'd done. It took days to get rid of the smell of that green dog's mess from my hand!

From the age of five I'd been attending Todd's Nook School, but when Snow Street School re-opened sometime after the war, I was moved there. There, when I was nine years old, I fell in love with Margaret McConnell. I envisaged us walking down life's rich path together with me carrying her satchel and pushing her on the swings till we were old and grey, but it only lasted until she saw Billy Darling.

Fancy being given a name like that, I mean, you were half way there with a name like Billy Darling. Being a wonderful chap, I took it like a man. And when the tears were dry I realised that there was more to life than silly old Margaret McConnell — there was Sheena Cuthbertson.

Despite the extra-curricular activities, I passed my eleven-plus, much to my parents' satisfaction, and after another brief encounter with Todd's Nook (which is Northumbrian for Fox's Lair) it was on to Rutherford Grammar School, where I started the same day as a chap called Bruce Something-or-other.

Holidays for the Rankin family were usually spent at Rosyth in Fife, which is on the north bank of the River Forth — just south of Dunfermline — as my uncle, Bob Turner, worked in the shipyards up there. In those days, of course, there was only the railway bridge over the Forth linking the north side to Edinburgh and the south, as the road bridge wasn't completed until 1964. Uncle Bob eventually moved to Portsmouth and later took a pub there. I suppose it was his own fault: if he hadn't lived a seagull's wing away from sea he wouldn't have got lumbered with us! I do remember the dartboard he had in the garden which my brother Joe and I would lean against the wall and throw a few blunt darts at until we got fed up. Now I probably had many infuriating habits, but Joe's worst were lingering in front of the board while removing his arrows, and walking in front of me just as I was about to have my throw. Obviously realising I was the more talented player, he designed these feeble ploys to put me off, but one day it got too much for me, and I hurled a dart just as he walked in front of me, to prove how dangerous it was. It was! It went straight into his leg and stayed there! My not unreasonable plea that he'd obstructed my throw and I really ought to have that dart again was completely drowned out as he brought half of

4

Portsmouth to a standstill with his screaming. As I was usually such a placid child, no one dreamt that I could have committed such a foul deed, and my parents thought that there had to be more behind the darts incident than met the eye. 'The eye,' they thought. 'That's it. Maybe his eyesight's not A.1 and he didn't see Joe walk in front of him.' The next thing I knew I was trying to locate a card on the wall that was supposed to have letters on it, and a man in a white coat was guiding my head towards a point above his mantelpiece. I refrained from the usual gags like 'What wall?' etc — on the whole these don't go down too well with opticians. At last, with a little assistance, my eyes focused on the card, digested the first three or four letters, sent them down to my brain which digested them and performed a quick translation for my mouth. On the fifth and sixth words I struggled, and then ground to a halt. Only nine years old and my increasingly noble features were to be covered up with a pair of those round revolting National Health specs. What would my mates say!

Being good lads at heart, my cousin Michael and I joined the local scouts, although they were a little sneaky 'cause the whole troop had to go to church regularly — we knew there'd be a catch somewhere. We must have been terribly impressionable as the talking point in church was always the vicar's robe. When he told us it was worth £6,000 we went round with mouths wide enough to catch the entire plague of locusts for weeks. He was obviously pulling our legs — maybe to keep our interest, but in any case it worked. We became regular churchgoers for a few months, if only to boggle at his coat of many colours. His words obviously didn't fall on stony ground. Our days as boy scouts came to an end when we were told we had to wear shorts. Shorts! We'd just started wearing long trousers! Sorry, Baden-Powell, we were not prepared to bare our knees. So we looked for excitement elsewhere.

And talking of excitement, one of the highlights of the year for us Newcastle kids was the annual fair (known as the Hoppins) on the town moor. It was somewhere you could have a good time without spending too much money. I spent what little I had on the dodgems — that was as near as you could get to driving a car at that age.

Fairgrounds in those days seemed much more romantic than they do now; the kids who worked on them never seemed to go to school, and the whole way of life appeared very attractive to blokes like me and Bruce who were still bound tightly by school rules, discipline and time-keeping. The whole idea of travelling around from town to town with no routine was really appealing to us. Perhaps the will to lead that kind of life-style was a contributing factor in our success,

5

although the harsh reality of a lengthy tour of one-night stands wasn't as glamorous as it had seemed during the planning and dreaming stage, despite the fact that it was an integral part of our chosen profession. The words in Ricky Nelson's *Teenage Idol* summed it up pretty well:

> Some people call me a teenage idol, some people say they envy me,
> I guess they've got no way of knowing how lonesome I can be.
> I travel around from town to lonely town,
> I guess I'll always be just a rolling stone.
> I get no rest when I'm feeling weary, I've got to pack my bags and go.
> I've gotta be somewhere tomorrow to smile and do my show.

It obviously applied to the fairground people as much as to the showbiz ones. Songs that I remember from the days of hanging around the Hoppins in 1955 were things like the Stargazers' *Twenty Tiny Fingers*, Frankie Laine's *Cool Water* and Mitch Miller's *Yellow Rose of Texas*. It wasn't until the following year that the tinny fairground speakers rang out over the town moor with music that teenagers could really adopt as their own, rather than share the music with people of all ages, as had been the case up until then. And with the new music came new fashions. No longer were young people automatically dressing like their mums and dads as soon as they were sixteen. It was in 1956 that teenagers really started getting their own identity, the most outlandish I suppose being the 'Teddy Boys' with their drainpipe trousers, thick crepe-soled shoes, long Edwardian-style drape jackets and greased-back hair piled up on top of the head, with long sideboards. An amazing thing was that similarly styled gangs of youths mushroomed almost simultaneously around the world. Japan had the *Taiyo-Zoku* (children of the sun). In Germany it was the *Halbstarken* (half-strong). Their Swedish equivalent were the *Skinnuttar* (leather jackets), many French teenagers became *Blousons Noirs* (blackshirts) and Russia had *Stilyagi* (style boys).

This almost global phenomena is difficult to explain, except that it was maybe a social backlash after the years of World War II. After all, the Teddy Boy gangs had been on the streets of Britain since 1954, perhaps inspired by the sullen, 'angry young man' image of James Dean, who seemed to epitomise everything that youths of the time apparently felt. He symbolised speed, fast cars, violence and, above all, contempt for a life-style that conformed to the pattern dictated by society. Heady stuff! But many thousands of teenagers who'd sat through Dean's films — *East of Eden, Rebel without a Cause*

6

'In the beginning' — Hank, Bruce and George Williams,
'The Railroaders'. November 5th 1957, Newcastle University

Hank aged 7 with brother Joe and
cousin Evelyn (Hank's the one in
the middle)

Hank with Mum, Dad and
young brother Joe

and *Giant* — were very definitely affected by his image.

So as the strings of coloured bulbs blazed out from the fairground lighting up the Newcastle dusk, there'd be many swaggering Geordie versions of James Dean, Marlon Brando, and later Elvis Presley strutting through the fairground with their thumbs characteristically jammed into their waistcoat pockets, ready to take on the world!

I wasn't quite ready to take on the world, but I did fall foul of our local vicar one day after Sunday school, when my cousin Michael and I went off to play in the graveyard! When you're a kid things like that don't seem to matter, but think of the rumpus if a couple of 62-year-old company directors were caught chasing each other giggling and laughing around the gravestones! They'd probably get two years each. We got a good hard slap round the face from the vicar, and ran off feeling angry and confused. Can you imagine a man of the cloth doing that in the 80s? Not only would the lads' parents be down on him like a ton of bricks, but he'd probably be defrocked and fill a good few column inches in the *News of the World*. The 50s were difficult, though — there was a lot of pre-war and wartime discipline still hanging around. If a teacher whacked you — your bottom or hand — it hurt, and that was it — you knew what the consequences would be if you did it again. Or if the local bobby clipped you round the ear, you didn't rush home and tell your dad or he'd clip the other side so they matched!

I was becoming more and more interested in music, but as there was no pop radio all day, listening was restricted to either going round to David Horsey's house and playing Fats Domino, Elvis and Little Richard records, or Radio Luxembourg, the station that everyone traditionally listened to under the bed-clothes. I'll bet if they'd done a survey any time during the 50s as to where most youngsters listened to Luxembourg, the answer 'in between the sheets' would have come out top. Another friend, Brian White, who for some obscure reason was called Jim, actually *gave* me a wind-up gramophone! That was it — I was hooked. I bought my first record, *Flamingo* by Earl Bostic, after hearing Richard Lyon from the famous *Life with the Lyons* comedy series choose it as one of the records he'd like to take to a desert island with him. I used to play it to death on my gramophone at full volume, which was achieved by pushing a sliding door to expose the horn, and then opening the window to expose the neighbours to what I thought was a really cool piece of music.

I drove most of them mad, except for Dougie six doors up who was a bit older than me and allowed to make expeditions to witness stars like Frankie Laine and Dickie Valentine at the Newcastle Empire. Fancy actually being allowed to see them in *person*! I'd be all ears when Dougie gave me a minute by minute account of the show the following day, demonstrating most realistically how Johnny Ray had cried or narrowly missing my ear with a high-kicking Frankie Vaughan impression.

Mind you, there was a guy around who was *trying* to kick me, bash me or do whatever he could to make my life a misery, and all because I was going out with his sister! At fifteen, Muriel Miller was my first real crush, and everything was rosy until I realised she had an older brother, Jackie, a couple of years above me at Rutherford Grammar, who was after my blood for daring to fancy his little sister. Fortunately I had loyal classmates who helped me to do a pretty good impression of the invisible man. After all, there were plenty of places to hide in the old Victorian building that was my daytime home for five years. Rutherford had a *Tom Brown's Schooldays* feel about it with its large old classrooms, well-worn stone stairs and our headmaster, Charlie Hall, strutting about like a Dr Arnold hovering hawk-like, waiting to pounce on some unsuspecting Flashman-type character. And there were a few of those! Muriel's brother for example, who at seventeen seemed like an all-in wrestler compared with the slender young Rankin. But I couldn't run forever and the day of reckoning came one bleak day when we met face to face! There was a lot of verbal, and even the old shoulder charge accompanied by the traditional schoolboy challenge of 'Yeah?' to which the other would reply 'Yeah?' with an even bigger question mark at the end.

This was, of course, the usual weighing-up process while you were thinking, 'Has he got the measure of me, or could I get away with thumping him first?!' A little audacity often goes a long way, but on this occasion my natural Geordie charm and logic seemed to win him over and Jackie realised I was genuinely fond of Muriel! The things you do for love! Well, that was one problem off my mind, the only other headache was coping with school and my increasing love of music at the same time. I was still only fourteen when I got my first instrument in 1955. It was a Windsor G five-string banjo that I bought from one of the Rutherford schoolmasters, James Moody, for the heady price of two pounds ten shillings. Being a decent sort of chap he let me have it on easy terms, so we agreed that I'd pay him half a crown a week out of my pocket money and he'd let me have the banjo immediately. This was a great step for me, as I'd been really getting into Chicago-type jazz, New Orleans jazz and folk music. I'd hang around the shops that sold that type of music and not only read all the jazz columns but cut them out and stick them in a blank school exercise book which I started in October 1955. Initially it was filled with tickets from concerts I went to, like George Melly and Lionel Hampton; newspaper cuttings of jazz greats Fats Waller, Benny Goodman, Jack Teagarden and Baby Dodds; blues artists Ed 'Noon' Johnson and Billie Pierce and later a few autographs, like the picture I got of Chris Barber's Jazz Band after I went to see them at the City Hall in 1956 — they all signed that picture to Hank! (Everybody by now knew me as Hank — there were dozens of Brians littered all over the school and it got a little confusing. I think virtually every Brian ended up with a new name — Brian White became Jim, Brian Armstrong got tagged Pommy and I got stuck with Hank!) Monty Sunshine, who played lead clarinet on their classic *Petite Fleur,* autographed my picture and so did Johnny Duncan, who'd taken Lonnie Donegan's place when he left the group.

Johnny, of course, went on to have a massive solo hit with *Last Train to San Fernando.* I thought maybe if I learned to play the banjo well somebody would rush up and ask *me* to sign one day! But that was only a dream, the harsh reality was buying a tutor book and practising long and hard. I started with basic chord shapes and gradually taught myself to play in different keys, through the combination of buying a better tutor and spending as many evenings as I could at a local jazz club called the Vieux Carré down near the Tyne. It was run by a former public schoolboy who lived in a caravan. I learned a lot from Big Pete Deuchar: he'd been playing the banjo since 1952, and had been driven so hard by his mentor, the legendary trumpeter Ken Colyer, who incidentally was the leader of Britain's first ever skiffle group, that he was now a first-rate player.

We certainly didn't appreciate how lucky we were to be able to go along and not only see guys like Pete and other great musicians but chat to them and learn from their experiences. Far better, we assumed, to be somewhere like New Orleans, where you could get to watch and talk to the real old American legends. But we only realised there was more to being in New Orleans than meets the eye, when Pete Deuchar went out there to spend some time with one of his heroes from the world of jazz, George Lewis. Our natural envy turned to surprise when we heard of problems hitherto unknown to us jovial friendly Newcastle lads who didn't care whether the guy we were drinking with was yellow, black, green or purple! Because George was a Negro and Pete was white, there was virtually no chance of a social evening, as they weren't allowed to travel together on any form of public transport and they couldn't eat or drink together in public. With those and many other weird cultural traditions to conform to, it was no wonder they channelled everything into music. At least we could all mix together in our British establishments and hear each other's music.

The Vieux Carré was *the* place to be, but after a while a new jazz club sprang up next to the old Rutherford Grammar School. I say old, because at that time the school had been transferred to a new building on the north-west side of Newcastle. It was there that my playing career really began. Despite an initial leaning towards the clarinet, which I'd always liked for its fluidity, agility and tone, I got stuck into playing not only the banjo but also the guitar, as a mate of mine, John Tate, would often lend me his machine to hurt my fingers on!

Schooldays are the stage of a would-be musician's life when his dreams, frustrations and plans for the future often manifest themselves in guitars, lists of songs and intended personnel for his first group being doodled all over his rough exercise book, and I was no different. Just as thousands of blokes who followed the Shadows during the late 50s and early 60s would draw Fender Stratocasters, Telecasters and Fender Bass guitars on the back cover of their maths book, so I would do the same with the instruments associated with a skiffle group, my books being full of inky sketches of washboards, double basses, acoustic guitars and banjos, trumpets and clarinets.

And my very first plan for my first ever intended group in 1956 not only found its way on to paper, but miraculously still survives with the sloppy schoolboy scrawl, revealing that my brother Joe despite his tender years had been designated to play bass, John Tate and Derek Johnson were to be on guitars, the role of mandolin player was to fall to Mal Malarky, the washboard would be scraped by Howard Muir, and rather inevitably I was down for playing my five-string banjo. Variations of this outfit would often have a bash down at the new club, in the hall next to the old school banging out numbers like *Go Down Old Hannah* that we'd heard the Ken Colyer Skiffle Group do so well, *Rock Island Line, John Henry, Railroad Bill* and a song which I sang called *Ice Cream*, which just about summed it up!

Throughout 1956 and into '57 skiffle really came on strong and although it was a fairly short-lived phenomena compared to the longevity of other musical styles, its real service to the history of British music was as a catalyst. It really speeded up the process for up and coming musicians to go from buying their instrument and learning a bit to getting up and having a go. You suddenly didn't need to be a talented player of many years standing to have a chance. Skiffle was real do-it-yourself music — if you had a feel for the rhythm you were away.

11

As the craze came and went within a relatively short time, many young people not unnaturally ask, 'What was skiffle?' I think someone better qualified to explain than I am is Chas McDevitt, who not only led his own group, but had one of the biggest ever hits to come out of the skiffle era, *Freight Train*, which was also the name he gave to the coffee bar which he started in London a little while later, where Bruce and I were often to sing for our supper.

Skiffle started in the 1920s, when a lot of itinerant musicians were attracted to the boom towns of Kansas City and Chicago, along with the migrant labourers. As they were financially unstable, they tended to band together, and to help pay their debts, they would hold what they called 'rent parties', where friends would turn up bringing food, money and instruments. Those people who had no real instruments made use of anything that came to hand: washboards, suitcases, brushes, comb and paper and tea chest basses, all of which helped to create happy music — skiffle. Skiffle was a fusion of the country musicians' art with that of the city musicians — folksongs with a beat, where songs of the boll weevil and the plough gave way to the rougher tales of the big cities — sidewalk blues and streamline trains. The musicians of the period had names as colourful as their music, like Washboard Sam, Tampa Red, Leadbelly, Blind Blake and Big Laces Merryweather!

British skiffle differed from the original in two ways, really: first, the British combos rarely used a piano, and secondly they didn't rely on big-city blues for their repertoire, but incorporated mountain ditties, songs from the west about bad men and gamblers, negro spirituals, work chants, and even some popular and jazz standards. So really a *new* musical form had been developed within our shores, and the decadent youth of Britain was creating something worthwhile. We thought then that one thing was certain: as long as people wanted to be happy, skiffle would flourish! Maybe they didn't want to be happy after 1957.

Words of wisdom from Chas McDevitt, star of *Saturday Morning Skiffle Club*, on the light programme, which evolved into *Saturday Club*, on which we would play countless times in the years to come. In early 1957 the group whose names I'd scribbled in my book that we were vaguely planning to call the Riverside Skiffle Group became the Crescent City Skiffle Group instead, when we realised there was already a fairly well-established ensemble playing under the former name! We decided on Crescent City because that was the musicians'

Hank's schooldays scrapbook

name for New Orleans, and we thought added a little bit of weight to things!

By May we felt the world was ready for us, and entered a skiffle contest run by the South Shields Jazz Club whose president was none other than the great Chris Barber, which seemed impressive at the time but he was probably president of dozens of jazz clubs who thought it'd look good to have his name gracing their note paper! Fred Rowe, the club secretary, wrote back to me with details of the competition.

Dear Hank,

Very pleased to receive your entry for the Skiffle contest. Just a reminder that it will be held in the Pier Pavilion, South Shields (near the lifeboat) on Saturday 18th of May, so could you try to be there about 6.45 p.m.

Tickets are available at 2/6 or 3/6 or pay at the door if there are any tickets left.

I am enclosing the complimentary tickets to admit each member of your group.

The whole contest is being recorded and copies of any group will be available if you want them. So far we have had entries from:

Team Valley Skiffle
Peter Bond Skiffle
Rumjunglers
Brian Vainbridge Skiffle
Santa Cruz Skiffle
Saints Skiffle
Black Cats

Tickets are on sale at 'Jeavons' Bigg Mart. See you on Saturday and here's wishing you the best of luck in the concert.

Well, we were in, but up against some stiff competition and there would doubtless be some last minute entries as well. So it was heads down for two or three days of furious rehearsals!

By seven o'clock that Saturday night the atmosphere at the Pier Pavilion was positively crackling with excitement, as the nerves and enthusiastic pre-contest chatter gave way to the event itself. Group after group went on and gave their all, plucking and hitting, singing and shouting through the one song each group was allowed. An interval filled by the music of the Rivermouth Jazz Band gave the judges, who included Big Pete Deuchar, the banjoist from the Vieux Carré club, a chance to assess the evening's talent, confer and have the thankless task of telling all but one of the groups that they hadn't

14

come first! Now during our number *Stack O Lee* I played a banjo solo, which was an idea I'd nicked from watching Ken Colyer, and we were sure that had clinched it for us. Then came the announcement: 'Fourth — Team Valley; third — Pilgrims; second — Peter Bond Skiffle . . . and tonight's winner — the Crescent City Skiffle Group!!' The words rang in our ears. It was us — we'd actually won! We'd blooming well come first! Whoopee! Good old May 18th 1957! I felt ten feet tall, and I thought the whole world should be rejoicing.

It was during the summer of 1957, while eager optimists were poring over the very first premium bond draw, and Professor Bernard Lovell was banging the last few nails into what would be the world's largest radio telescope, at Jodrell Bank in Cheshire, that Bruce and I became quite friendly at school. We'd been aware of each other before, but it was our mutual interest in music that brought us closer together. He'd bring his 'National' guitar to school (an American built, steel bodied guitar) and I'd join in, picking out tunes and gradually developing an ability to play single lines that I'd learned from listening to guitar solos on the radio. At the time Bruce was in a group called the Railroaders and I guess I must have impressed him enough for him to ask me to join.

As the Railroaders, we played mainly in working men's clubs and similar establishments. We even did a week at the Newcastle Palace, which wasn't really big league stuff but was certainly a step in the right direction. On the opening night I went on stage proudly sporting my sixteenth birthday present around my neck — a lovely Hofner guitar that my Dad had bought for me, complete with electric pick-up so I could deafen the whole of Stanhope Street with one chord. That night it nearly deafened *me*. As I strummed the guitar I also touched the microphone stand, and thanks to somebody's wiring expertise nearly became the first Railroader in space. There was an almighty bang — a black singer who was in the show leapt into the orchestra pit and I was stunned. Sparks flew from the guitar, and a couple of Geordie sparks came rushing on stage armed with the tools of their trade. In that split second I realised that I had broken three strings and thought, 'So this is what happens when you break a string on an electric guitar!' Remember it was the first time I'd played one — I assumed that the broken strings were the cause of the explosion rather than the result.

The Railroaders were initially myself, Bruce and George Williams on guitars, a bloke called Jim on drums and a tea-chest bassist, but as we added rock 'n' roll songs to our repertoire, a guitarist called Eddie Silver joined us, and George switched to bass. By late '57 we were becoming pretty popular around the local clubs and actually starting to make a bit of a name for ourselves. It was at one Railroaders gig on Guy Fawkes night 1957 that I had the most sobering experience of my life. I got blind drunk! We were playing at the university, the booze was flowing, and we even had the renowned jazzman Monty Sunshine sitting in with us on stage for a few numbers. The combination of playing with the stars and signing hundreds of autographs afterwards, plus the atmosphere and excitement obviously heightened the effect of the vast quantities of cider I'd been knocking back and I was violently sick. My face alternated being a somewhat pallid green and a rather attractive off-white, while my mind slipped in and out of consciousness for several hours. No doubt about it — I was absolutely smashed, and judging by the vast numbers of inert bodies littering the floor of the university hall the following morning, the old west country apple juice had had the same effect on everybody. Sharing my plight with dozens of others was cold comfort as I crawled home past buildings that gradually became recognisable as Newcastle through a cold grey dawn that still had streams of sulphur from the previous night's fireworks clinging to it. I just wanted to crawl home and die quietly! It wasn't worth getting a taxi as it was only a short crawl! That experience almost put me off heavy drinking for life.

It was George Williams who first noticed the announcement of the talent contest in a music paper, just before Christmas 1957. It sounded good. It would mean going to London, but as Bruce had been going on for quite a while about trying our luck in the capital, it seemed as if the time was right. A contest in London would undoubtedly be vastly different from the sort of competition we'd been up against in the Newcastle area and we fleetingly thought we might be wading out of our depth. But all such gloomy conjectures were soon dispelled, and before we knew it one of those great old London North Eastern region locomotives was hauling the Railroaders, complete with guitars and drum kit, to a new horizon — Kings Cross! At least that's what we hoped, but the shadow of one of Britain's most horrific train crashes was still very much in the minds of most people in the country. Only a few days earlier, ninety people had been killed in the fog in a railway accident at Lewisham in south London, resulting in the tragedy and ensuing chaos being reported in the daily papers for the next few days. Sitting on a train reading about fatal rail accidents is as bad as learning of an air crash while glancing at the news 30,000 feet up. Little did we know that we'd end up flying to virtually every country in the world. Anyway, we got to Kings Cross safely with our guitars and drums intact, stayed in a hotel for the weekend and played well enough in the contest to win a place through to the finals in April. In high spirits and obviously wanting to make the most of our weekend, we spent one evening at a club near Shaftesbury Avenue called the Nucleus, where Robin Hall and Jimmie McGregor were playing. It was magic to see them playing live, as opposed to on television, but we weren't quite so thrilled with the transvestite community at the Nucleus. Once we'd explained to the more naive Railroaders that a transvestite was a chap dressed up as a lady, and that it wasn't a fancy dress night we decided to do the decent thing and slip out — just as some bizarre creature called Angel with flame red lipstick shining like a beacon out of his five o'clock shadow started doing weird things on stage. Pleased to be out in the comparatively fresh air of the Metropolis we strolled slowly back towards our hotel. Maybe it was just the reaction of coming out of a club into the cold night, but my nose started to run, nothing startling in that, but I couldn't catch it! Ah yes, I had the same devastating wit back in 1957! Anyway, being a far-sighted sort of chap for someone so short-sighted, I'd brought my trusty handkerchief and after I'd been sniffing for a few minutes the other lads started encouraging me to use it. My hand only stayed in my pocket for a split second, and they probably heard my scream as far away as the banks of the Tyne. While we'd been in the club, some wise guy deciding that I was a country yokel had kindly slipped a lighted cigarette into my pocket. I ripped my flaming duffle coat off and did a Zulu war dance on it, much to the delight of the others.

Partly because of my slavish devotion to music, I lost Muriel Miller. Two years of seeing my back disappearing down the road with my instrument case under my arm must have been enough for her, and she started going to dances with her friends or on her own. I think one night my absence virtually pushed her into the arms of another sixteen-year-old Romeo, while I was busy being a Railroader in another part of town.

Bruce didn't come back to school for the first term of 1958 — in fact he didn't come back at all, and as we were both determined to be professional musicians I joined him, a little prematurely, in the ranks of the school leavers just a couple of months later, although the school did encourage me to enter the commercial art world. The only job I ever had before making music my living was cycling around Newcastle delivering electrical parts for a measly two pounds ten a week minus my national insurance stamp. The job only lasted for four weeks, and I wasn't going to get rich that way, not at the speed I rode the bike anyway — I was certainly no Reg Harris.

March 1958, and the only vague glimmer of hope on the horizon was the final of the talent contest in London. If that didn't work out, my bicycle clips might become a more permanent feature in my life.

2 / Bruce's Story

(1941 — Spring 1958)

It's a pity that in 1941 there were no polite cover-up names for being illegitimate. In the early 80s you're a 'love child' — in the early 40s you were a bastard. A pretty unfair start to life!

I was born by the seaside at Bognor Regis, and had three years of infancy, oblivious to World War II raging away, getting my lungs full of fresh Channel air — although with the sewage outlet just a mile out to sea I'm not sure that it was all *that* fresh!

My dad was Stan Cripps and my mum was Grace Welch. They never got married but they had me, so I guess they must have loved each other. I've tried many times over the years to discover more about those early days, but I've nearly always drawn blanks; it's strange how Victorian attitudes to things like that still prevail in many families. I discovered I was illegitimate by accident when I was seventeen. It hurt a lot more finding out that late, and it was to give me a permanent chip on my shoulder.

So a three-year-old Bruce Cripps and his mum took off to the north-east. Stan stayed in Bognor, but Mum apparently decided it'd be a good idea to move up to Chester-le-Street and stay with her mum and her sister Sarah. I never really knew my mum — she died of T.B. aged thirty two years later when I was five. Sadly I have absolutely no memories of her. The tragedy is that they can cure it these days, with modern drugs like streptomycin, and mass radiography centres where you can have regular check-ups. In the 40s it was different. Either you were lucky and got over it — or you didn't. All I have now are a few very old but highly treasured photographs of her.

If you take the A167 out of Durham and head north, towards Gateshead and Newcastle, a few miles up the road you'll drive in to Chester-le-Street. That's where my first recollections of the world come from. Although relatively famous for its sand workings, clothing and confectionery industries, the town has always been overshadowed by its more famous neighbours. I suppose in the 40s there weren't that many cars around, travel took a lot longer, so people couldn't whizz around the country like they do today — the war had just finished and there wasn't the money to do it. The only way that people knew of places, unless they'd been there, was if they had a football team! And the north-east had some famous teams!

When World War II broke out the 1939/40 season had barely got under way, but although the league was frozen after a handful of games, it remained alight inside the hearts of millions of football fans via hastily organised leagues and cups that lasted through the war years until things got back to normal for the 1946/47 season. The north-east had Sunderland and Middlesborough in the first division, Newcastle in the second division, Gateshead, Darlington and Hartlepool in the third division (north), and Bishop Auckland were one of the country's top amateur clubs. Names on the tongues of schoolboys all over England. But Chester-le-Street? Where was that, France?

So at the tender age of five, Cripps, B. joined the ranks of the terrified and wary at Red Rose School near the cemetery, making the short round trip from 15 Broadwood View every day. There was just me and Auntie Sadie (I'd always called her that, she'd never been Auntie Sarah to me at all) but she did have friends who popped in to see us, and it was one of those friends who gave me my first musical instrument. His name was Uncle Norman. In those days anyone who had trousers longer than knee length, had a few hairs on their chin and drank beer you called Uncle! There wasn't the familiarity that there is now, where you even get parents encouraging their kids to call them by their Christian names. So Uncle Norman gave me a ukulele — I couldn't play a note, but at least I was musical enough to know that I wasn't doing it right!

Sadly a few years later we had a flood and it got ruined, but I often wondered whether the guy who wrote the hit tune *He played his Ukulele as the Ship went down* was looking through our window when the inspiration struck him!

When I was eight three things happened — love struck in two different ways, and I saw my dad for the first time that I can remember. Sadie got me dressed up in the way usually reserved for Sunday, although why you should dress up on the day of the week that not so many people saw you was beyond me, and took me along to Newcastle Central Station. I knew it was going to be something pretty exciting considering the fuss, but it was some chap and his new wife.

He was introduced to me as my father, but it didn't mean that much to me — there was hardly a joyous reunion with tears and violent emotions, but he seemed OK because he took me fishing!

20

Grace, Bruce's Mum

'Dodging Hitler' — Bruce with his Mum in Bognor Regis (even then I had a weight problem!)

'Me on the wagon — gotta lotta bottle!'

Stan, Bruce's Dad

I went on the train with them, the few miles north to Berwick-on-Tweed, the last town in Britain before you trip over the remnants of Hadrian's Wall and into Scotland. The fortnight which was to be the longest I ever spent with my dad in my life was a fairly memorable one, full of fish, water, rods, entangled lines and stilted conversation. On reflection it was also a sad two weeks. From Berwick you could (and still can on a clear day!) see Holy Isle, which used to be Lindisfarne, connected to the mainland by a stretch of sand at low tide. The Abbey founded on it in 635 A.D. was the first establishment of Celtic Christianity in England. And there we were, two people who should have been so close, a father and son destined always to be complete strangers to one another, a stone's throw from what was to some people the start of the strength in the family unit in England. I didn't see him again until I was seventeen and that was only briefly.

Two happier notes were struck around 1949 — I fell in love with Anne Usher, she must have been eight as well, but she seemed so elegant to me. I did at least talk to her, but my vocabulary and courage weren't really up to pouring out my feelings to her on the swings. I didn't even know what my feelings were, but their house did have a garage and that had to count for something, and as it backed on to the school playing field, I could feel closer to her by just looking at the house any time I felt like it!

The other love I encountered around that time stayed with me a little longer than Anne Usher, in fact it's still with me today — music!

There I was in the back row of the local cinema when it hit me in the shape of the evergreen *There's no business like show business, there's no business I know.* Wow! That was for me. I knew there and then that there were 'no people like show people', and my mind was made up.

In 1951 Aunt Sadie and I moved in with her Indian boyfriend, which meant an upheaval and a new home at 126 Elswick Road, Newcastle, a large flat above Nazam's fish and chip shop. Inevitably it led to me working in the intoxicating atmosphere below, gutting fish and chopping chips when I wasn't at school. It was great in the winter wrestling with frozen corpses of cod while trying to endure the arctic conditions in the shop!

Nazam obviously had a nose for business — with meat, butter, bacon, cheese, sugar and sweets and tea still rationed, fish was a good line to be in! The vision of a new found affluence in the post-war years still hadn't materialised, in fact things got worse. The meat ration, which had been one and sixpence a week in 1945, was

22

Hop-a-long Welch aged 8

Bruce saying goodbye to Hank's Mum
the day he and Hank left for London
in April 1958

Bruce at Red Rose School, aged 8 (back row behind the teacher)

reduced to eightpence in 1951, as a result of a verbal bust up with Argentina or something, so it was lucky we didn't live above a corned beef shop! Despite the animosity that I suppose must have been aimed at the man organising the country's money, the Chancellor of the Exchequer, the fact that he and I shared the same surname didn't really lead to any unpleasantness at school!

Unlike Bruce Cripps, already a strapping schoolboy for his tender years, Sir Stafford Cripps was once described by Prime-Minister-to-be Harold MacMillan as 'a strange, monastic-looking man, emaciated and said to live off watercress grown off the blotting paper on his desk!' About as far removed from the rapidly filling out ten-year-old gannet from Newcastle as you could possibly get. Money was tight, though; income tax, although it didn't worry me much, was nine and six in the pound, and allegedly in 1951 only seventy people known to the Inland Revenue earned more than £6,000 net! No wonder Nazam had the odd little business on the side!

I passed my eleven-plus and moved to Rutherford Grammar School, starting the same day as Hank, although he was known as Brian Rankin then. Two new boys, Cripps, B. and Rankin, B.R., little realising what lay ahead.

To make ends meet, and in Nazam's and Sadie's case to make ends fish, my Indian 'uncle' was dealing (off the top and bottom of the pack) in nylon stockings as a market trader. He'd buy a job lot of seconds and muggins would sit for hours turning them into firsts by matching them up. There was the added problem of trying to do two jobs at once, gut fish and match nylons. If you didn't wash your hands really thoroughly after the first you'd get smelly seconds. I actually invented a new fashion before it came into existence — fishnet stockings!

Despite a growing dislike of Nazam and my new surroundings and an increasing passion for music, I went to all the local markets with him and Sadie to peddle our wares! South Shields, the Quayside, Stockton, Morpeth and even back to good old Chester-le-Street. Time at Elswick Road was spent either playing in the back alleys or indoors listening to the radio. I loved *The Goon Show* with Spike Milligan, Harry Secombe and Peter Sellers, and equally adored the parts in it where Ray Ellington and Max Geldray would bash out a favourite tune or song of the time. You'd have a sketch about something totally idiotic like 'Napoleon's piano' and suddenly Max Geldray would launch into a harmonica version of *Aint't Misbehavin';* then it was back to more insanity, broken by Ray Ellington singing *Don't Roll Those Bloodshot Eyes at Me.* I adored the classic kids' radio programmes like *Journey into Space* and Charles Chilton's *Riders of*

24

the Range. I liked *Take It From Here* and *Life with the Lyons* a lot, but I was always a bit baffled by *Educating Archie* — how could Peter Brough get away with being a ventriloquist on the radio!

Some of the first ever songs I remember were in 1953 — I think my ears were late starters! The stand out tune for me then was Guy Mitchell's *She Wears Red Feathers.* Maybe it was the line from that song 'She lives on fresh coconuts and fish from the sea' that brought it near to home for me!

By now I was arguing with Nazam quite a lot of the time because I thought he was working my auntie too hard, like seven days a week — and I wasn't going to have that!

At school things were so-so. Some teachers I liked, some I hated, like Mr Calrow. He seemed about eight feet tall and was the sort who'd send you up a ladder just so he could feel your bottom on the way down. Pa Brown, the French teacher, once found himself on the receiving end of the famous Cripps left hook, when he made a rather untimely remark about me having been dragged up by my mother. That was it, I saw red and whacked him! I was a big lad for fourteen, but not so big that the headmaster didn't give me a good thrashing across the backside with a strap that was made out of some fearsome forerunner to seat-belt webbing.

Mr Grant took art, and Mr Nimmo took rugby. Now I wasn't bad with the old oval ball, in fact I eventually made the first team, and might have gone on to captain Hull Kingston Rovers reserves or something if an untimely kick in the crutch hadn't finished my career. 'To hell with the career,' I yelled as they carried me off, 'what about my future married life?' Schoolboys have an unkind way of making light of a moment which could affect the rest of your life!!

At least as long as no one kicked me in the ear I could still listen to music. In 1956 the flickering glow of musical interest in me burst into flames as Lonnie Donegan crackled over the radio with a new brand of music that you could apparently make at home with a few improvised instruments — skiffle had arrived!

A tea-chest with an old broom handle stuck in it and a piece of string stretched tautly between the top of the broom and the box acted as a double bass; a washboard, normally used for scrubbing grubby shirt collars and cuffs, became a drum substitute when played with thimbles over the thumb and fingers; all you needed was a cheapo guitar and you were on your way. I was inspired to dash out and buy a £4/19/6 guitar at the local sports and music shop. I was really chuffed, but it killed my fingers! While I was trying desperately to master my new instrument, I was listening to a lot of trad jazz records at home on the wind-up gramophone, like Chris Barber and

Monty Sunshine. I suppose with Newcastle being a university town trad was very big in the area, and a lot of us were affected by it. I was also quite affected by a girl called Edna, who I used to take for romantic walks in Elswick Park where we'd hold hands and gaze at each other! If your relationship was platonic it was Elswick Park, if it looked like being anything else it was a trip up to the town moor. I was definitely a park man! But even half-hearted, clumsy attempts at kissing members of the opposite sex in the Disney-like setting of pre-fabs and bomb sites full of rose bay willow herb, were beaten into second place by our newly formed skiffle group. I think we must have taken the name the Railroaders from the fact that we'd often congregate in the little cafe at Newcastle Central Station.

We had a crack at what they called 'go as you please' talent competitions in local pubs. Although we were under age the glittering prizes of five pounds, three pounds and two pounds were a golden enough carrot to make it worth taking the risk. We did *Bring a Little Water, Sylvia, Oh Mary Don't You Weep, Rock Island Line* and loads of other Donegan-influenced material, including songs by singers that were his favourites. We assumed that if Lonnie liked them they must be great, so we set about the Leadbelly and Big Bill Broonzy song books with great enthusiasm.

Although things were looking bright on the music front, home life became increasingly intolerable. Nazam was ill-treating my auntie, and on many occasions I pleaded with her to leave but she obviously loved him a lot. One day it all got too much for me. I hit Nazam and threw him down the stairs. It was clear I couldn't stay in the flat any longer or I'd have put my fish gutting experience to good use on Mr Din, so I moved into one of the boarding houses he owned. Sixteen, and living on my own! I went mad and started eating things like egg and bacon that I hadn't tasted for years, as my diet had mainly consisted of curry since the age of eleven, because of Nazam's religious beliefs.

With not all that long to go to school leaving age Hank joined the Railroaders from the Crescent City Skiffle Group for an undisclosed fee! He'd been endowed with the name Hank because there were a million different Brians in his class. He actually looked like a university student in his specs, college scarf and a duffle-coat with those little wooden pegs down the front! Like Hank, I'd often hang out at the local fair ground to hear all my favourite records of the summer of '57 for nothing, like Johnny Ray's *Yes Tonight, Josephine*, Little Richard's *The Girl Can't Help It*, the Diamonds' *Little Darlin'* and Elvis' *All Shook Up*. Magic days. Charlie Grace's *Fabulous* had just hit the charts, so I tore off to Newcastle Empire to see him. Slim

Seventeen was a very good year

Whitman I went to watch, and the legendary Johnnie Ray, just sitting in the audience dreaming of the future.

After the shows I invariably went round to the stage door to queue for autographs, just one more eager face in the crowd keen to go home with another name in the book. Of course at the time it doesn't dawn on you that artists have tight schedules to keep and get plagued by a million sixteen-year-old Bruces, Charlies and Horaces, so it came as a great surprise to me when after waiting for what seemed like hours at the side door of the Empire I came face to face with the legend himself — the man who'd inspired me to pick up the guitar and play — the one and only king of skiffle — Lonnie Donegan! I nervously handed him my autograph book, and he spoke to me. Even now I can remember my hero's words like it was yesterday. 'Fuck off, son, I'm in a hurry!' I was choked, absolutely choked. I was a broken adolescent for ages after that.

Mind you, whenever I've bumped into him since I've reminded him of it and we've had a good laugh.

Later in 1957 I went to see Jim Dale just as he was breaking big with *Be My Girl*, and the atmosphere was tremendous. The place was packed and the screaming rose to fever pitch. 'Wow,' I thought, 'this is for me,' and I resolved really to do something about it. All the late nights at various venues absorbing music weren't exactly helping at school. It's not that I didn't want to learn, but I was asleep for most of the lesson!

When I wasn't being strapped or snoozing, non-academic time was more often than not spent with a ton of other lads, all crowding round certain books we were keen on. Well not exactly books, more educational publications really — for naturists! They were called *Spick and Span*, and were allegedly for deep thinking people to study the pleasures of the human form. To us they were plain old 'nudie books' and we all gathered around to learn more about the opposite sex accompanied by much sniggering, a lot of bragging and the odd smattering of rapier-like schoolboy wit. I always used to notice the pictures where the ladies wore black stockings — I knew my training under Nazam would stand me in good stead one day!

The Railroaders were still steaming along. I continually badgered Hank to play more rock 'n' roll and eventually it paid off as we started learning Elvis Presley numbers like *Paralysed*. I changed to a bigger cello-type guitar and we auditioned for the Saturday morning radio show *Skiffle Club*, but the producer Dennis Main Wilson decided that we hadn't got whatever it took, so that was that — but was it? Some sort of drive and determination stirred within me, so I made a reconnaissance trip to the legendary 2 Is coffee bar in London that

I'd heard so much about. After the brief visit to London I was convinced — that was for me. Hank and I both left school and entered the Railroaders for a talent contest we'd seen advertised in a music paper. London here we come! We were praying that there would still be a little of the famous gold left on the pavements for us as 1957 became 1958.

3 / Rockin' at the 2 Is

(Spring — October 1958)

I go home every night,
I make myself some tea,
I rush into the bedroom,
Put on my old blue jeans.
Back down the stairs
I say goodbye to mum,
She looks at me and says
'Where you going son?'
'Going rockin' at the 2 Is
We won't be home tonight.'

April 6th 1958. Perry Como's *Magic Moments* and *Catch a Falling Star* had been at Number 1 for five weeks, and an Easter parade of stars invaded Britain. Fellow passengers on BOAC flight 550 from New York on Good Friday were Pat Boone (here to headline a *Sunday Night at the London Palladium* show) and rock 'n' roller Charlie Gracie who'd spent forty weeks in the British charts during 1957 with songs like *Wandering Eyes, Butterfly* and *Fabulous.*

Hard on their heels on the London Airport arrivals list from New York was a lavishly dressed pianist who graced our Sunday afternoon TV sets with his smoothly extrovert style candelabra and constant references to 'Brother George'. Liberace had two sets of ivories, one on the piano and the other which he revealed when turning the ladies on with his winning smile.

April 6th wasn't a great day for rock 'n' roller 'Wee Willie' Harris, the zany singer with the shock of brightly coloured hair, who invariably popped up on the telly singing someone else's songs: he was fined five pounds as plain old Herbert Harris at Otley in Yorkshire for using a car with inefficient brakes. The price of fame, eh?

Jim Dale (who stars in virtually every *Carry On* film there is) and the Vipers were doing a week in Bradford — the teenagers went wild, completely jamming Quebec Street and battering down the doors to the Gaumont Theatre in an attempt to get at their idols. There were so few British singers and groups of this type that almost anybody could get screamed at! Anyway Jim and the Vipers were besieged wherever they went in Bradford by hundreds and hundreds of fans. If you had the money and fancied looking like your heroes, the papers were carrying advertisements for 'The Rock Suit': 59/6d, low-fronted trousers with thirteen-inch bottoms and a four-pocket jacket — as worn by the stars — so tantalisingly worded you almost tore your trouser pocket to get the money out!

April 6th was also the day that two sixteen-year-old guitarists, Hank Marvin and Bruce Welch from Newcastle-on-Tyne, were in London for the final of a talent competition. Hank called himself Marvin after Marvin Rainwater, who had a Number 1 hit in this country in 1958 with *Whole Lotta Woman*. Bruce changed his name by deed poll, reverting to his mother's name for personal reasons. They'd won through a couple of preliminary heats, but this was the big one for the Railroaders, so there were two days of heavy rehearsing prior to the contest for Hank, Bruce, guitarist Eddie Silver, bass player George Williams and a drummer called Jim.

One of the other groups in the competition that April night were the Velvets from Palmers Green, a four-piece guitar/drums/bass outfit. As Hank and Bruce sat in the stalls watching the north London group rehearsing they commented to each other on how the man beating the skin sounded incredibly like Buddy Holly's drummer Jerry Allison. Over four years later Brian Bennett was to join them in one of the most successful groups Britain has ever produced.

So it was as a five-piece that the Railroaders lined up for the final on April 6th 1958. They came third. A panel of experts placed them behind a jazz band and the ultimate winner — a Malayan opera singer!

Despite a good placing in the contest, the Railroaders ran out of steam. George Williams went off to manage Eddie Silver, who as a solo singer released several records on the Philips label, and Jim the drummer went back to his job as a coalminer. This left Hank and Bruce to team up with some other guys they had met at the talent competition who were playing together. They were Neil Johnson, trainee chemist Gerry Furst and drummer Pete Chester, whose father Charlie was a household name because of his numerous appearances as a wireless comedian.

Hank was pretty impressed with their newfound friends.

As we were only sixteen they seemed pretty grown up to us — they all drove cars. Gerry often appeared behind the wheel of his father's Ford Consul. Neil drove a Wolseley. Pete had an Austin convertible in which he tried to teach Bruce and myself to drive.

31

With the other three being mobile we used to head north to Pete's house in Vivien Way, Hampstead Garden Suburb, where we would rehearse and where we started our first attempt at writing songs. So within a fortnight of the demise of Railroaders we'd become two of Pete Chester's Chesternuts.

After the competition the manager of the Regal Edmonton, a kindly Scotsman called Mr Livingstone, had telephoned a landlady he knew in Finsbury Park to try and get us a room for the night. Yes, she had the attic spare, she said. So it was in Mrs Bowman's boarding house that two thrilled but exhausted Geordie lads collapsed in a heap in the room that was to become their base for some while. Mrs Bowman specialised in renting rooms to people in showbusiness, so that the house was full of actors, singers and dancers — in fact singer Leapy Lee, who went on to have a massive hit with *Little Arrows* in 1968, lived in the next room.

To counteract any apprehension their relatives might be having about Hank and Bruce's new way of life they'd write letters home that weren't exactly full of the truth but would hopefully allay any fears for their health and general sanity! One epistle from Bruce ran:

Dear Auntie,
    Things are great in London, we've got a lovely flat, food is good
    — it's marvellous here!
Love Bruce.

At least some of my letter was true — we *were* in London, although in reality we were all skint, and it was the accepted practice to sneak downstairs at night and pinch a bottle of milk or a couple of eggs from the fridge. The problem was trying to keep the dogs quiet — if they started barking you could be caught redhanded halfway up the stairs. It was safest to nick the apples from the garden — nobody minded that very much. You know some days we'd just exist on one apple — shared between us!

Hank recalls with embarrassment the day he unwittingly became an accomplice to a crime.

There were a couple of real rogues staying at the boarding house (not Bruce and I, two other rogues!) and one of them said to me one day, 'Come and give me a hand on my car.' Having all day at my disposal, no money and nothing to do I forced myself out of bed and went outside. He seemed to be having a problem with his number plates, he apparently didn't like the old ones and was putting new ones on. Would I help him? 'Course, I didn't think the old ones looked very good anyway, the new plates had a far nicer number! I might have been naive but I was very kind-hearted in those days! I realised a little too late that of course he'd stolen the car. Not only that but even though his mate couldn't drive I remember him jumping in, starting it up, catapulting along the pavement, nearly mowing some people down and finally smashing his way into a shop — through the window! Still the other guy was OK (despite being a bit of a villain). I vividly remember his fancy embroidered American shirts and snazzy black and white shoes. Also he was the one who brought rare records back from the States, like old Sun singles on that famous yellow label with black writing. I remember the words 'Jerry Lee Lewis and his pumping piano'. That line always gave us a great laugh. I think we conjured up an image of a demonic maniac hammering away at the ivories with his fists.

The American music that the two young Geordie lads were absorbing every day in that room in Finsbury Park had an undoubted influence on the songs they started to write themselves. As a group, the Chesternuts did very few gigs as they were not really a working band, but Bruce remembers one booking that turned the tide for them.

One of the few Chesternuts' bookings we had was backing comedian Benny Hill at a charity show in Stoke Newington. The song we played with him on was one he'd just finished writing, so the East London audience heard the first ever performance of a song that became Benny's debut chart record in 1961 — *Gather in the Mushrooms*. It was at that gig that we met impresario Leslie Conn who ran the British office of the American Carlton label, whose main artist was singer Jack Scott. Leslie was the first person to believe in us and to encourage us to write original songs. He even organised some recording time for us at Philips Studio in Stanhope Place, where, in the small amount of time allocated to us we put down two songs, *Teenage Love* and *Jean Dorothy*. The two numbers were released as a single on Columbia, but despite our appearance on BBC TV's *6.5 Special* it didn't set the chart alight. It was magic for us, though, making our first television appearance with such famous names as Don Lang, Tony Osborne, Pete Murray and Josephine Douglas. No record sales and very few appearances lead rather inevitably to a lack of the green folding stuff, so Hank and I began working at a coffee bar called the 2 Is in London's Old Compton Street, alternating between playing in the basement and working the orange machine. Hank was very proud of the fact that he was the first person to operate the machine just hours after it was installed!

The British rock 'n' roll scene started at the 2 Is in the heart of Soho. There are few who would deny that the little coffee bar at 59 Old Compton Street, with its cramped basement, was the first spawning ground for the new breed of musicians springing up, and a happy hunting ground, sometimes in both senses, for agents and managers eagerly pursuing new talent.

The 2 Is had been given its name by the previous owners, the Irani Brothers, and although it cost only two shillings to get downstairs, the front door was invariably guarded by 'Lofty', who'd keep a vague watch on who came and went, and a less vague watch on the scores of pretty office girls and nurses who'd flock in there every night, all dolled up in their pencil-slim dresses, lethal looking stiletto-heeled winkle-pickers and as much make-up as their faces would take. Many of the names that passed through the 2 Is are now legends: Cliff Richard, of course; Tommy Steele, the local lad from Bermondsey who made it to the very pinnacle of show business; Terry Dene, who had three big hits including the classic *A White Sport Coat* and went on to star in the film *The Golden Disc.* Wee Willie Harris of *6.5 Special* fame started there and stood out like a beacon around Soho with his flaming red hair. Like Tommy, he came from Bermondsey. His dad was a lighterman on the Thames and his mum was a chambermaid at the Mayfair Hotel in London's West End.

As well as the 2 Is, there was its rival, the Top 10 club in Berwick Street, which housed the daily market where a young Marc Bolan still in short trousers used to help his mum out on their stall; and the Bridge House in Canning Town where most of the Shadows-to-be played at one time or another — Bruce, Hank, Tony and Jet, as well as 2 Is regular Rick Richards and two guys called Bill Crompton and Thunderclap Jones who later wrote *The Stranger,* which became the B side of the Shadows' second hit single *Man of Mystery.*

One of the bigger London venues was the Trocadero at the Elephant and Castle, the stomping ground for many of London's Teddy Boys. Rick Richards remembers playing there with Cliff and Ian Samwell.

It was a talent contest, and I think we lost because our amps broke down, although the group that came first, the Vampires, did pretty good version of *Ghost Riders in the Sky.*

The 2 Is was not only full of budding *musical* talent. One regular was a lady who managed the ABC bakery along the road who decided that Hank was the guy for her.

Lofty, the 2 Is doorman, who's lost his roll of lino

Posing at the 2 Is — Vince Taylor, an American singer from Hounslow, Middlesex

Tony Sheridan, who recorded with the Beatles and later tried to sue them and failed. 'Nice try, Tony.'

She used to corner me in the darkest depths of the basement and start molesting me, but even in the half light and gloom the layers of make-up used to turn me right off. She even tried to bribe me with a bag of free doughnuts and pastries from her cake shop. I ate the cakes, of course, and then I'd wriggle out of the follow-up which was really the 'you've had the cakes now you can have me' approach — a bit much for a youth of sixteen! Although there were times when it crossed my mind that a bit of experience wouldn't go amiss, I never did anything about it with the lady who was as easy as ABC!

The place really attracted musicians, like moths to a flame, but in amongst them came an assortment of weirdos, like one guy who played the piano and had an even more acned face than the rest of us, who would drift down in the afternoons and start banging away on the piano like a maniac, pausing occasionally to enquire of a handful of uninterested customers, 'Would you like to hear my new song?' Despite the negative response, this character would launch into one of the songs he claimed to have written himself. It had a somewhat dubious lyric and was based on a real old Soho character who still popped up wherever we were playing, for several years, asking after Jet! She was an elderly Bohemian-looking lady who was very much out of step with the rest of society, I think she went off to Sweden eventually. 'Characters' are often OK in small doses, but they can tend to monopolise the conversation or bore the pants off you, so it's always useful to have your excuses to escape at the ready. The ideal excuse at the 2 Is was the juke box, which not only gave you a neat exit from a long-winded waffler but meant you could also drown out their conversation. The Everlys' *Claudette,* Marty Wilde's *Endless Sleep* or the Four Preps' *Big Man* were three that I played a lot on the juke box there during the summer of '58.

It was by the same juke box that Bruce met Anne Findley.

I fell for Anne seconds after a speaker fell on her. It must have gradually shaken loose from its wall mounting, which wasn't surprising considering the volume of the music down there, and whacked her on the head. Gallant as ever I rushed to the rescue and after a few well-chosen words of commiseration whisked her upstairs to the coffee bar to impress her with my wit and charm over a cardboard cupful of fizzy orange. It must have worked as she revealed all her innermost secrets to me that very evening — very personal soul searching things, like the fact that she worked for a linen company in Bond Street!

Brian with Wee Willie Harris down the 2 Is, 1958

'Licorice' Locking

Hank's first solo spot

Anyway, we started going steady, and in those days you married your steady girlfriend, which meant the awesome task of officially asking her father for her hand in marriage. Gulp! My prospects didn't look terribly good anyway, but when I was confronted with this ex-naval gentleman at his flat in Victoria, they seemed non-existent. I could hardly stand there and say, 'Well, sir, I'm an unknown, starving musician to whom your daughter has been donating two shillings a day to enable me to buy soup and sandwiches; my auntie Sadie occasionally sends me a couple of pounds; I haven't got a house, or a job, and only really own the clothes I stand up in and my guitar!'

With Welch cunning and guile I decided it would be best to wait for the right moment to ask him, or even *create* an opportunity! One came, sooner than I'd expected, when the film *The Battle of the River Plate* came to the cinema in Leicester Square. As Anne's dad was an ex-sailor, I thought he would be suitably buttered up if I took him to see the re-creation of this famous sea battle on the silver screen, then as we came out he'd be so pleased with my thoughtfulness and so overcome with nostalgia that when I asked him if I could marry Anne he'd clap me between the shoulder blades and say, 'Delighted, my boy.' Delighted he wasn't! It was only when we were decanted into the street after *God Save the Queen* that I realised he was crying his eyes out. Apparently he'd served on HMS *Hood,* which sank with all his mates on board, when he'd been on leave, and the picture had brought it all back to him! It would have been a little insensitive to ask him *that* night, so my carefully laid plans went as soggy as Mr Findley's handkerchief. The story had a happy ending, though, when he eventually gave his consent, and we decided to get married the following August.

Another young musician, Brian Bennett, the drummer from north London, had already met *his* future wife at the 2 Is.

I think it was her black stockings and nurse's uniform that first attracted me. In fact, she was the first girl I'd ever really liked. For obvious reasons we'd nicknamed her 'the nurse' and she'd turn up every Tuesday having made the trip across from Kensington. One of my earliest memories of the 2 Is was a guy called Mickie Most, who was working the Coca Cola machine at the time when I became resident drummer down there with the Tony Sheridan Trio, and Jim Sullivan, who played such great guitar that he went on to become one of the top session men in the business.

Without a doubt my drumming technique came from playing

Brian at the 2 Is

Brian with Licorice, 1959

down in Britain's most famous basement every night. At the time I was studying drums with an American teacher called Bruce Gaylor, so I had exercise books full of drum music, which I used to keep by the kit, read and put into practice while I was playing — I was virtually getting paid for learning! Tony Meehan was also becoming a familiar figure at the 2 Is, drumming briefly for the Worried Men. It was a really confusing network of musicians who'd sometimes be playing with several different groups at the same time, and you'd get people rapidly switching allegiance for a few extra pounds in their pocket. Those few pounds were pretty important then, so the scene was ever-changing and I'm sure some of the guys down there forgot who they were currently playing for half of the time! A brief spell in Scotland with a touring band called the Red Peppers, which involved singing, dancing and performing sketches, helped me appreciate the London scene, and it was back at the 2 Is that I teamed up for a while with singer Vince Taylor, who made some minor classics for the Palette label, all of which I played on. In fact they were my very first recordings. We did *Right Behind You Baby, Brand New Cadillac* and two other tracks, all of which were moderately successful in Britain. Vince eventually went off to France, where he really made it big alongside major French artists like Johnny Halliday and Les Chaussettes Noires. My first TV appearance was with Vince, on *6.5 Special* shortly followed by *Oh Boy* with Tony Sheridan which we did every other week opposite Lord Rockingham's XI, backing visiting American singers like Conway Twitty and Brenda Lee, who needed a small, tight musical unit rather than a large orchestra.

The impresario Larry Parnes — 'Mr Parnes Shillings and Pence' as we called him — frequently came on talent spotting missions to the 2 Is, often organising a whole tour on the strength of his findings in the small, dark basement beneath Old Compton Street. Larry used me many a time to help him out by doubling up as compere on a show, but my performance left a lot to be desired: I'd rush on and in my confusion mix up the next artist's name with the last like, 'Thank you, that was great, please show your appreciation for Duffy Gentle and now would you please welcome Johnny Power!'

There was one guy, though, who was secretly pretty pleased at my inability to act as master of ceremonies as it enabled him to get his start in showbusiness. He ventured backstage one night and asked if he could compere, little knowing that some twenty-three years later, after two decades of success, he'd steal the limelight at the Royal Variety Show — to think it could have been me out there doing the announcements instead of Jimmy Tarbuck!

Vince Eager was another singer I backed for a while who started at the 2 Is, and many a night we'd have three different London gigs. We'd start off with a session at the 2 Is from seven till ten, then rush round to another club, Winston's, for ten o'clock and finally dash to Churchill's night club for the 1 a.m. show — it was hectic but fun.

At the time I had a flat in Kensington that I shared with a guy who'd played bass alongside me behind Vince Taylor and Tony Sheridan, and who was eventually to become a member of the Shadows when Jet left — my old mate Licorice Locking, whose real name is Brian but who got the Licorice tag due to an early flirtation with the clarinet, commonly referred to as a 'licorice stick'. Licorice and I were very close, that's why we worked well together, on bass and drums, because, like me, he was a totally dedicated musician and used to practise at least five hours a day. It was never our ambition to be rich and famous, just to be great musicians — that was what really mattered most. But we'd often forget one important point — we still had to eat, and musicians are often apt to forget so we were really grateful to our 'meals on wheels' lady — my Margaret! When Licorice and I moved into a larger flat in Queensgate she was still working for an MP called Philip Goodhart as a children's nurse and when she was off duty would turn up with big juicy steaks which she'd cook for us. There was a bit of a rumpus (not rumpus steak) when Vince Taylor saw these great meals that were being cooked, and there was a heavy scene for a while, after he'd suggested that 'the nurse' should cook for everyone.

The main feeding place for the 2 Is crowd was the Act One Scene One across the road where you could have milk and a dash with cheddar cheese on French bread for half a crown. It was quite posh really, and if we saw any of our lot in there, we knew they must have cracked it, and have some good gigs coming in!

Other establishments frequented by the famous of the future included Russell Quay's Skiffle Club in Greek Street where Hank and Bruce first met Adam Faith, when as Terry Nelhams he was fronting the Worried Men; the Bread Basket, the Top Ten, Chas McDevitt's Freight Train and Chaquito's, where Hank and Bruce would often go through their repertoire as a duo, harmonising on all the Everlys' songs they knew, with Hank demonstrating his ability to play all Buddy Holly's guitar solos note for note. These gigs supplemented the meagre sum they earned working the orange and Coca Cola machines at the 2 Is, which it turned out was even more meagre than it should have been, as Hank realised years later.

Tom Littlewood, who managed the 2 Is, used to pay us eighteen shillings a night. We used to accept it without question, but it turned out that he was ripping everybody off by taking ten per cent commission out of everybody's wages — how mean can you get! Actually he still works in a sandwich bar in Soho — maybe I ought to go round for my pile of florins, although to be honest we were all on the fiddle in a way. Tom foolishly used to work out how much orange had been sold by the number of paper cups that had been used, so it didn't take all us bright sparks who worked the machine very long to come up with a good system for making a little bit of extra cash — we simply got our mates to bring their cups back and we used them again! Come to think of it we probably owe the owner of the 2 Is, Paul Lincoln, some money. Realising that we'd do anything for a few silver coins or a bit of folding green stuff, Paul used to pay Bruce for helping him erect wrestling rings. It nearly killed him, but as Paul wrestled under the name of Doctor Death Bruce rarely complained! Sometimes you really had to be careful who you were talking to, as there were some quite heavy blokes around Soho — in fact, the daughter of one of the most famous gangland characters of the 50s, Jack Spot, used to be part of the 2 Is crowd.

On reflection, it was a pity that the Chesternuts thing didn't work out. Bruce and I would really have liked it to be a successful outfit, especially after Pete's mum had kept us from fading away with malnutrition by feeding us up with poached eggs and crinkly chips! Those crinkly chips really impressed me. I'd never seen anything like them in Newcastle!

Scrimping and saving included the old 'dodging the tube fares' sketch. There were no barriers at Finsbury Park, so we'd just breeze on to the station promising we'd pay at the other end — which, of course, we never did. The tried and trusted 'food on the slate' and 'bus hopping' also helped our financial situation.

Despite the differing opinions of Church leaders, parents, teachers and even some young people who were wary of rock 'n' roll, the new music was clearly here to stay. There was a new harder edge creeping into the charts, and not only via American artists who were genuine rock 'n' rollers as opposed to skifflers. Marty Wilde hit the Top 10 in the summer of '58 with his version of Jody Reynolds' *Endless Sleep*, and Cliff Richard, backed by Terry Smart on drums, Norman

Mitham on guitar and Ian Samwell on bass, was going down a storm at the 2 Is coffee bar. It was there that Bruce first heard Cliff. Hurrying back to their lodgings at Mrs Bowman's after a hectic night working the orange machine he told Hank, 'There was a guy down the Is tonight went down a bomb — he looked a bit like Presley actually.'

It was during the summer of 1958 that they first met Jet Harris, whose bass guitar (one of the first in the country) was heralding the arrival of new-look groups. The makeshift one-string tea-chest bass of 1957 and 1958 had been fairly short-lived, and it now looked as though the popularity of the cumbersome double bass might also be on the wane.

Also during that summer a white-faced youth with a cap perched on his head got up at the 2 Is to have a bash on the drums. Bash? He was only fifteen, but Tony Meehan played like a professional. So it came to pass that during those few months in the middle of the year a group without a name or a leader would often play together down in that Old Compton Street cellar as a four-piece: Hank Marvin, Bruce Welch, Jet Harris and Tony Meehan. Tony remembers it well:

> Those were good days — a Crunchie in the back of the cinema watching Charlton Heston and Yul Brynner in *The Ten Commandments* or *Cat on a Hot Tin Roof* with Elizabeth Taylor, Burl Ives and Paul Newman. Pop films were still a bit on the slushy side and one of the slushiest of 1958 was *April Love* starring Pat Boone and Shirley Jones — as the *Daily Mirror* put it, 'Teenagers' record-romeo Pat Boone sings some pleasant songs which will have you floating in the aisle!'
>
> But us kids who threw caution to the wind sneaked out to buy the controversial book by D.H. Lawrence, *Lady Chatterley's Lover*. Full of jolly rude words, it was even more difficult to conceal in the house than it was to buy!

If Tony's library wasn't expanding, his musical horizons certainly were — one temporary move was to drum with Wally Whyton. Wally Whyton's group the Vipers had had three sizeable hits during 1957 — *Don't You Rock Me Daddy-O* and *Cumberland Gap* both made Number 10 in the chart and *Streamline Train* got into the Top 30 — but no chart success in 1958. As summer rolled into autumn, well over a year since their last hit, the Vipers had a re-shuffle, resulting in Hank and Jet joining the group. Hank lasted a week: 'After seven days in Birmingham I realised I just didn't click,' but Tony Meehan went in on drums.

Another 2 Is regular was singer/guitarist Tony Sheridan, a semi-permanent fixture in the Old Compton Street basement, who was several times to stand at the very brink of the big time, only to be left behind as stardom called to those around him. Tony was later to perform and record with the Beatles in Hamburg before they went on to conquer the world, as well as missing out on becoming a Shadow.

For Hank and Bruce the parting of the ways with the coffee bar that had become like a second home to them was just around the corner, and became reality the day that Cliff's manager came down to the 2 Is to check out Tony Sheridan as a possible guitarist for the Drifters. Cliff was undoubtedly on the way up, but John Foster, his manager, was having problems with his backing group.

> We'd lost the lead guitarist we picked up during our stint at Butlins and desperately needed a replacement. The obvious person to me was Tony, so I caught the bus down from Hertfordshire to London and popped in to the 2 Is to try and track him down. Tom Littlewood, who managed the place, told me that Tony was due in later that afternoon and if I wanted to I could go and wait downstairs. That meant you were really one of the in crowd, if you were allowed to go down into the basement during the afternoon! Eventually a few of the people hanging around had got wind of the purpose of my visit and started offering advice!

Rick Richards suggested a guy from Newcastle who'd impressed him a lot — Hank Marvin and his sidekick Bruce Welch.

> I pushed *both* of them to John Foster, because they were a pair, inseparable. They not only complemented one another on guitars, but they sang great Everly Brothers harmonies. Hank's technique was so good that blokes would sidle up to me and say, 'What sort of guitar is Hank using — it makes a great sound?' And I always gave them the same answer, 'It's not the guitar, it's the guitarist.' As well as recommending Hank and Bruce for the Shadows I also lent my name to Cliff, only he dropped the 's' and made it Richard. And just to confirm what sounds like a tall story, I still have the picture he signed in 1958: 'Rick — sorry I pinched your name — Cliff.' As well as playing down at the 2 Is I was also the unofficial photographer and captured many of the off-stage casual moments of that era, at the coffee bar where it all started.
>
> Ian Samwell — 'Sammy' — called me up one day in a very agitated state. 'I'm sure they're going to get rid of me. I can feel things aren't really working out and I'm positive they're after somebody else to take my place. What shall I do?'

My advice was probably the same that anyone would have given: 'Ask Cliff outright, "Am I in the group or do you want me out?"'

The outcome is history. Ian was to leave the Drifters at the end of the year but stayed long enough to play on Cliff's first two singles *Move It* and *High Class Baby*.

Yeah, I played on those two tracks. I played rhythm guitar on *Move It*, Terry Smart played drums, Frank Clarke was on double bass and Ernie Shears played lead guitar. Frank and Ernie got a six pounds ten shillings session fee each.

It became obvious that Cliff Richard was destined to become a major star, and that meant having the strongest line-up available to support him — which necessitated the departure of Sammy Samwell. However he needn't have worried, as songs with a winning formula for that era were to flow freely from his pen. Classics like *Dynamite, Never Mind, Mean Streak, Fall in Love With You, Gee Whiz It's You* (which he wrote with Hank), added to a string of songs which appeared on what was arguably Cliff and the lads' finest album together, *Me and My Shadows*, must have been more than ample compensation for losing his place in the Drifters. Sammy's finest hour, though, must have been the now legendary tale of how he composed what has become recognised as the first ever genuine rock 'n' roll song written by a Briton — *Move It*, which was born on a Green Line bus from Cheshunt to London. Drummer Pete Chester was another 2 Is regular who went on to write successful songs like *Don't be a Fool with Love, Lonesome Fella, Saturday Dance* (with Hank), *Tell Me* (with Bruce) and *Left Out Again*, the last two again from the *Me and My Shadows* album. Pete's most successful effort was a song he co-wrote with Bruce, *Please Don't Tease*, which held the Number 1 position for Cliff and the Shadows in the summer of 1960.

As well as playing at the 2 Is many of the musicians down there would join together to do one-night stands at other venues. Hank remembers a typical one at Bromley in Kent.

The particular booking was for a trio which comprised me on guitar, Jet on bass and a guy called George Plummer on drums. We were paid such a pittance that after our train fares we were left with one pound each. We often worked one particular London jazz club with the same line up. The place was full of beatniks with tight jeans and black sloppy sweaters — lots of the girls had pony-tails, and an abundance of facial hair seemed to be the order of the day for the guys. Just because we played a lot of rock 'n' roll music and didn't wear sandals they thought we were weird, but we did make some concessions like playing our version of *Swingin' Shepherd Blues* which had recently been a Top 10 hit for the Ted Heath Orchestra.

In September 1958 the music press published an exclusive interview with the guy they described as Britain's biggest teenage rock 'n' roll star, Marty Wilde. His records had sold in vast quantities — *Honeycomb* did 38,000 copies, *Oh, I'm Falling In Love Again* 70,000 copies, *Endless Sleep* 200,000 and his 3,500-strong fan club showered him with teddy bears, chocolates, sweaters and St Christophers. All this was sealed with every 50s rock 'n' roll star's proof of achievement — a 100 mph sports car. Not bad for a guy who a year before had been working in a timber yard for four pounds ten a week.

Although Marty was incredibly talented, his chart career as a rock star was to wane prematurely, as a new idol and his group hit the chart for the first time that very month, and a drummer who was shortly to join Marty eventually played a very important part in the Shadows history.

That same month, Cliff Richard made his small screen debut on ABC TV's *Oh Boy*, for producer Jack Good, and whether by coincidence or design, on the same day the *Radio Times* commented:

> Teenagers these days seem to have become very much a race on their own, and — if we are to believe certain adults — a rather mysterious and alarming race at that. They have their own peculiar clothes, speech, habits and plenty of money to indulge their tastes. One of their more persistent attitudes is a craving for rhythm which leads them to idolise certain pop singers, often as young as themselves, whose records they buy at the rate of a million a week.

A comment pointedly aimed at the likes of Cliff and Marty.

If you were a fan of the stars, chances are you'd be down to the newsagents for a packet of Woodbines, maybe a Palm Toffee bar to chew and the September copy of *Photoplay*, which for one and three pence revealed the secrets of 'Elvis in the Army' along with stories and pictures of your favourite stars, Tommy Sands and Joan Collins. Record shops were selling out of the favourites of the month like Connie Francis's *Stupid Cupid*, the Everly Brothers' *Bird Dog* and Ricky Nelson's *Poor Little Fool*, and the new breed of singers were rubbing shoulders with the old in a very mixed chart that not only took in Max Bygraves, Peggy Lee and Johnny Mathis but also comedians Bernard Bresslaw and Charlie Drake. And to play these hits, you could buy a brand new four-speed record player. If you

Jet obviously pleased with his famous
Framus bass

A pink sports coat and a
white carnation

couldn't afford it outright, then six shillings and fivepence a week for thirty-six weeks would secure it for you.

Laurie Henshaw in the *Melody Maker* reviewed the September new releases and tucked away in the middle was a new 45 by Cliff Richard and the Drifters.

> Cliff Richard makes a promising disc debut with *Schoolboy Crush*. This follows the tortured vocal patterns that seems to be the vogue these days. *Move It* is in the Presley idiom — but it lives up to its title.

Schoolboy Crush was originally intended as the A side, but when Cliff's producer Norrie Paramor took home an advance copy, his daughters raved over the British-written *Move It.*

In the meantime, back on a lonely barstool in the 2 Is, John Foster was still waiting for the arrival of Tony Sheridan when Hank walked in with his guitar, and started to have a twang. John thought he was good.

> He was as good as I'd been told, and although I had my heart set on Tony I would have missed the bus home if I'd hung around any longer, so I offered Hank the tour with Cliff and he agreed to do it if he could bring his mate Bruce along to play rhythm. I took the guys round to a tailor where Cliff was having a fitting for a lurid pink jacket.

> I thought they looked like a real couple of yobs, but John had assured me that this Hank Marvin guy could play like Ricky Nelson's guitarist James Burton, so I reckoned he couldn't be all bad, especially as he bore more than a passing resemblance to Buddy Holly.

> We went back to my place, had a bit of practice and it became obvious that Hank and Bruce were the right guys for the job, so we got ourselves to new Drifters. The 2 Is days were exciting times. We were all really the pioneers of British Pop.

4 / Jet's Story

(1939 — October 1958)

I was born Terence Harris on 6th July 1939 in Kingsbury's Honey Pot Lane maternity ward, where I was immediately turned upside down and smacked. I was the only child of Bill and Winifred Harris and the first home I remember was in Willesden, London N.W.10.

My big musical thing then was Winifred Attwell — I mean when she played boogie that really got me going so much I thought 'I've got to be able to do that', but I never could. I tried clarinet at first, then went on to bass to get a bit nearer boogie. It's not that easy trying to boogie on clarinet.

My parents never actually had the chance to say, 'Terry you're staying in tonight — you're not off out again,' because I kept *myself* in — locked in my bedroom every night. My mother would say, 'What on earth's that boy doing in there?'

I was making my own bass, not just an old tea-chest but my own four-string variety, and then I'd stay in night after night, week after week, just practising. I got involved in music at school, there was me, Peter Newman on saxophone, Ray Edmunds on drums and John Welsh on clarinet, all of us only thirteen or fourteen years old.

Eventually after much begging and pleading to my dad I was able to buy a proper stand-up string bass on the never-never — good old hire purchase that helped so many groups and musicians to get started. My first real instrument cost me £40.

It was hard — my fingers broke out in blisters and bled every time I played, and as I was only five feet seven it wasn't that easy to carry — maybe I should have persevered with the clarinet!

Anyway, I soon discovered, after some uncomfortable experiences on the underground, the best method of transporting a double bass. You tie a piece of rope around the spike at the bottom and the other end to the head and sling it over your back! From behind I looked like a walking bass — this enormous instrument with two little feet sticking out of the bottom.

Many nights Mum, Dad and myself would sit around the radio

and the Ovaltinies' tune would get imprinted in my head while we listened to Radio Luxembourg:

'We are the Ovaltinies, little girls and boys . . .'

There was no television, so radio programmes like *Journey Into Space* and *Riders of the Range* were the king programmes for a kid like me.

My parents were horrified when I said I wanted to earn my living as a musician! It was such an outrageous thing for the time. You work in a factory, you drive a bus, you work in a shop — but you don't become a musician.

I left home when I was about seventeen. Mum was in tears, and kept impressing upon me that there was no future in being a musician, but I had to go off and give it a go.

I went to live in a basement flat in Eccleston Square. I had some great flatmates: Elvis and 'Iggins, who were monkeys; a skunk called Sam who lived under the bed with my dirty socks; and a fox, Sandy, who had his own room in the cellar — at least he kept the floor clean with his brush! It was like a menagerie, and the whole bloody lot of 'em would often get taken on gigs with us!

I was playing double bass around the modern jazz clubs with a Willesden-based jazz trio called the Delinquents. One of the guys was Ray Taylor, I forget who the third member was — but it led to me being invited to join Tony Crombie's Rockets backing Wee Willie Harris. To me Tony was the guvnor — he was *the* jazzman for me.

One day he asked me, 'Have you seen this new invention?' — I said, 'No, what is it?'

'It's a new type of bass only it's shaped like an electric guitar.'

So I became the proud owner of the first bass guitar in the country. There I was on stage every night with this thing around my neck. There were no plectrums for them then, so it was back to the days of blood and blisters — and I thought they'd gone forever.

There were drawbacks to owning the first bass guitar in the British Isles — for a start I used to pluck it like a double bass because I knew no other way, and I was invariably knocked across the stage by electric shocks from the metal fingerplate!!

There were several London clubs we'd frequent and/or play in as well as the famous 2 Is. There was Sam Widges' which was quite near the Palladium; Ches MacDevitt's Freight Train coffee bar; and the Nucleus, where I went one night when someone had discovered pro-plus and preludin or something, and being a teenager and wanting to be 'in' with the crowd I took a whole tube of them. At five shillings a tube it seemed like a good value until they took effect a few

'Jet' Harris (the Vitapoint Kid)

minutes later when I was on stage. My body froze solid and I couldn't move a muscle!

There were the smokers down there too, but people have been smoking pot since time began — it's only the papers that blow it all up.

The Nucleus was in Endell Street, which runs from Long Acre to Shaftesbury Avenue. I'll never forget that because it was near the special clinic! Due to many a liaison with stage-door girls I made five appearances there, and in the end they gave me a membership card. I'm probably immune to penicillin now!

The Wee Willie Harris gigs were more variety than pop — you know, jugglers, acrobats, accordion players, and so on, but at least we were top of the bill.

After that I had a spell bashing the bass behind a guy who's now virtually a millionaire, Page One record label boss Larry Page. He was billed then as 'Larry Page the Teenage Rage'. He was the most awful singer I've ever worked with!

Other artists who were backed by the bass guitar work of Jet Harris were Don Lang, who'd had hits with *Cloudburst* in 1955 and *Schoolday* in 1957 and who regularly appeared on *6.5 Special*, and Terry Dene, famous for his big Top 20 hit for Decca *A White Sport Coat*.

In between times I was earning eighteen shillings a day working the Coke machine at the 2 Is with all the apple strudels and chocolate cake I could eat thrown in or thrown up. At night I'd play with whoever was downstairs in the black hole of Calcutta.

One night I was aware of being watched pretty closely by some guys, one of whom turned out to be the famous Wally Whyton, leader of the Vipers skiffle group. Of course the skiffle craze headed by Lonnie Donegan with its tea-chest bass, guitar and washboard had been very popular during 1957, borne out by the fact that the Vipers had three big hits and Lonnie himself had six. But although skiffle was on the wane, they were a big name earning good money and I jumped at the chance when Wally asked me to join them. The only tracks that went down for posterity with me in the line up were *Liverpool Blues* and *Summertime Blues*. Wally obviously was on the session and as far as *I* remember Johnny Booker and George Van Der Bosch. However, Brian Bird's 1958 publication *Skiffle* (published by Robert Hale) lists the personnel at that time as Wally Whyton, Johnny Martyn and Hank Marvin (guitar and vocals), Jet Harris (bass) and Johnny Pilgrim (washboard). The *Liverpool Blues/ Summertime Blues* session was produced by the man who'd already made a name for himself producing the Goons and other comedy

records, and was to guide the Beatles to great heights years later —
George Martin.

The rest of the story the history books must have related time and
time again. The offer came to join the Most Brothers, Mickie and
Alex Murray, on their British tour headlined by the Kalin Twins,
an American duo who'd just topped the charts with *When,* so I
joined up and found myself trekking around the country on the
same bill as a new young singer from Hertfordshire, Cliff Richard,
and his backing group the Drifters.

I don't think Cliff was very happy with Ian Samwell on bass, so he
asked me to join. Because I was the best bass player around I said I'd
think about it! My mind was made up for me travelling on the coach
to the next town. I opened the music papers and looked at the Top
20 and I saw Cliff Richard and the Drifters — Number 19. I thought,
'Get in there, Jet.' Apart from the success of the act, I could also add
the three pounds a night that Cliff was paying to the four pounds ten
that I was earning with Mickie and Alex. The crunch then came for
the Drifters drummer, Terry Smart, who was leaving to join the
Royal Navy — so I got Tony Meehan in.

To be honest, although they will admit to not being the world's
greatest musicians, I felt terrible for Ian and Terry.

5 / Tony's Story

(1943 — October 1958)

Daniel Joseph Anthony Meehan was born in the workhouse. Well, to be honest, it had already been transformed into New End Hospital, Hampstead well before my arrival into the world.

Actually, it still *looks* like a workhouse — an up-market one though! Well what would you expect, being in that area of London *and* next to Peter O'Toole's house!

Despite being born in London, my family are Irish through and through. My dad, Dan Joseph Meehan, is a Tipperary man and my mother, Mary Ann Donnelly, comes from Carlingford, Co. Louth. Carlingford is situated in the northernmost point of the 'Pale', a stretch of land extending fifty miles south and fifty miles north of Dublin to within three miles of the border. The 'Pale' was the area that the English controlled in Ireland for 500 years, from 1190 until William and Mary's time, and to venture out of the area was to go 'beyond the Pale', which gave rise to the famous expression meaning to go too far.

The Donnellys were a minor clan, but part of the O'Neill sept who ruled the nine counties of Ulster, and related to the great Gaelic warriors, the O'Donnells.

One of their traditions was for the eldest son of the clan chief to be fostered out to a trusted family from the age of twelve until he was eighteen. In those six years the lad would be taught the arts of being a man, which would include things as diverse as fighting and painting. People normally associate Scotland more with clans, but even the Scots clans originally came from Northern Ireland. The first Irish went into Scotland via the Mull of Kintyre about the eighth century. When I was a kid we spoke Gaelic quite a lot during the time I spent in Ireland. We were backwards and forwards between Northern Ireland and London a good deal when I was young; my grandfather had a farm in Co. Louth, and Mum and Dad were in the army in Dublin when they met.

I still remember a lot of Gaelic even now, one of the most common

54

greetings if you're passing someone in the street is 'Bal O Hdia Ar An Obair', which means 'God Bless the Work'.

In 1944 the Germans had a bash at the railway which was just behind us in Kilburn Park, in North London, resulting in our house in Iverson Road being bombed out, and my brother John, who at four was two years older than me, needing plastic surgery for the terrible scars he received. My earliest memories were montages of guns, explosions, uniforms and American servicemen. The six years after the war were more stable for the Meehan tribe; following the virtual destruction of our house, we moved to Cavendish Mansions, West End Lane, West Hampstead, where a third son, Keith, was born to my parents. We stayed there until 1951 when Kevin came into the world to complete a line-up of four boys for Dan and Mary Meehan.

Our next home was still in West End Lane, but in a new block of flats, Sydney Boyd Court, which had been erected on a levelled bomb site.

I went to the local school, Beckford Primary, which had its quota of 'gangs'. You had to belong to a gang, I suppose it was a by-product of the war, but we mainly used to play soldiers and cowboys — anything with guns and fighting. I loved military games, I was into those in a big way. In fact, I'd often spend my shilling pocket money on just two model soldiers; but with real dedication I'd sometimes save up and buy a small toy 'Howitzer' gun which had a ratchet that you pulled back, loaded the barrel with a matchstick and 'pow' down would go a couple of grenadier guardsmen that I'd lined up on the bedroom window sill. To be fair I didn't just 'zap' the British army, I'd stand the American soldiers on my fort and give *them* a taste of my Howitzer too. The models, of course, were all metal, none of your plastic rubbish then — so of course heads, arms and guns often broke off, resulting in the odd burst of tears until you realised that by sticking a matchstick into the headless body, you could leave enough wood showing to perch the head back on your soldier — a little wobbly certainly, but a small wedge of plasticine and he was almost as good as new.

I used to make up the most incredible fantasy games with my troops, which would end up with many a delightful anachronism such as the Cheyenne tribe fighting my Grenadier guards and American soldiers from World War II fending off the Apache in an old cowboy fort. It was to be another nine years before the most important Apache of all entered my life.

We had no television at Sydney Boyd Court, so the treat of the week was the trip to the Grange cinema in Kilburn for Saturday morning pictures, and the old blood and thunder cowboys versus Indians melodrama.

The hubbub from the crowd of excited kids often drowned out the sound of hooves as the good guys led by Roy Rogers or Tex Ritter pursued the bad guys across the range. Licorice was the order of the day for Saturday morning pictures, either straight or 'Allsorts'. Most of my mates almost lived on sherbet, but I could never touch the stuff. I preferred 'Spanish Wood', a sort of chewy stuff with a strange taste. If I spent my pocket money on the pictures and toy soldiers, money for sweets had to be raised elsewhere, so a gang of us used to spend hours going round the streets of West Hampstead collecting paper which we sold to the local scrap merchant. We'd often amass the grand total of tuppence each a day! Money was pretty scarce as the country was still counting the cost of World War II, so necessity really was the mother of invention for me and my mates. We made everything ourselves, we couldn't afford just to walk in to a shop and buy expensive toys, so we'd knock up primitive 'soap-box carts' from old prams, which we, along with kids in most other big towns and cities in the early 50s called 'trolleys'. Makeshift Indian headdresses created from pigeon feathers and a school belt were just as good to us as any that you could buy in the local toy shop, and the odd bits of clothes that our mums sewed together to make cowboy outfits turned us into characters from Kit Carson and Hopalong Cassidy annuals overnight.

Ration coupons were still in existence, so our main diet consisted of chops, mince and eggs done in so many different ways I'm surprised I didn't grow up with a little lion stamped on my forehead.

During the early 50s I spent quite a lot of time with green tabs in my socks chanting 'dib dib dib, dob dob dob' with the 11th Hampstead Scouts, and achieving a whole string of awards. I got badges as a swimmer, athlete, tracker, fire-fighter, path-finder, handyman, life-saver, master at arms, and to cap it all I was patrol leader of the 'Hawks'! Pretty impressive stuff, eh? *And* the scout shirt *still* fits me! I remember a moment in 1953 as being one of the most exciting of my whole life, that was going to a store called Blanks in Kilburn and putting five shillings deposit down on a little drum kit which comprised a cymbal, gong drum and a military snare. The complete price was five pounds, which I was religiously paying off until I came down on Christmas morning 1953 — and there it was, my first drum kit . . . a magic moment!

As if I wasn't busy enough with the scouts, I also switched schools, to Kingsgate Primary where I waded through my eleven plus and a year later, in September 1954, found myself as one of the learned herberts at Regents Park Central School in Lisson Grove, St Johns Wood. The Number 1 song the week I started was Kitty Kallen's *Little Things Mean A Lot*. Musically it was a time when about half a dozen top artists would all cover one song. Alma Cogan, for example, also did a version of Kitty's *Little Things*, and another song that was always on the radio in September 1954 was *Three Coins In A Fountain*. I think that Frank Sinatra's rendition of that just had the edge success-wise over the version by the Four Aces. A great favourite of mine was Frankie Laine's song *Champion the Wonder Horse* and luckily I was not only able to hear it every week as the introduction to the half-hour children's programme of the same name, but when the Hampstead fair was on, it would be blasting out all over the Heath.

My career as a budding Baden-Powell came to a grinding halt when I was fourteen. Our troop was camping at Goudhurst in Kent under an ex-army sergeant who ran the show like a full military exercise, you know, digging latrines, erecting bell tents, doing everything on the double and precisely to the minute, when I realised that my days in khaki were over — I fell in love with the scout leader's daughter! Nothing ever came of it, but it was the prime cause of me hanging up my woggle! I still think the scouts are great and scouting is a great hobby; it's healthy and it teaches you self-preservation and getting on with your fellow human beings.

I started to make some firm friends about this time. There was John Steiner, whose nickname was 'Frog', which turned out to be really ironic as he eventually joined the Israeli navy as a frogman! John, a chap called Tony Kessler and myself formed a skiffle group.

Tony and John played guitars, I played the washboard and my old army side-drum (which eventually got stolen from the 2 Is). We bashed out songs like *Rock Island Line* and *How Long Blues*, and as Tony played harmonica, we did a version of *Hava Nagila*. With John and Tony Kessler being Jewish and me coming from the Emerald Isle, we were undoubtedly the only three-piece, teenage Jewish/Irish skiffle group!

We were good mates, outside the group as well. We used to go camping a lot which was great, as they were a couple of years older than me and both Queen's Scouts! It was a big thing then, to be a Queen's Scout — you were quite a hero among your friends *and* you attended a special jamboree.

During the autumn of 1956 I attended a *lycée* in Paris for a while, but it didn't turn out to be the idyllic vacation that I'd envisaged, as trouble that was brewing in the Middle East eventually spread its tentacles as far as France. Despite President Eisenhower calling on Israel 'not to endanger the Peace', the Israeli forces invaded Egypt, resulting in England and France issuing an ultimatum to both countries to cease hostilities.

Inevitably, the French and the English both became involved. There were riots in Paris, with violent gun battles and vehicles being stopped, turned over and set on fire. Despite the problems in the city, I used to go 'over the wall' at night, braving the barbed wire that had been fixed around the top, to go to bars by myself; I must have been crazy — and only just out of short trousers! At least I wasn't involved in the conflict, but tragically a third of our skiffle group, John Steiner, was killed in action fighting with the Israeli navy.

Back home I started making music again with some special friends, Billy Flynn and Raymond Cleary, with David Rees on stand-up bass. It wasn't a rigid line-up though, I'd play with anyone who could get three chords together on their guitar, and loved to make traditional Irish music.

I'd often play at the Shannon Harpers in Carlton Vale in Kilburn, a club run by a guy called Butty Sugrue who was five feet tall, five feet wide and looked like something out of a medieval circus. His party piece was pulling actual railway engines with a piece of rope . . . held between his teeth! Nobody ever argued with Butty! Once a year they used to put on the 'Puch Fair', a primitive pagan festival where everyone went mad and ended up crowning a goat! We also played Irish songs at Brady's in Kilburn, where I'd join in with musicians of all ages, most of whom were far far older than me, but I'd listened to and absorbed music since I was a little kid so it came naturally to me. My mother was very proud. She used to come along to Brady's and bring her friends to see Daniel Joseph Anthony serving his apprenticeship!

Early in 1957, nearly fourteen and growing up fast, I became more aware of popular songs of the time. I think the two that really grabbed my attention during January and February were *Singing The Blues* and *Don't Knock the Rock*. I saw my first X-certificate film around that time, which might not seem such a big deal now, but during the 50s it was a terribly daring thing to do. If you went to school and told your mates you'd seen an X, you'd be the hero of the hour.

The film was *Love Me Tender*. It was Elvis Presley's first film, and it was only an hour and a half long. During that time Elvis sang four songs — *Poor Boy, Let Me, We're Gonna Move* and the title track — and got himself killed just before the end. Apparently 20th Century

58

Fox thought it was a good idea to have 'the King' die in the film, as adults who hated what he stood for, would subconsciously imagine that he'd really gone! After seeing *Love Me Tender* one critic apparently said, 'Presley is a pied piper who could lead his followers to an end more socially deleterious than their permanent disappearance in a cave.' I don't think my first X film did *me* any harm though!

As I got more interested in the drums, I used to spend whole woodwork lessons making drumsticks — not very artistic I grant you, but very useful and I saved a lot of money.

During 1957, Lonnie Donegan became even more successful, topping the charts with *Cumberland Gap* and *Gamblin' Man/Putting On The Style* and the skiffle craze continued, but the sound that Elvis was spearheading seemed to be sweeping all before it — everyone was buying Elvis records and during the year he made the hit parade with no less than thirteen different songs! As far as my mates and I were concerned rock 'n' roll was American and we assumed that no one was playing that sort of music over here — we were wrong!

One day early in 1958, my friend and fast-improving double bass player Dave Rees came out with what seemed like an outlandish suggestion at the time — going to Soho! Soho! Although it was just three or four miles south of us it was a great adventure for lads the tender age of fifteen, as the streets were full of people of all nationalities as well as villains, gangsters and prostitutes.

Chance brought us down Wardour Street and into Old Compton Street, where I was stopped in my tracks by this incredible noise coming from somewhere under the pavement. It seemed to be coming from a delivery chute, so I stayed to listen to what seemed to be a great record that I'd never heard before. I dragged the other guys to the door, desperate to go inside and listen to this music, but we got a bit of a shock when we realised that we really only looked what we were, naive schoolboys, next to the sophisticated clientele in the coffee bar. There was a guy on the door like Butty from the Shannon Harpers Club, only about a foot taller and six stone heavier! Bravely I asked him what was going on.

'Music.'

'Can we go down?'

'Cost yer.'

'How much?'

'Six bob.'

Six shillings! A fortune!

Somehow we managed to get downstairs, and fought our way through the crowd in the cellar to see what was going on. I was stunned — it wasn't a record, it was a group *and* they were British! I knew that because I recognised the blond bass player, as I'd once got his autograph after a show at the old Metropolitan in the Edgware Road. At that time he'd been playing a double bass, but now he had a guitar with four bass strings on it — my first glimpse of a bass guitar and my second of Jet Harris. The two guitar players with him were Geordies, but they were doing great versions of Everly Brothers songs. They were obviously into music that I liked, and as I'd become a big Eddie Cochran and Gene Vincent fan, I was wearing a cap just like Gene Vincent's Blue Caps wore, and thought that I looked pretty cool. Maybe it was that that gave me the confidence to follow up David Rees' suggestion to 'get up and have a go.' Not only was it the first time I'd ever seen a British rock 'n' roll group, but they actually agreed to me playing a couple of numbers with them!

None of us knew of course, that this temporary line-up including a fifteen-year-old schoolboy who'd come to Soho for a daring day out would one day top charts around the world and become the most famous group in Britain. That was the first time that Hank, Bruce, Jet and myself played together — in that dark, dingy cellar of the 2 Is. My fleeting appearance led to a couple of offers from guys who turned out to be conmen offering me the promised land, before I was offered the job as house drummer for fifteen shillings a night.

I raced off hot foot to my headmistress and told her I'd been offered a job playing drums in a Soho club, was it possible to take six months off? To my surprise, she said 'Yes.' I never went back.

Although I had some money in my pocket, and was doing what I loved best, I still lugged my drums around in improvised hat boxes. Night after night, I backed Mickie Most, Rick Richards, Wee Willie Harris, Vince Taylor, Vince Eager and Adam Faith, so I had to play every kind of music.

It was Rick Richards who actually offered me the job in the first place, so I have a lot to be thankful to him for. He did great versions of Hank Williams songs! It sounds rather glamorous, but I did have a personal helper, in the shape of a Russian duke who'd carry my drums for me. I had a vague idea why he lavished a lot of attention on me, but I didn't keep still long enough to find out! After I'd been playing at the 2 Is for a while I started backing Cliff Richard on some of his recordings for radio shows, which was a little awkward, as Cliff's drummer Terry Smart was also a great pal of his — a delicate situation! Although Sunday night was a scheduled work night for me down in the cellar, I never actually performed as I used to pay another drummer to sit in for me while I nipped off to six o'clock mass at St Patrick's church in Soho Square! Towards the end of 1958 the job with Cliff became permanent and I was Tony Meehan — Drifter.

Jet obviously not pleased with his famous Framus bass

Meehan with a few friends who dropped round

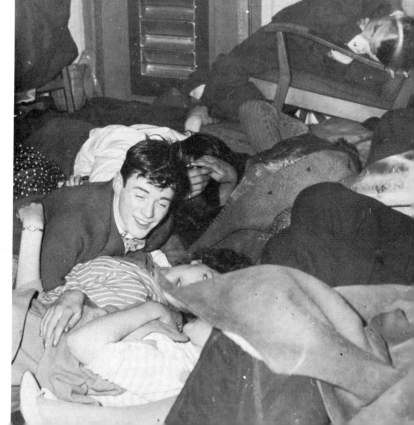

6 / *Drifting into the Shadows*

(October 1958 — Summer 1960)

Cliff and the Drifters' tour with Hal and Herbie, the Kalin Twins, and the Most Brothers, Mickie and Alex Murray, kicked off on 5th October 1958 at the Victoria Hall, Hanley, the same day that Her Majesty the Queen unveiled the Brookwood Memorial and Eamonn Andrews was on the radio confessing which discs he'd take with him if he was stranded on a desert island. Needless to say *Move It* wasn't among them!

Not only radio, but television and newspapers were slowly becoming aware of the popularity of rock 'n' roll music with the teenagers, but it was still condemned out of hand by most of the media 'establishment' and given very little exposure. It would be years before pop music was given national press coverage, with the exception of sensationalism when a personality had been killed or gangs of youths had rioted after a concert. Teenagers didn't want to be subjected to *Workers' Playtime* and *Mrs Dale's Diary* on the radio, nor did they care which cat was the grandmother in the Kit-E-Kat commercial or whether Philips stick-a-soles really did double the life of their shoes. They wanted rock 'n' roll, loud, and lots of it, and Cliff Richard and the Drifters gave it to them.

Hank's guitar technique was coming on by leaps and bounds. So much so that the Kalin Twins asked him to play lead with Eddie Calvert's group who were providing their backing. At the end of the tour Hank and Bruce went back to the Chesternuts, and Jet went back to the Coke machine and apple strudels at the 2 Is. Ian Samwell had decided to stop playing and concentrate on writing and Terry Smart was toying with the idea of vacating his drum stool and joining the Navy. Cliff made his radio debut on the BBC's *Saturday Club* on 25th October 1958, introduced by Brian Matthew. The programme had only had the new name of *Saturday Club* since 4th October, having previously been *Skiffle Club*. On the same bill between ten and twelve that Saturday morning were Lonnie Donegan and Alex Welsh, 'folk, skiffle and spasm music from Glasgow', a spot delightfully named 'Cats Call' and 'disc stars' listeners had requested. The two-hour show

Bruce, Terry Smart, Unknown, Ian Samwell, Hank 'Pretty Boy' Marvin

Hank obviously pleased with his Autoria. Bruce not pleased
with his Clifton

was sandwiched between *Uncle Mac's Children's Favourites* and school quiz programme *Top of the Form.*

Move It hit the number 2 spot in early November and while it was still well placed in the charts EMI released the follow-up, *High Class Baby*, featuring the same line-up as *Move It* — Terry Smart, Ian Samwell, Ernie Shears and Frank Clark — as it had been recorded before Ian's departure. Terry Smart did decide to call it a day and join the Merchant Navy, leaving the way clear for Jet, Bruce and Hank to suggest their mate Tony Meehan as drummer.

In January 1959, audiences at the Free Trade Hall Manchester witnessed Hank, Bruce, Jet and Tony all playing on stage together officially for the very first time, unaware of what the future would bring, but in a way not really caring as long as they were enjoying themselves — and backing Cliff they certainly were. The singer was pretty impressed:

> They all seemed to click together and for the first time I felt that the group up there on stage with me sounded right. Sadly there had to be a degree of ruthlessness in getting Ian and Terry out of the group which was extra difficult because they were mates, but what really happened was a natural progression. I suppose it would have been easy for us — a bunch of teenagers — to let the whole thing go to our heads, but the Shadows always handled the situation pretty well, which was amazing considering there were no footsteps to follow in like artists had in years to come. There were no guidelines for a lot of things we were doing, so we were virtually the pioneers of British rock 'n' roll. There was only really Marty Wilde, Billy Fury, the Shadows and myself, and that was it — there was no one to use as a yardstick and no one for us to be big time to really.

Hank thought the biggest show-off of all at the time was a monkey called Elvis.

> Jet's flat mate, Johnny Booker of the Vipers, had a big old American car and had agreed to drive us to some one-nighters in the London area. The first of these was in Slough. Our rendezvous was outside the Freight Train coffee bar in Soho, where I turned up wearing my new Ivy League jacket and trousers, thinking I was really cool. We soon discovered that the car boot wasn't big enough to take all of the equipment, so some of it had to go inside. As I leant in to put my amplifier on the back seat, a small, scrawny but thankfully caged monkey exploded into action and screamed at me, no doubt suggesting where the amplifier should go. 'What's

The Sex Pistols of 1958

The Drifters singing *Feelin' Fine. Oh Boy,* 1959

this?' I asked Johnny. 'That is Elvis.' After a few heated words it became clear that if Elvis didn't go, neither did we, so I said I'd have him on my lap in the back seat. He soon calmed down, and after a few miles I got the impression that he was quite taking to me. I felt a warm feeling spread over me — unfortunately it was also a very wet feeling. Elvis had peed. Hemmed in by amplifiers and unsympathetic comedians, I had no choice but to endure the wisecracks and my increasingly clammy clothing.

I was so angry about the state of my new clothes that at Slough I sought my revenge and in the dressing-room gave Elvis a taste of his own medicine. With great satisfaction I peed all over him. At least it was a new variation on the man bites dog story. Immediately I'd finished I was stricken with remorse and felt really sorry for the bedraggled little creature. He looked so helpless it had a profound and lasting effect on me, and to this day I have never again peed on a monkey.

Jet had problems with Elvis too, as more often than not he was at his flat.

We were in Worcester one night and Carol, my girlfriend, called me in a state of panic. 'Oh my God,' she said, 'you must come back at once.' Guessing that at least World War III had started or they'd decided to resume World War II I rushed back to find her distraught and screaming 'Elvis is up the drainpipe!' at me. He somehow wriggled up that drainpipe for five storeys, eventually emerging triumphant on the roof where he sat chattering for hours, refusing to budge, and screaming abuse at people. Gorilla warfare had nothing on Elvis.

In the first two months of 1959, Cliff's third single *Livin' Lovin' Doll* was released featuring Jet, Hank, Bruce and Tony, whose playing impressed producer Norrie Paramor so much that he arranged a record deal for them with Columbia, a move which Cliff wholeheartedly encouraged.

Although he had written Cliff's first two successes, *Livin' Lovin' Doll* was not one of Ian Samwell's songs, but he did come up with a number called *Feelin' Fine* which, with a Peter Chester composition *Don't be a Fool with Love* on the B side, became the Drifters' first single release in February, and to this day Hank is able to recall the sales figures.

I can never remember whether it sold eleven or twelve copies, anyway it cleverly avoided detection by the discerning record buyers, leaving us with a 'miss' record. To be honest it wasn't *that* good. I think if we'd *just* been the Drifters it might have brought us down a bit, but we were playing very much as a team with Cliff, so it didn't seem to matter that much; if it had been a hit it would have just been a bonus. It wasn't all glamour though — life on the road *was* a lot of fun, but it had its seedier side, like the night we played the Victoria Hall at Hanley. It was a bit of nostalgia for Bruce and myself 'cause that's where we'd first played with Cliff the previous October, but this time my digs for the night were several miles away from the gig (now that's organisation for you!) and I had to share a room with Tony and a guy called Dave. Dave's dad was the official guy who stood outside the theatre as the queues formed and yelled, 'Get your pictures of the stars here!'; 'Exclusive pictures of singing sensation Cliff Richard!'; 'Action shots of the Drifters — only a few left' — and Dave used to help him. Tony and I, like the decent, clean-living chaps we were, had retired early after the gig that night and were both slumbering away peacefully when the tranquillity only found in the land of nod was shattered by Dave, who'd ignored the door handle and crashed into the room the hard way. He'd virtually drunk himself senseless as he hadn't got a clue what he was doing and for several agonising minutes blundered around the room like a bull elephant on its last legs, until he collapsed in a heap somewhere near his bed.

We didn't notice the smell for ten minutes. At first we put it down to flatulence but half an hour later Tony said, 'It's getting worse, the rest of me is fast asleep but my nose is wide awake. I'm going to put the light on!'

We both wished he hadn't!

Dave lying unconscious on the floor was the very last thing we noticed — he'd been sick in the sink, on the bed, under the bed, over himself, over my bed, and horror of horrors he'd been to the toilet in more ways than one, literally everywhere! If Tony and I had had the presence of mind we'd have notified the *Guinness Book of Records* of our intended attempt on the world 'getting dressed' record. We got out so fast we felt like a couple of firemen who'd heard the alarm, and we were still putting our clothes on as we escaped into the pure, clean air of a Staffordshire dawn. We now faced a several mile plod to get back to the Victoria Hall. I felt sorry for Tony, he was only sixteen and struggling along with his bags, so I foolishly offered to carry them for him as well as mine, to which he agreed — and he didn't even offer me a tip as we came upon the theatre just as it was getting light. I helped shove him in through a fanlight so he could open the door, and we could have a couple of hours sleep until the coach arrived.

When Dave turned up at the rendezvous point the next morning he rounded on Tony and myself. 'Thanks for running out on me, guys, fine mates you are!' We just stood there open-mouthed, I mean he wasn't even embarrassed or apologetic, and when we got around to asking him what on earth the landlady had said, he really took the wind out of our sails. 'Oh I told her that you two made all the mess!' Our reply to this comment will be printed separately under plain cover.

One night in Manchester John Foster and Cliff were really stuck for a place to stay and had to sleep at the YMCA, but when there were no digs to be found it was all down to alternative accommodation — even for Cliff.

We'd invariably stay in the old Bedford coach if we couldn't find any rooms, so if anyone asked us where we were staying we'd say, 'Oh, in the Bedford actually,' and of course they thought it must be a posh hotel.

It was quite a long while before we got organised with proper accommodation on tours, basically because we just didn't realise in our naivety that it could be done very differently.

For a couple of years it was standard practice to disperse and look for the best boarding house deals as soon as we got to the next town. Jet would come back and say, 'I've found some digs for thirteen shillings but they're really near the theatre,' only to find Bruce or Hank had located a boarding house for ten and six a night *plus* a full breakfast of bacon and eggs There hadn't really been many acts touring Britain with an entourage in the way we were, and at first we were really making up our own rules as we went along. I suppose really we were laying the first shaky foundations for all future tours. Despite our thrift, the Drifters were also very generous lads. Many times I'd see them tossing coins out of the coach window, just to see passers-by scrabbling on their hands and knees to pick up the money before someone else got to it!

Although the Drifters' first allegiance was to Cliff, it was generally felt that if they were releasing their own singles as well, it would be a good idea to have a manager of sorts, which is how Ian Samwell became co-ordinator of the group's affairs early in 1959.

There wasn't really very much for me to do, as they were working with Cliff most of the time. My contribution was really very minimal, but I did organise the publicity side of things. To be honest, the best advertisement for the Drifters was the fact that they played not just as a backing group but as a team, with a successful singer who was having hit records, and it was initially because of that that I managed to get some good newspaper coverage. There was a young lady from Leeds . . . I know it sounds like the start of a limerick, but she posted herself to Cliff, and when this large box was delivered backstage at one of the gigs out popped this Yorkshire lass. She turned out to be a really nice girl, to whom I had to give ten out of ten for ingenuity, so as a way of thanking her for her effort I arranged to bring her to London and pay for her to stay at a top hotel, which *Valentine* magazine picked up on and did a nice little story.

Around that time, most of the group, and the rest of the world it seems, lived, or claim to have lived, at 100 Marylebone High Street and as Bruce remembers the size of the place it's apparent that the flat possessed some of the qualities of Dr Who's Tardis.

It had three bedrooms, a kitchen and a lounge and I think originally it was Cliff and John Foster's flat, but those two likeable chaps Hank and I somehow wormed our way in. We normally ate at the Wimpy Bar down the road, but when we stayed in someone would hastily prepare a delightful meal of tea and biscuits — which was our staple diet! Food wasn't that important, but getting about was, so we all bought scooters, although Hank didn't have too much luck with the black 125 Lambretta that he bought in Battersea and drove back for the very first time through the London traffic! He nearly made it, but being over-keen stopped abruptly in Marylebone High Street when the traffic lights were at amber and the car behind re-arranged the shape of his new pride and joy!

With his 125 back in shape Hank set off one sunny day for a spin with Jet — to Birmingham and Manchester.

Jet had Carol on the back and I was solo, but despite having the lighter load, my engine seized up and the back wheel locked solid — so I eventually traded it in for a Lambretta 175 with a big flashy aerial on the back.

It was wonderful driving then, as there were no parking meters, no traffic wardens and you could park right outside wherever you wanted to go. I thought I looked pretty impressive in my silver helmet and goggles, but Jet always reckoned I looked like a tortoise!

John Foster remembers the flat being over-run with singers like Billy Fury and Dickie Pride who often used to drop round.

One of our favourite games was cowboys. Believe it or not, we got a load of toy guns and we'd spend hours being utterly juvenile and playing cowboys and Indians. It sounds daft now, but we all used to play, even Cliff.

Cliff also remembers the popularity of that flat.

John and I actually had the flat, but some mornings I'd go into the living room and it'd be littered with bodies. You never knew who was going to be there, but they were good times. It was such a pity there had to be casualties like Ian Samwell, Terry Smart and John Foster — it would have been really great if we could all have grown together, but it wasn't to be and it's a real drag only bumping into them at functions where you never have time to chat properly.

In May Cliff made his screen debut in the film *Serious Charge* with such eminent folk from the acting world as Anthony Quayle, Andrew Ray and Sarah Churchill. It was also a first for the Drifters. Although not featured personally in the picture, they recorded an instrumental called *Chinchilla* for the sound-track.

The following month Jet took the plunge and married his girlfriend Carol Ann DaCosta.

I met Carol in the bar at Finsbury Park Empire. She'd come to see the new craze — Cliff Richard and the Drifters. I remember thinking, 'She's pretty,' then I found myself walking over and asking her if I could see her the next day. She said 'Yes' and that was it. We got married at Hounslow West Church and the best man was fifty per cent of the comedy duo Dailey and Wayne who'd been appearing on the same bill as us. I think Wayne was actually the best man but I thought about starting a trend that didn't get off the ground, by having them both as best man. Well it's different!

Cliff and Tony were on holiday in Spain but Hank and Bruce were at the wedding. We fought our way out past hundreds of kids who were screaming, shouting and taking pictures, and took off for an exotic couple of days in Grimsby!

Two months later, at 3.30 on August 29th 1959 a seventeen-year-old lad full of mixed emotions stood in front of the altar at St Stephens Church, Westminster. On Bruce's left arm was his bride-to-be Anne Findley and on his right the best man, Cliff Richard. Outside in the street there was a riot going on, with hundreds of fans trying to catch a glimpse of their idols, but the bridegroom's happiness had been tempered by the discovery of his illegitimacy when he had tried to

Jet telling the boys how pleased he is with his famous Framus bass

obtain his birth certificate a couple of weeks before, and the bitterness it brought with it was to dog Bruce Welch for years to come. Directly after the service the Shadows and Cliff had to rush down to the BBC's riverside studios to record *Drumbeat* — not much of a honeymoon for Bruce, the first night of which he shared with Hank.

> Anne and I had only been in bed for a short while when there was an almighty battering on the door and it sounded like a real emergency, but when I flung the door open there was Hank grinning like mad, hanging on to his girlfriend Billie and gleefully announcing, 'Sorry Bruce — forgot my key!' Some start to a honeymoon!

Encouraged by Cliff and Ian Samwell, Hank, Bruce and Jet started writing more following the release of *Feelin' Fine* which resulted in one number of Jet's, *Jet Black*, and one of Hank's, *Driftin'*, being included on Cliff's first LP recorded in front of a live audience at Abbey Road studios. Whilst *Driftin'* tore along at a great rate of knots, *Jet Black* was unique in as much as Jet's bass guitar was the lead instrument.

> I felt like a million dollars standing up on that stage at Abbey Road with my bass and blond quiff. I think I was too busy looking at all the girls down at the front in their 'A-line' dresses, I think they were called, to concentrate properly on what I was playing.
>
> I'd written *Jet Black* on the coach on the way to a gig in Grimsby, but when we came to re-record it for our second single, as the live version wasn't really good enough, it took over ninety attempts to get it right!
>
> We'd also run into a problem in the States, as the American Drifters had slapped an injunction on us to prevent us from using their name, forcing the record company to withdraw *Feelin' Fine* only two days after its release.
>
> So when *Jet Black* came out over there, we went under the name of the Four Jets, but that wasn't a permanent solution to the name problem as it would have created all sorts of chaos: 'Which one's Jet?' 'He's Jet.' 'No I'm Jet.' 'Only one of us is Jet.' 'We're all Jets really.' . . . With a combination of the American situation, Cliff's runaway success (*Living Doll* had by now sold over one million copies in Britain alone) and a bit of nudging from Norrie, we set about finding a permanent name, which arrived out of the blue one summer's day in July 1959 when Hank and I took off on our scooters up to the Six Bells pub at Ruislip.
>
> Jet and I were prepared for one of those three-hour long

discussions that you always have when trying to choose a group name, but we were aware that it had to fit in with the mood of the time and style of music as well as fitting in with Cliff's name.

Had it been 1963 we'd probably have come up with 'The Tynebeats' or something and in the psychedelic era we might have thrown up something like 'The Golden Egg Timers of Venus', but luckily Jet hit upon a name straight away. 'What about the Shadows?' The lad was a genius!

So we became the Shadows for the first time on Cliff's sixth single, *Travellin' Light,* and with our brand new name were keen to release another single ourselves.

I half remembered a good song that I'd written with Pete Chester called *Saturday Dance.* Well, I had the tune in my head but I couldn't remember the words. Luckily when I called Pete he still had them, and sent a copy over. We rehearsed a lot on the roof of Shepperton Studios during the shooting of Cliff's second film, *Expresso Bongo,* in which we made a fleeting appearance, mingling with stars like Laurence Harvey and Sylvia Syms.

Our first trip abroad was to Scandinavia and Germany, on an EMI promotion tour to plug Cliff's records. The only disappointment of the tour was Tony's absence or under the circumstances, Tony's abscess, as he was rushed into hospital to have his appendix out. But we took a very capable replacement, a young guy called Laurie Jay. It was only when we turned up at the airport that we all realised that none of us had ever flown before! We were still rehearsing *Saturday Dance* and the intended B side, *Lonesome Fella,* like mad, and still touring Britain with Cliff in an old coach.

Cliff takes up the story:

The Shadows and I had a driver at the time called Joe Lee, who, apart from being lumbered with dragging us lot around the country, owned a transport cafe on the A3, and had to put up with us singing our heads off to our current favourite records, one of which was Jerry Keller's *Here Comes Summer.* Now Joe knew that the Shadows were writing songs, and that we did quite a lot of our own material, so that, combined with the fact that he was not particularly aware of the Top 20, led him to believe that when we sang *Here Comes Summer,* we'd written it for him! It was crazy, everytime we sang it he'd beam all over his face and tell us what a great bunch of guys we were! It took a while to dawn on us that one of the lines in the song was 'We'll meet the gang at Joe's Cafe' and he assumed it was a number we'd written for him, with his transport cafe in mind! We didn't have the heart to tell him otherwise.

Joe Lee owned and drove the old Bedford coach which normally lived outside his place in Surbiton, and all of us remember it as being very draughty and very slow, especially as there were no motorways. It was always loaded down and someone would always want to stop every five minutes. We were forever chanting the magic words 'Tea Tea Tea' and poor old Joe would have to find yet another transport cafe. Len Saxon, who was my personal assistant and organised the stage lighting at shows, was often on board with us, and would help us humping our equipment which at the time comprised three guitars, three amplifiers, a drum kit and seven or eight suitcases.

The Grade Organisation eventually assigned Sid Maurice to them. He soon impressed the lads with his tales of the States and being on the road with Chuck Berry.

The often used pop star cliché of the 50s sent up so delightfully by Peter Sellers in the guise of teenage idol Twit Conway — 'Er, I wanna become an all round entertainer' — took another step nearer reality in December 1959 when Cliff and the Shadows appeared at the Stockton Globe in the pantomime *Babes in the Wood*.

A few weeks later Cliff and the Shadows were due to fly to the States, but while they were in Stockton a hitch developed when Jet crashed the car late one night, fracturing his shoulder which temporarily put him out of action. Jet's wife Carol was hurt and Hank was injured too, appearing on stage with one of his lenses blacked out and a plaster over his left eyebrow.

Fortunately Jet and Hank healed up sufficiently for the tour to go ahead, but they still had the prospect of re-living the accident all over again in the magistrates' court a couple of months later.

As well as the downs there were the ups, as Hank had his eye on a young Stockton dancer.

She was like a slightly rougher version of the late Grace Kelly, or was it Gene Kelly and I became quite friendly with her, but Cliff had also been giving her the eye. He really was a gentleman, though, and didn't go steaming in and beat me to it, which he obviously could have done, but approached me very politely and asked me whether I minded if he asked her out! How could you refuse such a genuine bloke, so sensing a deal I said, 'Sure, go ahead, but fair exchange is no robbery — can I borrow your car for the night?' — which meant that he couldn't take her anywhere, and as it was a flashy little two seater Sunbeam Alpine it would have impressed her no end. But he agreed and I shot off to Newcastle with Del, Cliff's driver, to show off to my old friends.

Stockholm 1961

Jet obviously pleased with
his hat. New York, January
1960

Snappy dressers! 'On tour' in the
States with the Greyhound bus

Cliff was really a very kind person even then, he had impeccable manners and would never have dreamed of hurting anybody's feelings.

In America Cliff and the Shadows were booked to appear on a *Biggest Show of Stars 1960 Winter Edition* alongside singers like Sammy Turner, Frankie Avalon, Bobby Rydell, Freddy Cannon and Johnny and the Hurricanes. The Boeing 707 touched down a few minutes before nine o'clock on the evening of January 18th with Hank, Jet, Tony, Bruce, Cliff's dad Roger, and his manager Tito Burns on board. Ahead of them lay the excitement of their first American tour and appearances on network TV programmes with Perry Como and Pat Boone. The first of the one-night stands meant a trip to Montreal on a coach so packed with stars that Tony couldn't believe it.

We were soon chatting with them all like they were old friends — it was great! The journey to Canada was long overnight haul, but well worth it when we saw the Forum, the ice hockey stadium, with 7,000 people packed into it — I reckon they were packed tighter than the ice! By the time we were due on I'd got through my third packet of cigarettes in four hours, but all the nerves went as we tore into *Forty Days* as an opener, and followed it with *Willie and the Cha-Cha, Living Doll, My Babe* and *Whole Lotta Shakin'*. The crowd reaction was amazing considering we were complete unknowns to them, they nearly brought the stadium down!

In the deep south, though, we came across the colour question, which created problems, as both our compere and our American road manager were black. We thought the two guys were great because they refused to let it upset them, and while he was in Norfolk, Virginia, Cliff announced that he'd never record in the States because the Musicians' Union wouldn't allow him to use his own group.

Bruce also remembers the song they used to sing over and over again on those Greyhound trips.

I was The Little Dippers' *Forever.* It had a grand total of eleven words:

> 'Hold me, kiss me,
> Whisper sweetly,
> That you'll love me
> Forever.'

We'd naturally sleep on the Greyhound bus throughout the morning and the afternoon, as it sped across the States at what seemed like the incredible speed of 85 mph! We visited Oklahoma City, Fort

Worth and the site of the famous battle at the Alamo where the names of the heroes who died fighting the Mexican Army are inscribed in plaques on the walls. There's Davy Crockett, Jim Bowie and twenty-eight Englishmen, although I reckoned one of them must have been Irish because when I went to the toilet at the bottom of the list it said 'Kilroy was here'!

During our brief stay in Minneapolis a magazine in a shop window caught my eye! It had the intriguing title of *Did the Devil send Elvis Presley?* which sounded so funny I had to go in and buy a copy, but what I didn't know was that the shop also sold nude pin-up books. I was immediately pounced upon by the owner who threw me out for being under age! He didn't realise I'd had my fill of nude books behind the bike sheds at Rutherford Grammar — and I never did find out whether the Devil sent Elvis Presley.

On the flight back from the States Ian Samwell, who was still acting as their manager on any non-Cliff ventures, was with them.

I sat next to Hank, and we had the guitars out just strumming quietly to ourselves, when one of the air stewardesses came down the gangway and asked us how we went about writing a song, so we said, 'We'll show you' and wrote an instant song for her there and then.

> 'Who's that walking down the street,
> Picking up her pretty little feet,
> Who's the one that catches my eye
> Every time that she walks by . . .
> Gee whiz it's you . . . . . .'

It was finished in ten minutes, found its way on to the *Me and My Shadows* album that summer, and got to Number 4 as a single the following spring!

On their return, Jet and Hank had to face the music of the aftermath of their car crash. Jet denied driving a car dangerously but admitted failing to display 'L' plates and driving unaccompanied by a qualified driver. Hank and the tour manager Mike Conlin were found guilty of aiding and abetting Jet, and were fined three pounds each.

Jet cheekily asked the chairman of the magistrates if he could pay half of his imposed fine of thirty-five pounds five shillings in court and the other half over the next two weeks. The startled magistrate, aware of who Jet was, expressed surprise that he didn't have a lot of money, as the group had only just come back from an American tour. Jet's reply stopped him in his tracks. He said, 'I spent a lot!'

During the spring tour of Britain the Shadows encountered

singer/songwriter Jerry Lordan, a meeting that was to accelerate their success dramatically. Travelling between towns Jerry would pass the time by picking out tunes on his ukulele and one day he played one that lured Hank away from his seat on the coach.

That was a good tour for us because not only had we got proper hotels organised for the first time, but Jerry Lordan played me a tune that he'd written called *Apache*. Even on his ukulele it sounded like a hit, and although he warned us that Bert Weedon had already recorded a version of it, it seemed he hadn't released it as a single, so we decided to record it. So it was back to Abbey Road with hope in our hearts, Cliff sitting in on Chinese drums and a suggestion from Norrie that we ought to get a proper manager who would be capable of handling us full time. Peter Gormley already managed fellow Australian Frank Ifield so his pedigree seemed pretty good, but nevertheless Jet and I went round to his flat to play him *Apache* and have a chat. We both agreed that Peter was the right man for the job and he in turn liked our single, although Jet was a little cautious and suggested a year's trial to see how things worked out. Peter told us that he needed more of a long term view, pointing out that he was not in the business to make a quick buck. And he really meant it, in fact we worked together for years without even signing a contract!

He bluntly told us that we weren't matinee idols and needed to get a career organised, develop the songwriting aspect of our talents and draw up a plan to make it in other countries. This was the sort of guy we needed!

With Peter at the helm things started to look good, but there was a small cloud on the horizon as it looked as though Jet would be called up to do his National Service.

I didn't fancy square bashing and polishing my boots every morning, and I was quite sure that a *real* sergeant major would make even Bruce look gentle and sweet natured, so armed with some advice from a friend, I set out to fail my medical! I drank a bottle of gin the night before, which was supposed to produce similar symptoms to sugar diabetes, and swallowed rolled-up balls of chewing gum which would show up on the X-ray as ulcers. When I took my seven and a half stone body to see the doctor the following morning, he looked at me wide eyed and said, 'Good heavens you're thin, and what's that on your head? Is it a wig?'

Not wishing to rub him up the wrong way in case he saw through my ploy for avoiding conscription I was ultra polite. 'No, sir, it's my hair,' I said. Anyway the trick worked and there were no bullets for me — at least not for a while!

Apache was released in July 1960 amid EMI advertisements adorned with drawings of Indians and cowboys with arrows through their hats, yelling the song title as a word of warning.

The EMI publicity boys had gone to town on one advert that had no doubt been inspired by 'Little Plum — Your Redskin Chum' from the *Beano*. It read, 'Hold on to your scalps! Here come the Shadows with their heap big hit *Apache*.'

It was the first of many feathers in their caps.

7 / *Apache to Kontiki*

(Summer 1960 — October 1961)

On Wednesday 20th July 1960, Hank, Bruce, Jet and Tony fought over the NME Chart to see if the excitement *Apache* was causing was reflected in the charts.

There were four new entries that week. Valerie Masters' *Banjo Boy*, the King Brothers' *Mais Oui, Because They're Young* by Duane Eddy and *Apache*, which was in at 19. They'd done it! But that was just the beginning. That same week Cliff took Bruce's *Please Don't Tease* to Number 1, where it stayed while the Shadows crept up to Number 7, then 5, then a three place rise to Number 2. They finally deposed their singer in the middle of August.

Their success raised the question of whether Cliff would now be featuring the Shadows more in his act, or replacing them with a lesser known group while the lads became an entirely separate entity.

All thoughts of replacing them were dispelled by Cliff, underlining, as he always had done, that he and the Shadows were a team and that's the way it would always be, but they had taken a joint decision that if they followed *Apache* with another hit they would earn their own spot on Cliff's bill as well as backing him during his, although he wisecracked, 'All right, if this happens again you'll have to go,' to which a grinning Jet replied, 'If this ever happens again we'll have to find a new singer . . .'

The boss of the company that published *Apache*, Bert Corri of Francis, Day and Hunter, celebrated by giving a special lunch for the lads and Jerry Lordan at Kettners Restaurant in Soho, just a stone's throw away from the 2 Is where it all started, but a far cry from having to borrow half a crown to buy some bread and cheese. Equally delighted with their success, Norrie Paramor and his wife Joan threw a beer and bangers party at their home in Hampstead, inviting the Shadows, Cliff, Jerry Lordan, Frank Ifield and musical director Geoff Love.

The Shadows' chance of having a hit with *Apache* in the States was thwarted by Danish guitarist Jorgen Ingmann. Ingmann had already

The Shadows sing (?) *All My Sorrows*

'A proud moment'. A gold disc for *Apache* presented by Norrie,
watched by Brian Matthew

recorded his new A side *Echo Boogie* and was looking for a B side when he discovered a white label record with just the word 'Apache' written on it. Not knowing where it had come from or whose it was, he recorded it. It turned out so well that it was made the A side, and with a tremendous promotional campaign by his US record company, became a monster hit for him in America.

On Wednesday 24th August the Shadows gave the first live radio performance of *Apache* on the BBC's lunchtime radio series *Parade of the Pops*. Committed to a long season at the London Palladium in *Stars in Your Eyes* with Cliff, Russ Conway, Joan Regan and Edmund Hockridge, they only had Sundays free to play elsewhere, with or without Cliff. At one Sunday concert they did in Blackpool Hank decided to have his own personal celebration for *Apache*.

> We caught the overnight sleeper, and we had a few beers to celebrate, and then a few more in the morning before tucking into breakfast in a local cafe. Even more glasses of beer passed our lips soon after we got to the theatre when the programme seller, Jack, insisted on treating us at one of the big hotels on the front. We had beer after beer until I suddenly realised that I was totally smashed. That's when I made the mistake of going to buy a present for a girl-friend. I staggered into a shop on the sea front with a veil of ale over my eyes and had a look around, but seeing nothing (literally) I reeled and lurched into the next shop. I thought I was going mad — there was the *same* assistant in the second shop. *Convinced* I was going mad I lurched into a third shop, looked at the assistant and said, 'You look exactly the same as the people behind the counter in the other two shops!' I felt a real idiot when I realised that it was all the same shop, with three different entrances!
>
> It was the most terrifying experience for me as I was not a drinker at all and only ever had the odd beer. I don't know how I made it back to the theatre but I remember the Blackpool Tower leaning first one way and then the other. I thought for a while that I was in Pisa, and judging by my condition maybe I was. By the time I got back to the dressing room I was so legless that I collapsed under a table totally unaware that Cliff had got his camera out and was taking some very candid birthday shots of me. I was like the Blackpool Illuminations that night — well lit up!

The arrival of *Apache* at the top of the charts brought many accusations that it wasn't the Shadows playing on the record at all but a group of session men. Hank found this very upsetting.

Somehow people just couldn't believe that a bunch of young

scruffs could make a Number 1 record. However, the success and pleasure it gave us far outweighed any problems it created. We'd been getting in some money from songwriting — maybe a hundred pounds here or there which was on top of our twenty-five pounds a week basic pay. It certainly brought about a gradual change of lifestyle — I even lashed out on an Ivy League suit and some brand new pointed-toe winkle-picker shoes. Things were looking up, we graduated from motorscooters to cars. I sold my old Vauxhall Velox and bought a Ford Zephyr convertible with a power hood. Bruce bought his first car at about the same time.

Yeah, it was an old 'sit up and beg' black Rover 75 — I think the first royalties from *Please Don't Tease* really paid for it. Jet had a Ford Consul with lots of impressive shiny chrome all over it, but Tony was still too young to drive. We made extra money by undertaking Sunday concerts and playing on Cliff's records. When we see the staggering amounts of money that are handed over to musicians today we realise just what a bad deal we got in those days. Standard money for playing on a Cliff and the Shadows single was a seven pounds a head session fee! The funny thing is that at the time we never really thought about money as such, but only that we could do things like change from our maroon stage suits to our first set of black mohair gear with black sealskin boots, blue button down shirts and black ties.

On Sunday 25th September 1960, the first ever Shadows variety appearance without Cliff took place at Colston Hall in Bristol.
Tony admitted to being very nervous.

It wasn't just me, we all were. We'd worked out a complete stage act but there were so many cues, beginnings and endings to get right. As it turned out, everything went fine except for one or two minor points we could brush up on for future appearances. The slapstick comedy routine worked OK and we did some vocal numbers with Bruce and Hank taking the lead.

Chas McDevitt and Shirley Douglas of *Freight Train* fame were also on the bill, along with Frank Ifield who'd just released a single called *Gotta Get a Date* and went on to have three Number 1s in a row a couple of years later. Michael Cox, who'd just had a big hit with *Angela Jones*, also appeared along with a group with the world's most inventive name 'Paul Beattie and the Beats' who were billed as 'recording stars from the programmes *Cool for Cats* and *The Jack Jackson Show*.' Our billing wasn't much better — for anywhere between three and sixpence and six shillings you could see the 'Disc Stars of the Hit Parade — in person!' What did they expect — cardboard cut-outs!

Young girls who spent some of their pocket money on *Boyfriend* that month were treated by Cliff to some one-liners on the Shadows.

Jet — 'He's where he is because he's a perfectionist.'
Bruce — 'When squalls blow up he sees they disappear in laughter.'
Hank — 'He has a keen eye for everything contemporary.'
Tony — 'He's the most honest person in the world.'

Somewhere between Cliff's comments and going into print the attributed quotes either got mixed up, or they all temporarily swopped characters!

As the album *Me and My Shadows* was released in October, the Shadows were voted the Best British Small Group in the *New Musical Express* polls and *Apache* was voted the Best British Disc of the year.

The problem of the follow-up was solved when they decided to record the theme music to the Edgar Wallace film series which had been written by the Leeds-born son of a prize fighter who'd been raised in Ireland and had a succession of jobs in the States as a bellhop, cowpoke, actor and stunt man before turning to songwriting. The writer of classics like *Hang Out Your Washing on the Siegfried Line, Does Your Mother Come From Ireland* and *South of the Border,* which the Shadows would record on their second LP, was, at 56, thirty years older than Jerry Lordan who'd written *Apache,* but nevertheless Michael Carr had some good tunes in him yet. The following year he provided them with their second Number 1, *Man of Mystery.* Hank remembers:

As soon as you got down to the lower strings on a guitar the comparison with Duane Eddy was inevitable, so we just had to try and achieve a different tone or style or use a different echo. We'd actually been to see him earlier in the year at the Edmonton Regal and renewed our acquaintance with his road manager Charlie Carpenter whom we'd worked with in the States. One of the main factors in Duane's success was the fantastic amplification system at that time. He had a large fifteen-inch speaker which gave what seemed like really full depth and power with an eight-inch speaker on top for the treble! It was all packed solidly with foam rubber and encased in a steel chassis, so the result was full volume without distortion. It seemed so incredible at the time that it inspired us to experiment with amplification and new sounds, as long as we could reproduce them on stage.

Jet and Tony obviously pleased with each other

We recorded *Man of Mystery* after a show at the Palladium one night, having convinced EMI that it would add to the atmosphere. The record company was a little shocked and bemused at a suggestion that would become commonplace for thousands of groups over the next couple of decades.

You see we were virtually making up our own rules as we were coming across new situations that neither we nor the record companies had experienced before. They weren't used to dealing with a self-contained unit like the Shadows, so at times they had to break down some of their old barriers and cope with four lads who were undoubtedly less conventional in their outlook and musical approach. Consequently, there were several raised eyebrows over our session at Abbey Road which lasted from midnight till four in the morning. We put down *Man of Mystery* in twenty minutes, *The Stranger* in one and a half hours and *The Theme from 'Giant'*, which eventually emerged on our first EP in January 1961 with *Shotgun, Theme from 'Shane'* and *Mustang*. *Man of Mystery* ended up with a wrong note being played in the solo — spot the wrong note folks and win a prize!

As *Man of Mystery* and *The Stranger* leapt into the Top 10, Frank Ifield gave Hank and Bruce their first cover apart from Cliff, when he released *That's the Way It Goes,* and one musical instrument company with an eye to the main chance soon jumped on the Shadows' bandwagon, marketing a guitar called the 'Apache'! For a mere £31/8/3 you could actually *own* the beige-tan guitar with a maroon scratch plate and two pick-ups, or if you wanted to be really flash and amaze your friends a tremolo arm would set you back a further £7/19/9!

At the tail end of 1960 Cliff's eleventh single *I Love You*, written by Bruce, was heading towards Number 1 and Bruce was again heading for the altar — this time as Hank's best man when he married Billie, the girl that he'd first met in the Freight Train coffee bar. After a brief honeymoon in Windsor, it was time to start thinking about another single which ended up as a team effort after a writing session at the flat rented by Bruce and Hank in Long Lane, Finchley. The result was *FBI* which became their third hit. Bruce recalls:

Hank, Jet and myself actually wrote it, but there were some contractual problems with the publishing, so Peter Gormley put his name on it, and when the royalties came in, he paid us. Sam Curtis, who was our roadie, was there when we were working the song out, and decided that if a bunch of idiots like us could do it then he could, and disappeared to write a song for his wife! When he re-emerged with a big smile on his face we could hardly refuse to listen to it, but it was so awful we had to stifle our laughter so as not to embarrass him. He'd put words to Russ Conway's *Roulette:*

'I love you Joyce,
You are my choice,
I want to be with you . . .'

and Hank came out with 'Play it again Sam . . . somewhere else!'

Well, I had to say something to cover up the embarrassment — it was so bad! I remember one night in Torquay when Sam and Joyce were going to give me a lift back to London. I heard someone banging on the door to be let in, so I opened it — and knocked him unconscious! Joyce started rushing around like mad, so I yelled, 'Quick, loosen his clothes', and the first thing she did was undo his trouser zip! At a moment like that too!

By the end of 1960 the singing sensation Dickie Valentine, former London Palladium pageboy, had notched up fourteen solo hit records, and his brother entered the lives and success story of the Shadows. David Bryce worked for Lew and Leslie Grade, and it was they who teamed him up with Cliff and his recently re-named backing group to act as general co-ordinator, flag-waver, morale booster and nursemaid!

The first encounter between the lads and their new found minder was in Allsop Place, just behind the Planetarium and Madame Tussauds. It was from there that most tour buses left, loaded with packages of pop stars off to play a string of one night stands around the country. Little did the majority of fans realise that the London Transport canteen a few yards along the road invariably played host to hordes of household names both American and British, wolfing down plates of beans on toast and mugs of tea, and swapping stories with the off-duty bus conductors. An autograph hunter's paradise if only they'd known!

David's first gig was in Portsmouth, and as they set off from Allsop Place, Bruce slid into the seat next to him and said, 'Here, how old are you?'

'Twenty-five,' was the reply.

'Cor, aren't you old,' exclaimed a wide-eyed Bruce. That remark probably contributed to David's initial wariness of Bruce!

He was also a bit arrogant, unlike Jet and Hank who immediately put me at ease with their friendly, easy-going natures. Tony was toffee-nosed, I reckoned, so I didn't take to him so instantly, but in general they accepted me as part of the team and I got on pretty well with them.

David wasn't particularly overawed at joining the Cliff and the Shadows set up, as he'd already seen more than his fair share of the music business. Apart from his brother Dickie being one of the most famous singers in the land, he'd worked with many visiting American performers.

I toured with Mario Lanza, the world famous tenor who sadly died in 1959. I seem to remember his real name was Alfredo Arnold Cocozza! Then there was Johnny Ray, 'The Prince of Wails' as they used to call him — he'd do his crying bit on stage and the girls would go mad, just as they would for Cliff years later. Touring with Bill Haley and the Comets in 1956 was an experience that'll always stand out in my mind — the scenes were so fantastic it's great to look back and say, 'I toured with him.'

The Bobby Darin/Duane Eddy tour in 1958 was a bit uncomfortable. Darin was topping the bill singing numbers like *Splish Splash,* which was his first British hit, but every night the audience would still be shouting for more twangy guitar numbers like *Rebel Rouser* during Bobby's opening songs. It was really embarrassing. All the lads would be on their feet chanting, 'We want Duane, we want Duane.' Eventually of course they had to take Duane Eddy off and give him his own tour.

Kathy Kirby supported him on that tour. Kathy of course was to make her chart debut some five years later with a vocal version of the Shadows' chart-topper *Dance On.* Funnily enough the number 1 remembered best from the Darin/Eddy tour was a number that neither of them performed on stage! Lee Hazelwood, who wrote for and produced Duane, kept playing this dreadfully morbid song he'd written about a girl who had been sentenced to die on the electric chair. It was called *The Girl on Death Row* and Lee was convinced it would be a big hit. It'd be a great story if I were able to say, 'That song went on to be an enormous best-seller', but it sank without trace. I think she got her sentence commuted.

Another group I worked with before teaming up with Cliff and the boys was Buddy Holly and the Crickets. It was possibly the jibes and teasing that strengthened me for the ribbing that I was to get in the early days from the Shadows. People say that Buddy Holly was ahead of his time. I realise now that it was not only musically, as he and Crickets Joe Maudlin and Jerry Allison coined a phrase that didn't fall into common use until the '70s. I suppose I can claim a little bit of the glory too, as it was my hairless head that put the idea into theirs. They called me a skinhead! 'Hey, skinhead, can you get some beers?'; 'Hi, skinhead, how're you doin'!'

So now you know how skinheads were invented. I was the original, and Buddy Holly coined the phrase!

I do vividly remember him insisting that he wasn't going to do any more touring after the scheduled American tour early in 1959. A decision that sadly became hard fact when he was killed in February during that very tour.

After *Apache* the Shadows' publicity had been entrusted to Leslie Perrin Associates, who were based in London's Denmark Street, long known as Tin Pan Alley. Determined to prove themselves, the hand-outs they ran up to publicise the Shadows demonstrated their keenness by including the words 'If we can help further please call us . . . day or night . . . the hour is of no importance . . . your story is.'

They also described the Shadows as the 'Awesome Foursome'! As *FBI* was released in February and voted a hit on *Juke Box Jury* when they were the surprise guests, one of the 'Awesome Foursome' became one of the 'Gruesome Twosome', as Jet's wife Carol was given special leave by the High Court to present a divorce petition within the statutory period of three years from the date of their marriage. In that direction things hadn't been going well for Jet for some while.

Cliff and my wife had been going together quite a bit and it was getting me down, so I started hitting the bottle, although I think Carol really encouraged him, so I never blamed our little bachelor boy really. It was another excuse for me to have a drink. It was bloody hard, standing up on stage every night behind Cliff thinking that he was having it off with your wife. I couldn't really stand the pressure, so I started drinking fairly heavily, until it became a state of mind. Bruce was always having a go at me about drinking! He was like a bloody sergeant major.

I had to keep on at Jet, because the more we earned the more he drank, but apart from that it filled him with a fighting spirit. Whenever we went to a pub he'd regularly have the mickey taken out of him for his dyed blonde hair — and a lot of guys thought he was bent. He was actually a really nice guy but even if he had just one drink he'd get really aggressive and threaten to take on any number of guys at once. Both Dave and Sam often whisked him away from a potential thrashing!

There was no doubt about it we were carrying a passenger — you can't drink *and* play. It was sad really because Jet was a better musician than I'll ever be. We'd always have to apologise for him on stage covering up with a few well chosen words about how unwell he was! There are some people we didn't fool though — a few hundred Liverpudlians who can tell the difference between a sick man and a drunk, with their eyes closed. A few months previously we'd been doing a gig at the Cavern Club in Liverpool, and Jet had really had a skinful by the time we got on stage.

During one number we were doing one of our cross-over step routines and Jet fell straight off into the audience! 'I'm sorry,' I said, 'Jet's not too well tonight,' to which the crowd howled back, 'That's because he's pissed.' You couldn't pull the vodka and beer over their eyes!

We were definitely moving in different directions in more ways than one — Jet adopted more and more of a 'couldn't care less' attitude when he was drunk, and I was becoming more obsessed with accuracy, even down to putting chalk marks on stage where we had to stand!

Jet had also started taking out a former beauty queen turned singer from Wakefield who he met when she toured with them. Patti Brook had been the winner of the 1960 Soho Fair Disc competition, and one of the judges, Emile Ford, had subsequently helped her with her first record *Since You've Been Gone*. The Shadows once smashed a couple of windows playing football in her mother's garden but they did in turn do Emile a favour one night in Ipswich during the early part of 1961. He didn't make it to the theatre, and the Shadows who were on the same show went on to fill in, singing songs like *Michael Row the Boat Ashore*!

Jet wasn't the only member of the group causing headaches, Tony's disastrous time-keeping was bugging Hank.

Whenever we went to collect him to go to a gig he'd still be in bed. Not only that, but he'd get shirty when we woke him up, never apologise, and be totally unrepentant.

Tony had always been very composed and self-assured even when he was fifteen or sixteen, but it was slowly starting to get up our noses. I had a terrible fight with him in the dressing room before a show one night when he sank his teeth in my finger right down to the bone. I panicked for a while, as there's not much call for three-fingered guitarists, but it didn't drop off! He actually had no respect for his elders at all, in fact he always displayed such arrogance towards Sam Curtis that one day Sam saw red, turned Tony upside down over his knee, pulled his trousers down and gave him a good spanking! Tony celebrated his eighteenth birthday as the group flew off to tour South Africa, Australia, New Zealand, Singapore and Malaya and Peter Gormley celebrated becoming Cliff's manager as well as the Shadows'.

It was the third time that the Shadows had left England, but Bruce remembers them having to hold back their excitement for an unexpected four hours.

We'd arrived at London Airport only to find that the plane had been delayed, so Hank, Jet, Tony, Cliff, Cliff's mum and I went into Hounslow where we ended going to the cinema to watch *Dr Blood's Coffin*. Eventually we had to make a mad dash back to the airport and a short while later were all safely on our way to South Africa.

We couldn't believe the reaction to our arrival in Johannesburg. Thousands of fans rioted outside the hotel and brought the traffic to a standstill. Our visit there also brought home to us the value of personal appearances — as our tour there resulted in us having two Shadows singles and four Cliff and the Shadows singles in the Top 10. We did our first ever live recording during that trip, at the Coliseum where we recorded *Shazam, Sleepwalk, FBI* and *Guitar Boogie*. We were promised Vox amps for the tour but we ended up being given Gibson amps which of course had to be used for the live recording as well. This was the only time that Vox amplifiers weren't used on our recordings.

The weather was great — I got second degree burns in Johannesburg, Jet who couldn't swim was pushed fully clothed into a swimming pool in Durban and Cliff had to jump in and save him, and the locals in Cape Town put us off having a dip by recounting horrific but true tales of swimmers returning to shore minus a leg or two after bathing in the shark-infested waters!

We travelled from South Africa to Rhodesia where we played Bulawayo and Salisbury. The day we left Cliff had four records in the Top 10 and we had two! Mind you, we nearly didn't leave. Tony's early morning call had gone unnoticed, us banging on the hotel door only produced a minor stirring from the Meehan pit. I was sharing a room with Tony and knew that getting up in the morning wasn't his strong point but this was really pushing it, we'd all finished our breakfast and the taxi was due to arrive in a few minutes to take us to the airport. I tore back upstairs to discover Tony sitting on the edge of the bed — nothing strange in that only that he was fast asleep! I grabbed hold of him, gave him a good shaking and told him we were leaving for the airport in three minutes, which at least got him into the vertical position. Nevertheless Tony still managed to move at his usual pace. He got up, stretched a few times, yawned, sauntered over to the window, shuffled over to the washbasin and with all the grace of a flower opening in slow motion passed the flannel gently over his face. Several minutes later he still hadn't appeared so I rushed upstairs to tell him we were leaving there and then. He was fast asleep. I was livid. I yelled, 'There are your tickets and there's your passport — see you in London.' Tony's attitude really was annoying the group more and more. He had this amazing pomposity and confidence for a seventeen-year-old and used to adopt such an incredibly superior attitude towards other people that it was embarrassing to be in his company when he was behaving like that. Tony was great at avoiding any extra work if he possibly could. In fact we were so used to his attitude that once in 1959 we ignored his pleas to be let off carrying the equipment after a gig as he said he didn't feel too good.

Yes, I felt really bad that night. We'd just done a gig at Cliff's old school and I complained to Hank, Bruce and Jet that I was feeling really rotten and asked them if they could pack my drums away and load them into the van for me, but they totally ignored me — that is until I collapsed!

Hank was full of remorse:

Poor old Tony, because he was always pulling strokes we totally ignored his moaning for about an hour until we realised he'd passed out on the floor. He always had a very pasty complexion, but that night he looked like an advert for that extra white washing powder that was around at the time, you know the one that goes, 'Someone's mum just doesn't know what someone's mum really ought to know . . .' We felt real heels when he was rushed to hospital with severe appendicitis.

Meanwhile on the music front, *FBI* had been a Top 10 hit for the Shadows and *The Frightened City,* which was the title theme that Norrie had written for a film, was heading in the same direction. And, on the personal front, Bruce's son Dwayne was born on 13th June.

On their return from Africa it was all down to the Associated British Picture Corporation Studios to shoot *The Young Ones.* There had been some talk of the Shadows having speaking roles in it with Hank playing the part that became Richard O'Sullivan's and with Jet taking the part that Melvyn Hayes eventually got.

To be honest I think I didn't get the part because of the old alcohol. I'm sure the important people on the film were all saying to each other, 'Jet's a drinker — let's not take the chance.' Filming *The Young Ones* really bored me so Hank and I used to sneak off

Tony learning to knit

Gotta Funny Feeling from *The Young Ones*

and catch newts that were in an enormous tank that had been used in the film *The Cruel Sea*, based on the book by Nicholas Monserrat. We were picked up by a big flash Bentley at about 6.00 am, dumped at the studio and by seven we'd be plastered in make-up and surrounded by a sea of Kleenex tissues. Then there was nothing to do for hours so we used to go newting — great crested newts they were — until we were called.

We'd go in the studios to do the club scene and get choked to death. The chemical smoke apparently wasn't having the desired effect, so the director went in for a bit of reality and he got the technicians to burn cardboard boxes! Luckily we were able to escape for one weekend at the end of June and that's when we did one of our strangest gigs!

Advertised as 'Rock Across the Channel', we twanged our way from Gravesend to Calais and back with what seemed like a dozen other groups. I'm not the greatest traveller on air or sea but Hank enjoyed himself chatting to the other groups.

There were the Shades, the Rockfellers, the Tremors and the Paramounts who had a hit two and a half years later with the old Leiber and Stoller classic *Poison Ivy* that was popularised by the Coasters. The Paramounts were a Southend-based group who later became Procul Harum selling albums by the ton and having a massive Number 1 hit with the classic *Whiter Shade of Pale*. I think they, like us and two thousand people on the jaunt across the Channel, spent the whole trip feeling like that title. Maybe the trip inspired the song which was to come six years later.

Perhaps the excursion was equally prophetic for us, as our next single was about an epic voyage on water, *Kon-Tiki*, and that topped the charts as well. The third group on the *Royal Daffodil* that day who got to the very peak of the Top 20 was the Searchers. Exactly two years later they entered the charts with *Sweets for My Sweet* and went on to notch up fourteen hits including three Number 1s.

It must have been a lucky boat. The only reason we were able to do the gig in the first place was that we had a couple of days off from filming *The Young Ones*.

We'd played a Saturday dance at Dreamland in Margate the night before and being the organiser of our road affairs and therefore endowed with more than his fair share of grey cells, David Bryce suggested (forcefully, of course) that we head straight off to Gravesend and stay the night there so we'd be fresh in the morning! Were we *ever* fresh in the morning? Sam Curtis and Dave bundled

With Gene Vincent on his first visit to this country in 1959.
We travelled to Manchester especially to meet him

Gendarmes holding back the crowd at Calais

all the equipment into the van, and a short while later a bunch of dishevelled, tired-looking wrecks turned up at the hotel in Gravesend. It looked more like world's end to us! After we'd battered on the door, a cheerful night porter with a big friendly grin on his face pressed his nose against the window and beamed at us with his sunny smile: 'Clear off you yobs or I'll call the police.' He was clearly in a good mood!

Needless to say, we were the very last group on board the *Royal Daffodil* the following morning. Jet was pretty disappointed when he discovered that Gene Vincent, who was due to appear, had had an accident a few days before and couldn't make it — he'd always been a great fan of Gene's, and the news wasn't helped by the fact that Jet actually felt seasick before we even set sail!

After picking up more teenagers at Southend we were well and truly into the party spirit! Two thousand young people hell-bent on having a ball, some of them dressed in crazy costumes, fancy dress and of course a lot of Teddy Boys and Girls. Among the crowds were Cliff's sisters Joan, Jacqueline and Donella, rocking and jiving with the rest of them.

We opened our set with *Shazam*, which was relayed all over the boat as the screaming, whooping hordes yelled their heads off! The trip to Calais took five hours, but they must have heard us coming for at least four of them.

The reception committee at Calais was headed by the mayor and a cast of civil dignitaries — there to greet and welcome the youth of Britain. And meet them he did, as dozens of blokes who'd been at the duty free alcohol on the way over teemed down the gang plank, like a drunken rabble (which they were) throwing up and heaving all over the quay. Terrific for Anglo-French relations!

It was in our contract to play on an open air stage in the local square, which sounded OK until we realised that there was no dressing room! Good organisation, eh? Eventually we changed a few hundred yards (or its French equivalent) down the high street in a little bistro place, with the gendarmes holding the crowd back. No doubt keeping them at gendarme's length!

Another thing ze French 'ad forgotten was zat ze mains was a long way from ze stage! Sacré bleu! (Whatever it means.)

Mais formidable, one of the groups on the boat with us lent us a long lead and we were away. The crowd erupted when we played *Apache* then *FBI* and *Man of Mystery* cross-over stepping like there was no tomorrow! There wasn't. Halfway through one number the lads we'd borrowed the lead from pulled the plug out and swiped the cable back! Quick as a flash — which isn't easy with the power off — David whipped a few pounds out of his pocket, did a deal with the group concerned and the power was back. The French and English youths became more frenzied and more drunk as the day wore on, so by the time the ship's siren sounded it had the same effect as a sheep trying to round up a whole bunch of dogs. With a schedule to adhere to, the captain of the *Daffodil* could only wait so long, and as the ship headed back into the Channel there were still several inebriated but irate British youths hopping up and down on the Calais quayside yelling obscenities at the captain. Everyone was ill on the way back.

The British papers were full of it the following morning carrying headlines like 'Rock 'n' Rollers invade France' and, in *The Times,* 'British youths shock Calais.' Actually it wasn't that bad, despite the boat having been insured for £10,000. Calais itself was insured for £25,000!

While the Shadows had been busy, *The Frightened City* reached Number 3 in the chart after its release in May, and stayed there for the whole of June, July, August, September, and into October! Jet, Hank and Bruce had written the B side, *Back Home,* with a commercial artist friend of theirs, Jim Goff, who'd drawn the *Apache* cartoons for the EMI publicity drive the year before, and who went on to publish a humorous cartoon book on worms in the '70s! Like *Man of Mystery,* the follow-up to *The Frightened City* was written by Michael Carr. *Kon-Tiki* was released in September, as was the Shadows' first album.

It contained one tune that was to pave the way for the Shadows' love of making a pun of the title, *Theme from a Filleted Plaice,* and a piano instrumental number, *Stand Up and Say That* by Hank.

That was the first time I'd ever played piano on a record — I suppose it was really inspired by Nashville's legendary piano player Floyd Cramer. When it came to the vocal numbers I'd always liked Dion and the Belmonts' version of *That's My Desire,* so we did that and the Crickets' *Baby My Heart.* The idea behind *Nivram* was to write a *Swinging Shepherd Blues* type melody, give it a jazzy feel and stick in a bass solo. That was the first ever pop bass solo. We didn't know the lyrics to *Baby My Heart* at all, so we just kept repeating them over and over again; and we used *Shadoogie,* which was a combination of Shadows and Boogie, as the opening track on the LP. Norrie suggested *Blue Star* because that was one of his favourite tunes, and we also did a version of Santo and Johnny's *Sleepwalk.*

It was during their six week season with Cliff at the Blackpool Opera House that Jet changed his hair colour from blonde to dark, and Tony's lackadaisical time-keeping and general unconcern become too much for Hank, Bruce and Jet.

Tony treated the other three to a repeat performance of a previous occasion when he'd turned up halfway through a gig in Leeds and just wandered nonchalantly on stage without even an apology. This time he was nowhere to be found as Hank, Bruce and Jet ran out to rapturous applause, and they'd finished *FBI* without drums, when Tony strolled on in his street clothes. In September 1961 they kicked him out.

On October 7th the Shadows performed a historical feat by topping three charts simultaneously. They were Number 1 in the singles chart with *Kon-Tiki,* Number 1 in the LP chart with *The Shadows* and top of the EP chart with *Shadows to the Fore!*

The same week they had another of their EPs in the Top 10 *plus* two of Cliff's on which they were playing, as well as appearing on another Top 10 LP *Listen to Cliff.* Pretty impressive stuff for a group who'd only had their first hit little more than a year before!

Their first album had been a long time coming as far as the fans were concerned, but the often critical pens of the music scribes were raving over the debut LP. Nigel Hunter, reviewing for *Disc,* summed it up rather well.

> It's been worth the wait. The LP is a mixture of their familiar brand of modern instrumental showcasing plus solo spots from Messrs Meehan and Marvin and vocalising from all four. Those additional attractions avoid the pit which the Ventures tumbled into.
>
> There is contrast and variety and no risk of boredom or monotony. Especially impressive is Hank Marvin's Nashville piano playing, and thank goodness for one drummer who can play an extended solo which is logical and relevant without losing himself.

Tony Meehan might have been a good drummer but he was no longer a Shadow, and a replacement had to be found to complete the tail end of the season at Blackpool. A phone call to the guy who was drumming for Tommy Steele at that time did the trick — Brian Bennett.

TOP TWENTY
Melody Maker charts service
Data supplied by over 100 record dealers

1. (2) KON-TIKI .... Shadows. Columbia
2. (5) MICHAEL .... Highwaymen. HMV
3. (1) JOHNNY REMEMBER ME John Leyton. Top Rank
4. (4) WILD IN THE COUNTRY / I FEEL SO BAD
Elvis Presley. RCA
5. (6) JEALOUSY .... Billy Fury. Decca
6. (3) YOU DON'T KNOW .. Helen Shapiro. Columbia
7. (13) WALKIN' BACK TO HAPPINESS
Helen Shapiro. Columbia
8. (8) GET LOST .... Eden Kane. Columbia
9. (7) REACH FOR THE STARS / CLIMB EV'RY
MOUNTAIN .... Shirley Bassey. Columbia
10. (11) YOU'LL ANSWER TO ME .. Cleo Laine. Fontana
11. (10) TOGETHER .... Connie Francis. MGM
12. (12) HATS OFF TO LARRY .. Del Shannon. London
13. (—) WILD WIND .... John Leyton. Top Rank
14. (—) SUCU SUCU .... Laurie Johnson. Pye
15. (9) MICHAEL, ROW THE BOAT Lonnie Donegan. Pye
16. (18) GRANADA .... Frank Sinatra. Reprise
17. (—) CHILI BOM BOM HARD HEARTED HANNAH
Temperance Seven. Parlophone
18. (—) MUSKRAT .... Everly Brothers. Warner Bros.
19. (15) WELL I ASK YOU .... Eden Kane. Decca
20. (14) AIN'T GONNA WASH FOR A WEEK
Brook Brothers. Pye

JAZZ TOP TEN

1. (1) THE BEST OF BARBER AND BILK, Vol. 1 (LP)
Chris Barber and Acker Bilk. Pye
2. (2) ACKER (LP) .... Acker Bilk. Columbia
3. (5) TIME OUT (LP) .... Dave Brubeck. Fontana
4. (4) BEAUTY AND THE BEAT (LP)
George Shearing and Peggy Lee. Capitol
5. (9) SEVEN AGES OF ACKER (LP) .. Acker Bilk. Columbia
6. (6) THE BEST OF BRUBECK (LP) .. Dave Brubeck. Fontana
7. (8) THE NUTCRACKER SUITE (LP) .. Duke Ellington. Philips
8. (7) A GOLDEN TREASURY OF BILK (LP) Acker Bilk. Columbia
9. (3) THEM DIRTY BLUES (LP) .. Julian Adderley. Riverside
10. (10) AT THE LIGHTHOUSE (LP) .. Julian Adderley. Riverside

TOP TEN LPs

1. (1) THE SHADOWS .... Columbia
2. (2) SOUTH PACIFIC .... Soundtrack. RCA
3. (3) G.I. BLUES .... Elvis Presley. RCA
4. (4) BLACK AND WHITE MINSTREL SHOW
George Mitchell. HMV
5. (5) HIS HAND IN MINE .... Elvis Presley. RCA
6. (6) THE SOUND OF MUSIC .... London Cast. HMV
7. (9) HALFWAY TO PARADISE .. Billy Fury. Ace of Clubs
8. (10) THE SOUND OF MUSIC .. Original Cast. Philips
9. (7) LISTEN TO CLIFF! .. Cliff Richard. Columbia
10. (8) OLIVER! .... Original Cast. Decca

TOP TEN EPs

1. (1) THE SHADOWS TO THE FORE ...... Shadows. Columbia
2. (2) THE SHADOWS .... Columbia
3. (3) THE BUTTON-DOWN MIND OF BOB NEWHART
Warner Bros.
4. (4) SUCH A NIGHT .... Elvis Presley. RCA
5. (6) CLIFF'S SILVER DISCS .. Cliff Richard. Columbia
6. (5) ADAM'S HIT PARADE .. Adam Faith. Parlophone
7. (7) UNFORGETTABLE .... Nat "King" Cole. Capitol
8. (8) ADAM, No. 1 .... Adam Faith. Parlophone
9. (9) ME AND MY SHADOWS, No. 1 .. Cliff Richard. Columbia
10. (10) THE JOHN BARRY SOUND .... Columbia

Chuck who? (Hank learning to walk)

'The Savage'

8 / *Brian's Story*

(1940 — October 1961)

In December 1939 there were plenty of problems in the world. Italy left the League of Nations, Russia was expelled from it and His Majesty's cruisers *Exeter*, *Achilles* and *Ajax* took on the German warship the *Admiral Graf Spee* in the battle of the River Plate, which resulted in the *Graf Spee* scuttling herself in the entrance of Montevideo harbour just before Christmas, and Hilda Bennett was seven months pregnant with me! I eventually took my bow on the 9th February 1940 in London only to get evacuated fairly swiftly to Nottinghamshire to be a milksop in Worksop! My father Laurie had been building up a printing factory for the six months prior to World War II, but Hitler's invasion of Poland had stemmed his creative potential a little, and instead of stamping his dyes he found himself stamping his feet in the 57th Wessex Regiment, who were bundled off from Worksop station to join the 87th Army for the African campaign, leaving my mum and me waving goodbye on the station with one handkerchief between us.

After six months up there we went back to London and rented a house in New Southgate — a little closer to the war, and even closer to the Standard Telephones building, which was being used as a munitions factory, a prime target if ever there was one! One of my earliest memories was of my mum and myself standing at the window watching the searchlights picking out the enemy and my mum gazing at the sky saying, 'He's got a lot of guts, that guy up there, German or not.' Little did she realise it was the first of the 'doodle bugs', and there was no pilot, just an eerie whining sound, which would cut out suddenly and the whole area would hold its breath 'cause you hadn't got a clue where it was going to land or whose home would be reduced to a pile of rubble next. Lots of people had air raid shelters in the garden, but we had an Anderson shelter made of iron with a wire covering under the stairs, so we'd sleep there every night. To us local kids — we were only very tiny — it all seemed unreal, a bit like a game, really, as we demonstrated the day a Spitfire crashed in the field behind us, and all the excited lads in

Brian with Mum, aged 4

Brian with Dad, 1949

On your bike!

the neighbourhood dashed across and started clambering over it. We obviously knew no fear then, as we'd been weaned on the war; it dominated conversation, news, and the sky!

When you're young, radio news bulletins seem not merely boring but also exceedingly long, so it was to my enormous delight one day in 1944 that I heard what was apparently the Glenn Miller Orchestra coming over the wireless live from London's Aeolean Hall. From there it was one short step to locating as many of my mum's pots and pans as I could, turning them upside down and bashing the living daylights out of their bottoms with a couple of spoons. And Hank and Bruce never believe me when I tell them that British skiffle started in our kitchen in New Southgate in the mid-40s.

I was six when my dad came home from the war, to be faced with the daunting prospect of looking for a home. The lady we'd rented ours from had beetled off for the duration of the military punch-up, and as the dust and smoke settled over Europe she came scuttling back to claim her little piece of New Southgate.

For a while my parents and I crammed into a council house in Farndale Avenue, Palmers Green, along with my aunt, uncle and a couple of cousins, but to save it bursting at the seams the three of us later transferred ourselves to a very small flat in the same road. Saturday was the big night out for us: after my face had been scrubbed to make me a cherubic pink colour, and I'd made exaggerated sound effects in the bathroom to give the impression that I was cleaning my teeth, I'd be off to the Capitol Cinema at Winchmore Hill. As with most picture houses in those days, there was a fantastic restaurant where you'd order up expensive looking cakes, toast and tea cakes and be served by waitresses in smart hats and black and white uniforms. Then with your tummy almost bursting through your blazer buttons, you'd be plunged into the subdued lighting of the cinema, to the strains of an old boy pounding away like the Phantom of the Opera on the theatre organ. They were magic, those nights at Winchmore Hill!

By now I was at Hayzelwood Lane School, Palmers Green, and my dad was getting the printing works in Arnos Grove back on its feet. It was called, not surprisingly, the Arnos Press; my dad was obviously gifted at choosing names, but less bright in other ways, like letting me help him out during summer holidays!

Still, it must have been nice to have the patter of tiny prints around the place! When we weren't at the factory we'd toddle off to sunny Westgate for our hols, and it was there that I was influenced by a holidaying violinist from one of the London orchestras, who'd play his instrument for hours on end for a wide-eyed nine-year-old

102

Brian Bennett from north London.

He must have had the patience of a saint, which was more than I had, as after a few lessons my mind wandered back to the upturned pots and pans. I'd fleetingly had some toy drums, but in true Keith Moon style they were demolished by my cousin at Christmas. One of my best mates at Hayzelwood Lane School was a guy called Quinton Pope, who occasionally invited me to spend some of the summer holidays at his aunt and uncle's farm in Somerset, where we'd work during the daytime (well, as much as small boys ever do), and listen to the radio in the evenings. The old wireless was one of the important things in my life at this time, as I'd discovered 'The Voice of America' radio station in Tangiers, where every Tuesday I'd be glued to Willis Conover's *Jazz Hour*, eagerly devouring music by legends like Count Basie and Stan Kenton.

After failing my eleven-plus, I went on to Winchmore Hill School, where I found more and more people had got the music bug. There were the traditional boys who liked trad jazz and then got into the very early forms of skiffle; the moderns, like me, who used to listen to the likes of Kenton, Oscar Peterson, Basie and Ellington, and drummers like Gene Krupa, Buddy Rich and Shelley Mann and the real modern music; and two other friends, Richard and Maurice Watson, who had a huge collection of classical music which we'd often sit and listen to round at their house.

Spurred on by listening to the 'greats' I was determined to pursue a musical career, and to that end procured myself a small drum kit, comprising snare drum, bass drum, a high-hat and one cymbal, praying that the saying 'From little acorns . . .' would one day come true. I joined the school orchestra (well, not too many people had drum kits!) and also the Hayzelwood Lane youth club band — after all, the more outfits I was involved with the more practice I could get.

The Esquires dance band, which I also played for, had the amazing luxury of a bass player — now that was big time! Any additions to the drum kit had to be saved for, so as well as earning a bit working at the printing works, I tore around on my bike at the crack of dawn delivering papers. In fact one house that I regularly delivered to in Winchmore Hill was the first home that Cliff ever bought some eight years later!

During 1952 and 1953 I started going down to the West End every Saturday to Doug Dobell's Record Shop in the Charing Cross Road and would end up buying a couple of second-hand 78s for about two bob, after spending the whole afternoon going through all their American imports. I bought some Lionel Hampton stuff after seeing him in concert when he first came to London in the early 50s. Hampton was the sort of bloke whose name was much-revered in music circles, having been a member of the famous Benny Goodman Quartet along with Gene Krupa, Teddy Wilson and of course Goodman himself.

Steered by a driving force that said, 'You are going to be a professional musician', I left school completely unqualified in 1954 at the age of fourteen, and formed my own group — 'The Tony Brian Trio, piano, guitar and drums — 125a Farndale Avenue, Palmers Green, N. 13 — Telephone PAL 7987.'

You know how people are, they get a business card, keep it for years and when an anniversary crops up they'll remember that little bit of paper tucked away in their wallet or wedged under the tea caddy in the kitchen and decide to try and book the act concerned, who've invariably been scattered to the four winds long before.

The bloke living there now has probably got wise, formed his own Tony Brian trio and is currently taking bookings for twenty-firsts, working men's clubs and silver weddings. A neighbour of ours in Palmers Green, Frank Horrocks, was the pianist with the Ted Heath Orchestra, and he used to take me down to the Tuesday night swing sessions at the Aeolean Hall in Bond Street. To see a big band like Ted Heath's in action, performing numbers like *Hot Toddy, Dragnet* and *Vanessa,* cemented my determination to be a big band drummer. *Dragnet* was the title theme from one of the most popular TV detective programmes of the 50s. Its start was heralded by four notes which must have been uttered many millions of times by schoolboys of that era and later as they played detectives, pretending to be the hero, Sergeant Joe Friday, who every week attracted most of Britain to their black and white sets perched next to the budgie in the corner of the front room with the never-to-be-forgotten words, 'This is the City — I'm a cop . . .' If *Dragnet* commanded one of the biggest audiences on the small screen, then *The Glenn Miller Story* attracted crowds to the cinema all over the country to watch, damp-eyed like me, the story of Miller going through the lean times to the point where he got his big break in 1939 through working at the Glenn Island Casino with its ten weekly radio broadcasts. I remember the cinema was filled with more sniffing when Miller volunteered for the armed forces in 1942, and after a short but amazingly successful career leading a wartime band most people were glad of the darkness of the Winchmore Hill cinema to hide their tears as his plane disappeared without trace en route to Paris one foggy day in December 1944. I discovered something that night — there's nothing tastes as bad as a salty choc-ice!

104

Brian's first group, 1954

Brian wishing he'd taken up the flute

The
TONY BRIAN TRIO
PIANO — ELECTRIC GUITAR — DRUMS

125a, Farndale Avenue,
PAL. 7987   Palmers Green, N.13

On my personal musical front I met a couple of local guys, Eric and Michael Milton, who knew a bloke called Steve Murray, who had a skiffle group that was about to embark on a summer season in Kent on the Costa del Ramsgate! In 1956, ten pounds a week for working a couple of hours a night seemed like a pretty good deal, so I found myself playing on a bill with people like Jim Dale, Ricky James and Rory Blackwell. During the day, to make an extra few pounds, we'd go off cherry-picking and hop-picking in the fields of Kent, and on some free evenings I did the odd gig at the local pub. I might have been mad but there was no doubting my keenness. In fact I hardly even noticed girls in those days, I was so absorbed in my drums.

After the summer season I worked for Ricky James for a while, as he'd helped me buy a new kit, and as I was virtually back in my home territory I asked my mum to come along to the opening night of our week's residency at Collins Musical Hall. Either my family were proud of me or inquisitive, as along trooped not only my mum, but aunties, uncles and cousins to see the lad in action. I must have been pretty naive, as it was only when I got on stage that I realised what sort of show it was and my parents and the accompanying relatives were stunned as several well-endowed ladies followed each other on to the stage and stripped off!

I was still playing with the Milton Brothers when they evolved into the Velvets who were the two of them, myself and a guy called Errol Hollis. We were promised this and promised that but beyond a lot of rehearsals we didn't do an awful lot except for entering a talent contest which was being held just down the road in Edmonton. The group were really into Buddy Holly numbers, so we decided to play *Peggy Sue*. We were running it through during the rehearsal when I noticed a couple of guys who were also in the contest staring at me. Although I didn't know it at the time it turned out to be Bruce and Hank from the Railroaders, who apparently were marvelling over my authentic Jerry Allison drum sound on *Peggy Sue*.

Over the next couple of years, 1957 and 1958, I spent most of my time down at the 2 Is. 1958 seemed fairly to gallop into '59, as in January the music papers announced a new line-up of Cliff Richard and the Drifters which I noticed included Tony Meehan and Jet Harris along with Hank and Bruce; and I was invited to join Marty Wilde's Wildcats along with Licorice Locking, Tony Belcher on rhythm guitar and Big Jim Sullivan on lead. Almost immediately we went into the studio and covered Dion and the Belmonts' American hit *Teenager in Love*. Craig Douglas also did a version of it, but our interpretation won the day, when some months later, in the summer

106

of '59, we got to Number 2, fending off the other recordings. Craig and Dion eventually made Number 12 and Number 28 respectively. We would have had a Number 1 if it hadn't been for those other blokes who used to play down at the 2 Is, but there it was at the top of the charts — Cliff Richard and the Drifters' *Living Doll*. They were having a good run, and it was great to see some of your old acquaintances doing well.

We toured a lot as the Wildcats as *Teenager* was Marty's third hit and he was rapidly establishing himself as one of Britain's most popular singers. Being an astute sort of chap, it was during a summer season at Blackpool that year that I noticed my drum kit was getting bigger, as I was adding to it all the time. I foresaw many problems ahead of me trying to lug it around on buses the whole time, so I took my driving test in the bracing seaside air of north-west Lancashire and passed. After I'd treated myself to a celebration stick of rock, one of those little light bulbs suddenly lit up above my head just like they do in cartoons, and I went in search of a phone box, located one, inserted my four pennies, dialled a number and pressed button A.

'Hello, could you put me through to Larry Parnes please?'

'I'm afraid Mr Parnes is busy.'

'It's Brian Bennett here from the Wildcats.'

'I'm sorry but . . .'

'Tell him I've got a proposition for him.'

'Hold on a moment, please.'

(Click, click, click, mutter, mutter, click, click)

'Brian, what can I do for you?'

'It was just an idea I had, you see I've just passed my driving test and I need a bit of extra money so I thought I'd offer to drive the group's Dormobile.'

'It's a bit much driving the van and playing the drums — how much would you do it for?'

'Well . . . er . . .'

'I'll give you an extra tenner a week.'

'Thanking!'

'Right, I'll have a word with the driver and dispense with his services. Give my regards to the lads.' (Click.)

It was probably one of the daftest things I'd done. For months I knackered myself, and more than once nearly killed the lot of us by falling asleep at the wheel, while the lads were snoring their heads off in the back of the van. I must have been crackers! During 1959 we recorded two more songs which became Top Tenners, *Sea of Love* and *Bad Boy*, both of which were in the chart on 12th December 1959, the day I married Margaret, my 'nurse' from the 2 Is, with Tony Belcher as my best man. Marty got married the same month, so of course we were at each other's weddings — his reception was at the Lotus House and mine was at the Palm Court Restaurant in Palmers Green.

I decided to get married in my stage suit as it undoubtedly qualified as the most respectable piece of cloth hanging in my wardrobe, and while I was at it, I thought, I might as well go the whole hog and wear my stage tie and socks — at least I'd stand out. As it happens we all stood out. Four Wildcats, wearing identical blue suits with matching ties and socks — it was pretty hilarious. I'm sure the minister thought Margaret was marrying the lot of us. Even if he did, it was only me that married her, and only me that drove her off in style for a honeymoon in the New Forest.

We occasionally backed other artists as well as Marty if he was involved elsewhere. I was delighted at getting the chance to play with Gene Vincent and Eddie Cochran when they came here to tour in the early spring of 1960. Eddie was a great guitarist, he taught Big Jim a lot and showed me quite a bit about playing rock 'n' roll drums, as he'd beaten the skins on several of his own records. Eddie and Gene were the first real loonies that I'd encountered — they were so much fun and had such a great sense of humour that when Eddie told me he was coming back to tour Britain later that year I was overjoyed at the prospect of working with him again. I wasn't playing drums on his last gig of the tour at Bristol's Colston Hall, but I knew he was being diverted straight off to the airport to go back for some TV and recording commitments in the States. I was sitting in the flat when I heard the news. 'American rock 'n' roller Eddie Cochran has died in hospital following head injuries sustained in a road accident.' I couldn't believe it. I was shattered, totally shattered. Gene Vincent, who had also been a passenger in the taxi along with Eddie's fiancee, songwriter Sharon Sheeley, ended up in hospital too, and the last thing he remembered was Eddie singing Freddie Cannon's latest hit, 'California here I come, right back where I started from . . .'

That summer we were heading back in that direction for a season in Bournemouth, where Marty and I and our wives shared a lovely little cottage and spent many a summer's day driving round in his open sports car. We weren't so lucky with the Dormobile — it decided to conk out and we had to summon the local garage man, whose eyes widened in amazement when he saw the van. He muttered something that sounded like 'Oh . . . er . . . er . . . um,' and then scratched his head in amazement. 'Oive got to be honest with you, I ain't never

108

Brian with Eddie Cochran

Brian, Margaret, Marty
and Joy Wilde.
Bournemouth, 1960

The Krew Kats

seen one o' them before, guvnor.' You'd have thought he'd just encountered a man from Mars, by the look on his face. I didn't meet any Martians on tour, but we did work with a lot of stars, like Bob and John, the Allisons, who were to represent England in the following year's Eurovision Song Contest singing *Are You Sure?* and Ronnie Carroll who'd had a minor hit during 1960 with a cover version of Steve Lawrence's *Footsteps*.

By the autumn, Marty was becoming increasingly involved in other projects — he not only made a film, but also went into the London stage musical of *Bye Bye, Birdie*, which left Jim, Tony, Licorice and me a bit high and dry.

We decided to try and strike out on our own, but Larry Parnes refused to let us use the name Wildcats so we changed it slightly to the Krew Kats and went into the studio, to record a Chet Atkins instrumental called *Trambone* which despite only reaching Number 33 loitered around the chart for a remarkable ten weeks.

We'd backed a few singers for Radio Luxembourg broadcasts and met Norrie Paramor, who'd suggested our session at the Abbey Road studios which produced not only *Trambone* but *Samovar*, one of Jim's tunes *Peak Hour* and a number I wrote, *Jack's Good*, dedicated to the TV producer of the same name! Good bit of crawling that!

The four of us often played as session musicians for artists in Joe Meek's stable in his upstairs studio above a shop in the Holloway Road. Joe was quite a character, having served his apprenticeship at the IBC studios as engineer on sessions from Chris Barber to Tommy Steele before eventually starting up his own production company, RGM, and one of the first independent record labels, Triumph. The label was fairly short-lived as it was soon swallowed up by Top Rank, but not before Joe had notched up a couple of hits, one by an instrumental group who became known for taking old tunes and twanging them up, the Flee-Rekkers, and another by Michael Cox. He was a hot property after his hits with *Angela Jones* and *Alone Came Caroline* when we went in to back him on his next single. Big Jim Sullivan was messing around in between takes with a version of Chuck Berry's *Sweet Little Sixteen* when Joe Meek yelled out, 'That's it, that's the one, let's do it,' and it became Mike's new 45.

He was a very positive character, Joe, I'm sure it was his great drive that brought him so much success both as a producer and a songwriter. His record speaks for itself when you look at the charts for the early 60s. John Leyton, Mike Berry, Michael Cox, the Outlaws, Heinz, Iain Gregory, the Honeycombs, the Cryin' Shames, Peter Jay and the Jaywalkers, and of course the Tornados, with my mate Clem Cattini on drums, for whom Joe wrote and produced

110

Telstar which not only topped the charts here, but became Number 1 in America and at *that* time a feat like that was extraordinary! We were pretty friendly with the Outlaws, and Geoff Goddard who went on to write several early 60s classics like *Johnny Remember Me* and *Wild Wind* for John Leyton, as well as two fine tribute songs *Tribute to Buddy Holly* and *Just Like Eddie.* I think Geoff and Joe were fairly obsessed by Buddy Holly, and for some reason in 1967 Joe killed himself with a shotgun on the anniversary of Buddy's death.

Another real character was music publisher Eddie Rogers, who was looking after the Krew Kats career, or at least was supposed to be, but he'd invariably turn up to see us a little the worse for the booze. Not surprisingly the work petered out, and an attractive offer of a summer season with Tommy Steele was enough to turn the heads of Messrs Locking and Bennett towards Yarmouth! A few days later I was bundling my drums, Margaret, myself and a few clothes on to a train bound for David Copperfield country where we took a little flat over a bar. I decided I'd struggled on and off trains long enough and it was time to think seriously about a car, so Margaret started working evenings in the bar downstairs and was soon shown the tricks of the trade like accepting a gin and tonic from a customer, only having the tonic and pocketing the money for the gin! It's a good job it wasn't sloe gin or it might have taken us longer to save for the car!

Although we were based at Yarmouth, we'd often fly off with Tommy in his little six-seater Dove aircraft to do one-nighters in other parts of the country, but wherever we went we were potential targets for his practical jokes. On one trip back from Bournemouth there was a violent storm so we couldn't land at Yarmouth airport and had to be diverted by ground control to a nearby military base where we came down in driving rain, only to find there was no transport to get us from the plane to the nearest building. Eventually an old military fire engine was rustled up, but it was a really ancient old thing with a long ladder jutting into the air. Any port in a storm though, and as this particular part was being treated to diabolical weather of monsoon proportions we gratefully made a dash for the fire engine to discover that it could accommodate all but one of us. The one of us just happened to be the man who was organising Tommy's gigs, yes Mr Parnes Shillings and Pence!

'You'll have to hang on to the ladder, mate,' yelled the driver through the pouring rain.

Larry had no choice — either drown slowly or quickly — so he hopped up on to the ladder. As we started heading towards the group of buildings at the perimeter of the airbase a wicked toothy grin spread over Tommy's face as he pulled a pound note out of his pocket and pressed it into the driver's hand.

'Go on, mate,' he said, 'once round the airfield!'

We were in hysterics in the cab as we careered around for a good ten minutes while Larry was being blinded by the rain and could only jump off at the risk of breaking his neck! I guess he never had the urge to ride shotgun on a fire engine again! After the show we all used to eat at a great restaurant in town called the Savoy. It was run by a guy called Mr Lucas, and despite having played all night I invariably used to cart my drums down there, Licorice would take his bass and we'd play jazz with a guy called Alan Hawkshaw who was bashing the old keyboards down the road at the Aquarium Theatre for Emile Ford and the Checkmates — we must have been gluttons for punishment, and if Mr Lucas' clientele didn't like it, it was also punishment for gluttons! Alan and I became great friends after that and worked together on many occasions. Both Licorice and myself were pleased to see Hank, Bruce, Jet and Tony doing well for themselves backing Cliff, especially as he'd been at Number 1 with *Please Don't Tease* that summer from the middle of July until the middle of August, but when we saw a copy of the *New Musical Express* on 17th August and saw the headline 'Cliff Richard Sensation — Dethroned by his Shadows at Chart-Top' it really increased our incentive to get back in the studio and create a hit record.

We called Big Jim Sullivan, booked Abbey Road studios and organising hiring a car. Then a few nights later Licorice and I tore back to London after an exhausting evening in the orchestra pit backing Tommy, recorded four titles during the night including one called *Jungle Drums,* and drove back the following day in time for the next night's show. Hectic stuff!

There was a show in the West End of London at that time called *Stop The World, I Want To Get Off.* The drummer for the show was Andy White, the guy whom George Martin was to rope in the following year as drummer for the early Beatle sessions at Abbey Road, before he realised Ringo could play a bit! Anyway Andy revealed that he was planning to leave the show around Christmas so why didn't I come and check the parts out? Wow, this was the ultimate for me, the West End *and* twenty-five pounds a week — it sounded fantastic, so I went along one day in September to discuss the ins and outs of the job, and as we stood in the pit going over the score Margaret phoned with a message. I excused myself from Andy to hear the words, 'Bruce Welch has just called, and he'd like you to join the group — it's the Shadows you know . . .'

'I know it's the Shadows but I'm still with Tommy, and I've been offered a good job in a pit band in the West End!'

I spoke to Bruce and he asked me how much I was getting. I told him twenty-five pounds, so he said they'd double it! Fifty pounds a week — it seemed incredible! I talked to Larry and Tommy who both tried to talk me out of it but I felt I couldn't miss an opportunity like that. Before I knew it Peter Gormley was driving me up to Birmingham to join Hank, Bruce and Jet for an appearance on the TV show *Thank Your Lucky Stars*. I certainly thanked mine.

9 / *Shadows to the Fore and More*

(November 1961 — Summer 1962)

On 12th October 1961 *Kon-tiki* was knocked off the Number 1 spot by the Highwaymen, five students from the Wesleyan University in Middleton, Connecticut with their arrangement of the traditional song *Michael Row the Boat Ashore.*

Among the new releases in October were Ben E. King's *Here Comes the Night,* Johnny Burnette's *Setting the Woods on Fire* and Eddie Cochran's *Jeannie Jeannie Jeannie* — none of which could be heard on *Housewife's Choice.* On Radio Luxembourg Peter Noble took over the *Honey Hit Parade* and one of the top London Ballroom DJs was none other than Ian 'Sammy' Samwell, resident twice a week at the Lyceum, as well as appearing regularly in Basildon, Norwich and Stevenage as a front man in Mecca's plan to launch more and more disc-jockey sessions.

The *New Musical Express* started advertising its 1962 'All Star Calendar' with the birthdays of 435 leading British and American disco stars for only three shillings, available just too late to record Cliff's twenty-first that month, which was celebrated on the plane to Australia, Brian's first trip abroad with his new group.

The party was great. Because Cliff was famous, the airline had organised a special commemorative cake, and we celebrated for most of the 38-hour flight! When we arrived down under we went straight from the plane, into a taxi and off to smile and be bright for a 9.00 am chat show with a DJ called Bob Rogers, who was a top radio personality in Sydney. Like Hank and Bruce he was a very keen fan of the Goons — and of course, also like Hank and Bruce, he was a keen Shadows fan!! We did several shows with Bob over the years — I think Hank liked him particularly as he always used *Nivram* as his signature tune!

We were so young and eager then that we didn't even stop to think about being tired, it was such great fun! The only thing that was slightly disconcerting was the fact that the Australians and the audiences in the Far East were obviously not aware that Tony had

114

Dan Farson meets the Shadows
(an early TV show)

Cheap at half the price

left the group as they kept shouting his name whenever I did a drum solo. Mind you, people still do that today, twenty-two years on, they'll say, 'Hello Tony . . . er . . . I mean Brian.' To some people I'm still the new boy! I preferred to stay very much in the background in those early days; I'd hate talking on the radio as I'm a terrible speaker and if a camera with a red light on it even *looked* as if it was going to point in my direction I'd feel uncomfortable!

I felt a little more at home when we stopped off in Kuala Lumpur on the way back, to go on safari. Cliff and ourselves dressed to the nines in khaki and pith helmets, crawling through the undergrowth with pots and pans, in an unsuccessful attempt to flush out a wild boar or two.

Back in England, EMI also threw a twenty-first birthday party for Cliff — he was presented with a camera, which he used immediately to record for posterity the new Shadows line-up. Ex-Drifter Ian Samwell and ex-Shadow Tony Meehan were among the guests, along with an all-star line-up which included Marty Wilde, Helen Shapiro and Frank Ifield as well as DJs Pete Murray, David Gell and Ray Orchard.

During a previous visit to Scandinavia the Shadows had had their first taste of cabaret audiences and that, coupled with having seen such artists as Peggy Lee and Sammy Davis at work, brought out a great desire to have a go at that form of entertainment. Bruce even recalls taking dancing lessons.

We thought it would be great if we could suddenly take our guitars off and launch into a song and dance routine, and as Cliff was taking lessons too, we thought that we could also work out some on-stage routines with him. We didn't really like the cabaret idea, although our management were pretty keen on it, but our album did include a wide range of styles so we could incorporate those, a few connecting links, some dance routines and we'd have the basis of a show. We'd also started writing songs in a slightly humorous vain, like *Stars Fell on Stockton* complete with lots of whistling bits! That was the first number that Brian Bennett ever recorded with us.

Not only was it the first time I went into the studio as the Shadows' drummer, but I'd even co-written the tune. The A side, *Wonderful Land,* was done before I joined, and Norrie Paramor had added a great string and horn arrangement to it, which was revolutionary for the time. I found it easy to work with Norrie

On safari

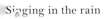

Singing in the rain

Learning the words

because of our previous relationship when I'd been with the Krew Kats, but according to Peter Gormley I wasn't going to find it so easy working with Jet.

One of Peter's first questions to me on joining the group was, 'Do you drink?'

'Well, yes, I like a few beers now and then.'

'Well, don't get involved with Jet.'

When I first met Jet in Blackpool the first thing he did was ask me out for a drink!

'Harmless enough,' I thought. 'Where shall we go — one of the pubs on the front?'

'No, can't do that, Bruce'll see us,' and with that he proceeded cautiously down the corridor from the dressing room, eventually stopping outside the gents. He gave a furtive glance over his shoulder and said, 'Quick, in here!' Once inside the apparent safety of the toilet he pulled a couple of cans of beer from under his coat, and handed one to a very bemused young drummer!

'Do you always drink like this?' I asked him.

'Sometimes. Bruce hates drink — he goes potty if he thinks I've had too much!'

For all Bruce's regimental attitude, he was a vital ingredient in the Shadows for his stabilising influence and his capacity for being a good anchor for the group. He was always on top of the situation, and he used his strong personality to insist on things being done to absolute perfection!

While the Shadows front line was going through a sticky period personnel-wise, with Tony leaving, Brian joining, and increasing clashes between Jet and Bruce, one of the men behind the Shadows' (and Cliff's) success talked about their good points. Like Peter Gormley, Norrie Paramor never sought the limelight and was happy to be the producer without making a big song and dance about it:

Now there's a quartet of characters for you! A really happy, mischievous bunch, who it's always great fun working with especially as they're such practical jokers and keep the studio technicians in fits of laughter. This gaiety is an essential part of the Shadows and their music. The quartet's attitude of complete abandon is reflected in their happy sound and it's true to say they play very much for kicks. Despite the fact they can't read music they are terribly inventive and imaginative musicians and their talent is by no means confined solely to rock 'n' roll.

Norrie's own ability to diversify and adapt to different musical

118

Hank and Carole

The Marvin family

Ben, Tahlia and friend

Bruce and Lynne

Bruce, Jason, Lynne, Mary (Lynne's mum) and Dwayne — 'the family', wedding day, August 1979

A chip off the old block — Dwayne Welch

Bruce's Aunt Sadie

Brian at work in the office at home

Margaret and Sarah

Bennetts junior — Jonathan
and Warren

'We're all going on a summer holiday.' Athens 1963

Right, above Cliff and the Shadows relaxing with their new
ATV camera

Right, below The Ants — all we need now is Adam

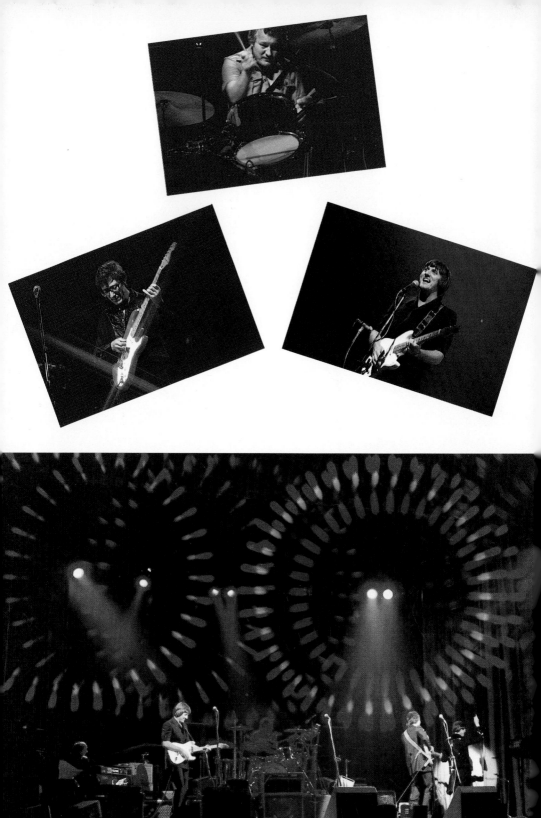

Paul McCartney relaxing as Hank Marvin (photo by Linda McCartney)

1961. The Shadows, Cliff and Princess Margaret — what a line up!
(We're the ones working)

We are not impressed!

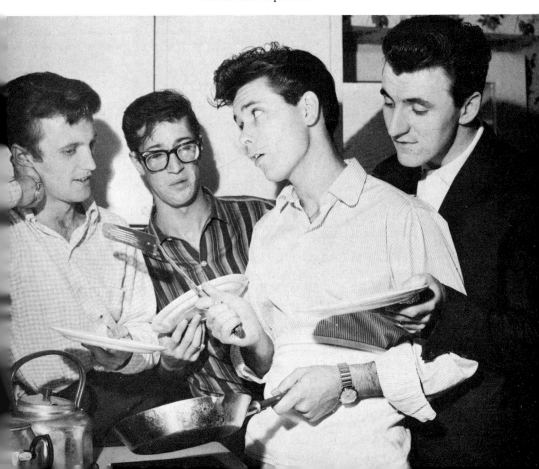

styles is borne out by the wide range of different artists he'd produced. As well as the Shadows, Cliff and Helen Shapiro, there was Big Bopper sound-alike and ex-Covent Garden porter, Tommy Bruce; Welsh singer of *Tell Laura I Love Her* fame, Ricky Valance; established artists like Michael Holliday, Ruby Murray and the man with the golden trumpet, Eddie Calvert; and Australian Frank Ifield for whom Norrie would produce three Number 1s on the trot during 1962.

Both sides of the Shadows' sixth hit were written by Norrie, *The Savage* and *Peace Pipe*, although Hank didn't feel it was right for a single.

> Bruce and I felt really narked as up until then we'd been involved in the choosing of our singles, but *The Savage* was released without our knowledge while we were in Australia. As we were not consulted, Bruce and I didn't feel there was any harm in being honest to newspaper reporters when talking about the new single. This resulted in a very irate phone call from Peter Gormley who informed us that Norrie Paramor was very upset that we felt that way to which I replied, 'That makes five of us then, doesn't it!'

The Savage got to Number 10 in the chart despite the fact that Hank and Bruce weren't happy about its release, and was apparently even good enough to be borrowed note for note over a year later by a Swedish group. The Violents were Tonny Lindberg, Hans Rosen, Olle Darlington and Johnny Landenfelt. Like many other groups who'd formed in 1960, they'd modelled their style very much on the Shadows, to such an extent that in fact their first big hit in Sweden, *Ghia* had exactly the same tune as *The Savage.*

Whether the ultimate tribute or blatant plagiarism, the record helped them on their way to becoming the top recording group in Sweden during 1963 and 1964.

As *The Savage* was released, singer Eden Kane was in hospital undergoing a sinus operation, Hank and Bruce's 50s hero Lonnie Donegan was being presented with two gold discs by Bing Crosby for *Does Your Chewing Gum Lose Its Flavour* and *Rock Island Line,* American singer Dion was in England promoting his new single *Runaround Sue* and Billy Fury had his future revealed to him by a famous London clairvoyant.

The Shadows certainly needed no clairvoyant to tell them that 1962 would be a good year for them. In the NME points table based on the 1961 charts, where thirty points awarded for a week at Number 1 down to one point for Number 30, the Shadows came a very creditable third. Elvis had 1,525 points, Cliff 1,053 points and the

'Ba-oom-ba-dut-dut' — Sunday Night at the London Palladium

Shadows were breathing down his neck with 1,046, while their nearest rivals, the Everly Brothers, as fourth most successful act of the year, notched up just 815.

On 20th November 1961 the Shadows returned from Australia with Cliff all set to headline ATV's *Sunday Night at the London Palladium,* and to take part in discussions for their next film in which acting roles were scheduled for the Shadows. Tentatively titled *Summer Holiday* it was still in the early planning stages but one storyline had Cliff and the Shadows cast as young entertainers travelling across Europe in an old London bus. While discussions were underway regarding the Shadows' future contribution to the silver screen, reports came through from Australasia that following their tour record sales were already a hundred per cent up on the figures before their arrival.

As '61 became '62 *The Young Ones* had its première with resounding success; the Shadows embarked on a two month British tour with Cliff, the Two-Tones, the Trebletones and Patti Brook; *Wonderful Land* was released as the new single, and the future looked rosy. The only dark cloud on the horizon was the increasing problem with Jet which had been a nagging doubt in the minds of Hank and Bruce for some while.

Brian Bennett, partly because he was the new boy in the group and partly because it's his nature, found himself acting as mediator and general nice guy in an attempt to smooth over the abrasive flare-ups.

Jet would have a few brown ales and it would be all over, he'd get a stream of verbal from Bruce, and go on stage in a really black mood. As soon as Bruce was looking the other way, Jet would look back at me on the drums and mouth, 'The effing bastard,' to which I'd just shrug my shoulders and raise my eyebrows. I couldn't afford to take sides, but it got pretty awkward sometimes especially when he got really low, and dressing-room rows would end with Jet in tears. He'd be the first to admit, now, that things couldn't really have carried on the way they were.

It was just a craving I had for drink. I can't explain what the feeling is. It's a state of mind I suppose, brought on by personal problems. It was undoubtedly Cliff's relationship with Carol that started me on the bottle, although he would never have deliberately done anything to hurt anyone else, he was always too much of a young gentleman and a friend to do that. It was just one of those things — we were all young and the whole world had exploded around our ears, presenting us with all sorts of situations — and

Breakfast in Paris

Avez-vous — a Daily Mirror?

laid many temptations in our path. Heaven knows how most of the group emerged relatively unscathed.

In March the Shadows played the Paris Olympia and went down like a bomb from start to finish with Bruce attempting to make the announcements in 'Franglais'.

> We never really knew whether they understood us or not but they rarely complained at my improvised lines like 'Et maintenant notre latest disc est a numero one best seller — *Wonderful Land.*' At least *we* understood *them* at the end of the act when they stood up and shouted 'Un autre! Un autre!' We celebrated our Parisian success at an all-night restaurant in the meat market where the French porters all drink in their bloodied overalls. There were quite a crowd of us at the 'Pied du Cochon' — Peter Gormley, Norrie Paramor, our booker Eddie Jarratt, songwriter Jerry Lordan, a couple of journalists and of course 'nous'.

The part of the night that Jet remembers with most fondness was going on to a jazz club.

> We left the old 'Pig's Foot Restaurant' at three o'clock in the morning, and went to the Blue Note Club to listen to a great team of American musicians led by drummer Kenny Clark. He mesmerised me almost as much as the French billiards champion with whom I'd played the previous day. I actually played billiards most of the time while we were in Paris, and although it was weird having no pockets in the tables I found it just as interesting, especially when the leading French player was giving me a few tips on how to go and beat my mates back home. Being in France was a bit like a holiday really and *Wonderful Land* getting to Number 1 in Britain at the same time put us all on cloud nine.
>
> Apart from all the good things that were happening to the group, Bruce was pissing me off more and more — he was like a bloody robot. When Carol left me for Cliff, Bruce came out with a real classic line that really hurt me and has remained imprinted on my brain, 'What are you so worried about, Jet, she's only a bloody woman!' The crunch came at the NME poll winners' concert at Wembley. The bar was open all day for the artists, so by the time I met up with the lads, I'd had a few. Bruce just turned on me with six little words. 'We don't really need you, Jet.' By then I'd had a bellyful of him. I walked out and never went back.

124

The boys next door (depending where you live)

10 / *In and Out of the Shadows*

(Spring 1962 — November 1963)

Licorice Locking was sitting at home when the phone rang. The man on the other end of the line spoke with a slow, familiar, Australian drawl — 'Licorice, how would you like to become one of the Shadows?'

Well, dad, you could have knocked me down with a puff of wind — it was the greatest thing that had ever happened to me. I'd always been very friendly with Hank and Bruce and of course had known Brian as a close friend for many years, as well as having played with him in various groups including the Krew Kats, Tommy Steele's backing group, Marty Wilde's Wildcats and touring with Eddie Cochran and Gene Vincent. I'd always admired the Shadows as everything they do is sheer simplicity, methodical, yet at the same time one step ahead of anyone else. The fans were extremely kind to me despite Jet's departure, which must have been a real shock to staunch supporters of the group, and made me feel at home in my new surroundings. I had stacks of letters in the first few weeks and was particularly delighted by one from an ordinary working family in Liverpool which welcomed me as a new Shadow and ended simply 'You're all right, son!' It was a great honour to be invited to take over from such a well-liked artist and bass player as Jet, but the fans still had access to his talent via his new material.

While Licorice was settling into my old position as bass man with the Shadows, I went into the Decca Studios to put down some new tracks which included the Latin American standard *Besame Mucho* and a number called *Chills and Fever* that had been an American Top 20 hit at the beginning of 1961 for a guy called Ronnie Love.

Jet's recording manager Jack Good was really excited with the results as was borne out by his comment at the time:

Jet has a real cool voice, I think the best description of it is a sort of male Ann-Margret. We used two guitars, piano, bass, percussion,

126

'Willie and the hand jive'

On stage

a chorus of six voices and former Shadow Tony Meehan on drums on the session, which I feel really enhanced Jet's performance both as a vocalist and guitarist. With regard to other possible avenues, he could develop into a strong and natural actor given the right script, and there are already two film directors who are willing to screen test him as soon as possible.

Licorice's first appearance with the Shadows was at the British Songwriters Guild charity concert, 'Our Friends the Stars'. Cliff was also on the bill along with Eden Kane, Danny Williams, David Hughes, Ray Ellington, the Countrymen and Max Bygraves. The occasion certainly didn't overawe Licorice, as the press described him as 'confident and relaxed' and another critic remarked:

> Recent changes in the Shadows' line-up have done nothing to dim the versatility of the group, for they were in top form.

What better moment to join the country's top group, than at a time when they were right up there on top of the charts, with their third Number 1.

No other single could knock *Wonderful Land* off its perch for two months, so there it stayed at the top of the heap from 22nd March until 17th May, a remarkable achievement, only ever bettered by nine other acts in the history of the chart. It would be seven years before the Archies' *Sugar Sugar* equalled their run at the top, and nearly fourteen years before Queen bettered it by just one week when they took *Bohemian Rhapsody* to Number 1 for nine weeks. Human beings are strange creatures, though, and while the Shadows were enjoying this particular pinnacle of their career, some people had the audacity to write to the music papers suggesting the boys were slipping!

Although it currently seems fashionable for the press to join glee-fully in the swift demolition of any artist who's been successful, it wasn't the case in 1962 and the Fleet Street pen pushers leapt to their defence, albeit in the lingo of the time.

> Beginning to slip indeed! Since when has a disc in the Top 10 without fail meant that an artist was beginning to slip? Half the people who write these letters are doing so because they're fans of a rival group. Maybe it would interest them to know that hardly any groups (and certainly not the Shadows members) are not worried about competition. It's only when their second and third platters don't make the grade that they start to worry, but this hasn't happened to the Shadows and it's very doubtful whether it ever will. The Shadows are not going to rest on their laurels, in

other words while you are saying 'Isn't the Shads' latest waxing cool!', the boys are working on their next number or even the one after that. Naturally the interest in instrumentals may die off, but the Shadows will be prepared for such an emergency — and though this has not been decided, the day might come when they start using a vocal Jordanaires backing on their platters.

Some very pleasant and swingin' tunes can be made certain Number 1s through this method.

In the meantime Jet was in the chart with his first solo single *Besame Mucho,* released on Decca, which featured the distinctive sound of the six-string bass which was to become his trademark. Viewers eagerly glued to *Thank Your Lucky Stars* on 5th May saw Cliff and the Shadows being presented with gold discs, just prior to them flying off to Greece to film *Summer Holiday.* The picture only required the Shadows' presence for a fortnight, so there went Hank's free holiday!

At least we got a *couple* of weeks in the sunshine, the non-working hours of which were spent with Cliff and Una Stubbs, stuffing ourselves in restaurants at night and swimming by day — it was a tough fortnight!

The title track for the film had been written the previous winter by Bruce and Brian.

Bruce and I were together just running through some numbers when a script arrived for *Summer Holiday,* the picture we were due to be involved in a few months later. Most of the score had been written by Myers and Cass who always wrote quite old-fashioned songs — it seemed like a lot of writers were trying to make rock 'n' roll sound sophisticated.

Anyway at that time they hadn't written a title track, so Bruce said, 'Let's have a go,' picked up the guitar and immediately started singing, 'We're all going on a summer holiday, no more working for a week or two . . .' and it just came straight out. I went over to the piano and the same thing happened with the middle section. I went straight into, 'We're going where the sun shines brightly, we're going where the sea is blue . . .' and the whole song was finished inside twenty minutes.

We put it straight down on my Starlight tape recorder, and just over a year later it topped the charts.

The Shadows cropped up during the film in various guises, contributing three instrumentals to the soundtrack, *Round and Round,*

130

'I remember who!'

'Play back' in Barcelona with Peter Gormley (*left*), Malcolm Addy (*centre*)
and Norrie (*right*)

Les Girls and *Foot Tapper,* while the gang who'd been in *The Young Ones,* Melvyn Hayes, Richard O'Sullivan and Co., were joined by Una Stubbs and Laurie Peters, an American actress who'd previously appeared in the Broadway production of *The Sound of Music* and in the film *Mr Hobbs Takes a Holiday.*

When *Summer Holiday* was completed, it was found to under-run by several minutes and when the phone rang in Norrie Paramor's office in Upper Harley Street, Bruce heard a panic-stricken voice on the other end saying another song would be required — but pretty quickly.

> Cliff was there with me, so we just sat down for a couple of hours and by tea-time we'd written *Bachelor Boy* which was slotted into the film in a hastily shot sequence at Elstree, in which we had to perform some sort of dance. I know Hank hated that!

> It was a real wally dance, I mean it looked so staged and contrived we'd have been better off sitting around singing and playing our guitars!

During their time in Greece, togged up in Greek national costumes and playing bazoukas, the critics were reviewing their follow-up to *Wonderful Land.* One comment by a journalist, John Wells, said:

> Let's face it, *Guitar Tango* isn't obvious hit parade material. There hasn't been an unamplified guitar in the chart for years. They took a gamble and it paid off. A & R man Norrie Paramor deserves a big bouquet.

And Norrie's own comment was:

> I don't consider it to be as way out as people claim. I think it has tremendous individuality and freshness and shows the boys to be considerably more versatile than many realise.

But not everybody was enchanted by the tango rhythm played on acoustic guitars. In a letter to the *New Musical Express* a gentleman called Keith Conroy described it as 'a shameful example of their work' while another reader, N.W.L. Martin, thought it was 'a fabulous number performed magificently.' Disc jockey Keith Fordyce played safe with his comment that it was 'a very enjoyable disc' whereas one national press critic declared it to be 'the worst thing they've ever made' and *Juke Box Jury* compere David Jacobs confessed, 'I simply don't know what it's all about!'

Bruce knew what it was all about though.

It was incredible, really, we'd stuck to a particular style and sound for our previous seven records and quite a lot of people were accusing us of clinging to a tried and trusted format, but when we *did* try something new, they were the first to turn round and accuse us of forsaking the familiar Shadows sound!

For all the bashing it had from the critics, *Guitar Tango,* with Brian Bennett's 'Debs' delight' parody *What a Lovely Tune* on the other side, reached Number 4 in the chart — not bad for a tune which had its humble beginnings in a demo the Shadows had received from a French song-writer. While the Shadows and Cliff were appearing in the *Holiday Carnival* at Blackpool ABC, Jet Harris released his second solo single, *Main Title Theme,* in August, and the same month made his solo TV debut on Granada Television's *Spot the Tune* and his solo theatre debut at the Princess Theatre in Torquay.

In September Jet not only toured with Del Shannon, Freddy Cannon and Joe Brown but was also offered a dramatic role in an episode of AR-TV's *No Hiding Place.*

That same month guitarist Bert Weedon, who'd been voted Top Musical Personality the previous year, gave an interview which included some strong feelings about Jet and the Shadows.

At the risk of extensive criticism, I stick my neck out and say the Shadows should split up if they have a keen eye on their future. The worst thing in show business is to get a 'tag' — you become known by one section of the public only.

Soon I am sure Jet Harris will become a big star in his own right and people who watch television and go to the pictures will have his name on their tongues — but they wouldn't have if he had stayed a Shadow. Frankly I don't think Hank and Bruce will split up. They are inseparable as friends and together they have a powerful partnership as owners of the Shadows. Going back to Jet, I believe he has a wonderful future. I have been studying and playing the guitar myself since I was thirteen — so I should know a few things about it — and I think Jet is a very talented instrumentalist.

As *Main Title Theme* was nearing the end of its eleven week run in the chart, the album *Out of the Shadows* was released, featuring Jet playing bass on some tracks, Licorice on others and Brian drumming on a Shadows album for the first time.

My drum solo, *Little B,* was actually done in one take, with no overdubs or edits, the guys just put their instruments down and tiptoed over to the percussion instruments exactly as we did on stage. The jazz-influenced *Tales of a Raggy Tramline* I'd written with Hank and Jet before his departure. That was a great title — we've always had fun thinking up names for tunes, because you can call an instrumental anything you like. Cliff even contributed a number he'd written, *Some Are Lonely.* Around that time the EP from the film *The Boys* starring Jess Conrad was released, for which, in addition to the title track, we'd written *The Girls* and a slower version of *The Boys.* The fourth number was *Sweet Dreams,* which had been written by Bill McGuffie who'd scored all the incidental music for the picture.

By the beginning of November as *The Boys* climbed to Number 1 in the EP chart, and *Out of the Shadows* was at the top of the album chart, the *New Record Mirror* announced a fabulous 'Make a Star' contest with two exciting prizes — the Brian Matthew Cup for singers and the Bert Weedon Trophy for budding guitarists. Hank *didn't* enter the contest as they'd only just flown back from Memphis!

Elvis Presley's dad Vernon called us while we were there and invited Cliff and ourselves over to the mansion, Gracelands, which was a great thrill, but Elvis himself wasn't there.

While Hank, Bruce, Brian and Licorice were in the States, the Crickets, whose song *Baby My Heart* the Shadows had covered on their first LP, were in England — minus drummer Jerry Allison who'd been called up by the American army owing to the Cuban crisis — following up their success a few months earlier with *Don't Ever Change.*

Within days of flying into London airport, Cliff and the Shadows were rehearsing like mad for their second Royal Variety show, along with Andy Stewart who appeared in his kilt, Harry Secombe who went on stage dressed as a mountie, Eartha Kitt who didn't dress as a mountie, husband and wife team Johnny Dankworth and Cleo Laine, and Frank Ifield, who, like the Shadows, was managed by Peter Gormley.

Dance On was released in December 1962 having been recorded, like all the other Shadows singles, at Abbey Road, under the supervision of Norrie Paramor with an engineer called Malcolm Addy twiddling the knobs. Malcolm had been there since 1958 and was to stay until 1966 but towards the end of 1962 he was often assisted at the control desk by ex-research chemist Peter Vince.

I was virtually a tape operator and button pusher learning all I could from watching people like Norrie and Malcolm and listening to Cliff and the Shadows, little knowing that I'd become increasingly involved with them over the next two decades. The recording equipment at the time was fairly primitive by today's standards, and of course that applied to record players in the home as well, as most people still had 'Dansette' machines that only enabled you to control the bass, treble and volume. A four speed autochange model cost around twenty-four pounds in 1962 and for an extra two guineas you could have legs as well! There was a more basic model for about twelve pounds which most kids had as they didn't care too much about legs! Instruments were even fairly cheap for young people buying their first ones. I think Selmer did a Spanish guitar for about seven pounds and drum manufacturers like Dallas made kits which retailed from about twenty pounds.

Cliff's double-sided single *The Next Time/Bachelor Boy* held the top spot over Christmas '62 only to be knocked off in January by *Dance On*, the Shadows' fourth Number 1, which had been written by the Avons of *Seven Little Girls Sitting in the Back Seat* and *Rubber Ball* fame. Nobody was more delighted than Cliff, except of course Brian, Hank, Bruce and Licorice, as he paid tribute to them in the *New Musical Express* tenth anniversary book.

Hank is one of the nicest people you could wish to meet, and it's virtually impossible to get annoyed or mad with him. He's terribly easy going. Nothing ever seems to bother him and he takes life in his stride without ever a grumble or a moan. As a solo musician I rate Hank as one of the most inventive rock 'n' roll guitarists in Britain. Yet in a way he's only just starting. To my mind he's barely scratched the surface of his talent.

Bruce is the go-getter of the group, terribly reliable and a bit of a task master in as much as he keeps the boys at it during rehearsals until everything is perfect. You see perfection is Bruce's aim, and he spares nothing to achieve his goal. He's very very truthful, and whenever I want an honest opinion about something — for example a record — I ask Bruce because I know I will get a truthful constructive answer.

I've known Brian for a couple of years and he's a quiet guy who keeps himself to himself. He's an excellent drummer, but if a thing is bad he'll have no hesitation about saying so; similarly if something impresses him he really lets you know. More so than the other boys, Brian is very punctual, and I know I speak for all the group when I say that it's good to have him with us.

On 10th January, *Summer Holiday* was premiered simultaneously in

London and South Africa where the Shadows and Cliff embarked on a tour six days later which took in Cape Town, Port Elizabeth, Durban and Johannesburg as well as Bulawayo and Salisbury in Rhodesia and a charity concert in Nairobi organised by Kenyan leader Tom Mboya.

During the tour the *Daily Express* criticised Cliff for commenting on racial affairs in South Africa. Their attack evoked a swift reply.

> I agree that I'm not qualified to talk about it. The Shadows and I didn't go to South Africa to delve into the racial question, we went there to perform and entertain . . .

After the tour, there were only a few days' rest before the start of a six week British tour, for the Shadows to have some time with their families, see a few old friends or just sit around watching telly. So after a few short days catching up on the latest records and discovering that familiar programmes like *The Army Game, Armchair Theatre, Candid Camera* and *77 Sunset Strip* were still flickering cosily from the one-eyed monster in the corner of the front room, they were off again. New numbers and new movements were the order of the tour: their set included a Drifters song, *Up on the Roof,* which Kenny Lynch had just taken into the charts for a couple of months, and their new single *Foot Tapper.* For a whole month of the six week tour Cliff and the Shadows topped the charts. *Summer Holiday* was there for three weeks and *Foot Tapper* for one week. To celebrate the success of the remarkable achievement, Bruce lashed out and threw a party.

> I thought I'd give a party for Cliff and invite a few mates. The Vernons girls were there, the Beatles, Cliff and, of course, Brian, Licorice and Hank. Not being much of a drinker I went off to make a cup of tea, but I hadn't been in there a couple of minutes when the kitchen filled up with the rest of the Shads, Cliff and John, Paul, George and Ringo.
>
> I'd heard that the new Beatles single was supposed to be pretty hot and asked John what it was like. He immediately upped and went into the hall, located a guitar and reappeared a few seconds later to launch into a duet with Paul:

> 'If there's anything that you want,
> If there's anything I can do
> Just call on me and I'll send it along
> With love from me to you.'

By the end of May *From Me To You* was Number 1, and it stayed there for seven weeks.

136

Hank suggested we returned the compliment by inflicting our new number on them, so he and I treated the assembled company to *Atlantis* on two acoustic guitars, which was followed by Cliff and ourselves giving a deliberately out-of-tune take-off of *Please Please Me*. After that there was no stopping the impromptu battle of the bands, as John, Paul, George and Ringo gave us a Shadows impersonation complete with a wildly exaggerated leg-kicking cross-over step!

We continued singing together, the nine of us, mainly rhythm and blues stuff including the Beatles' rendition of the Chiffons' *He's So Fine* and the Isley Brothers' *Shout*, rounding things off with some Ray Charles classics as dawn was breaking outside.

It speaks volumes for the talent of Ray Charles that four weeks later Cliff and the Shadows flew to Paris in May specifically to see him in concert. Hank was ecstatic.

Charles was quite sensational; he sang and played with so much feeling it was a wonderful musical experience, and it's just as well he was so great, as we were all slightly disappointed with the sixteen-piece band he brought over.

Brian was of the same mind.

The band was a little disappointing, the only exception to me was the drummer, who was first class. Ray sang his current hit, *I Can't Stop Loving You*, but the one we especially liked was his version of *One Mint Julep* which had the whole place rocking.

Licorice had his favourite, too:

Hide Nor Hair went down very well, and he tore the place apart with his slow styling of *Georgia*. And the crowning glory came at the end of his act when he finished with *What'd I Say*. It was terrific.

Bruce still hadn't fully recovered from the experience.

He completely dominated the stage from the moment he set foot on it. We were shouting right along with the rest of them. I guess it was quite a new experience for Cliff to *be* one of the screamers!

By the time *Atlantis* was released in June, Licorice was becoming more and more interested in participating as a Jehovah's Witness and he talked at length to Hank about his beliefs on a plane journey that summer.

Licorice and I fell into an informal discussion about the various ideas on the origins of man and I suppose his explanation of the

137

Bible account of this aroused the first seeds of my interest in the scriptures.

Since his interest and associations with Jehovah's Witnesses he'd always led a very moral life and wasn't keen on raving it up at all, but he was a very amusing guy. His impression of Jacques Tati's famous character M. Hulot was brilliant, and when he decided to do his Zombie act, lurching around at airports and restaurants, he'd terrify the life out of people.

Ironically Licorice nearly had the life terrified out of *him* while they were in Greece filming *Summer Holiday*.

Hank, Bruce, Brian Bennett and a group of people working on the film decided to come swimming with me one day during a break in shooting. The sea was really warm, and a group of us decided to head out for a raft which we all reached safely, except for Bruce and the film choreographer, Herb Ross. Apparently, Bruce was not used to swimming long distances, and was floundering sixty or seventy yards away from our objective and getting quite panicky. Luckily, Herb heard his cries for help, swum out to him and somehow managed to get him to the raft. Just in case he was in a bad way, Brian and myself swam at high speed back to the shore for a paddle boat and successfully took a fairly breathless Bruce back to dry land.

On the morning of 1st June 1963, the Shadows and Cliff were relaxing in Lytham St Annes in preparation for a start that evening of a sixteen-week-summer season at the ABC Blackpool with Carole Grey, Arthur Worsley and Dailey and Wayne. The Beatles were at Number 1 with *From Me To You* and their summer date sheet took in Rhyl, Great Yarmouth, Weston-Super-Mare, Llandudno, Jersey, Urmston, Nelson, Liverpool, and at Blackpool the couple of Sunday concerts John, Paul, George and Ringo did on the Shadows' one night off a week seemed like another good excuse to get together. The crowd scenes outside the theatre were such that it appeared the Beatles were never going to get out alive until their roadies, Mal Evans, Neil Aspinall and Co., enlisted the help of Cliff and the Shadows' tour manager David Bryce and his crew.

We hatched up a devious plot for getting the guys out of the ABC involving a dramatic escape in our old Thames van, known affectionately by the Shads as 'the vomit box'. They had such wonderfully descriptive powers then! As Beatle fans were keeping an organised vigil outside most of the sizeable hotels in Blackpool someone obviously had to come up with an alternative destination.

Hank drew the shortest straw so it was everyone back to his rented bungalow for a party — the road crews, the Shadows and the Beatles.

With both groups having increasingly heavy recording, touring and personal commitments the chances of the Beatles and the Shadows meeting were few and far between, and became more impossible as time went on. According to Bruce the great thing was the lack of animosity or jealousy between the two groups, and their mutual respect, both personal and musical.

Brian, Hank and I even went to Paul McCartney's twenty-first birthday party. We travelled down by car from Blackpool and met Paul and his then girlfriend Jane Asher as arranged in the doorway of the Liverpool Empire, before following them back to the house. There were so many singers and musicians from Liverpool there that it was almost as if a Merseybeat Handbook on pop music had come to life. The Fourmost were there, so was Billy J. Kramer, Paul's brother, of course, Mike McGear, and John Lennon, who became increasingly the worse for wear as the evening wore on and ended up punching the Liverpool DJ, Bob Wooller (this of course was some time before he wrote *Give Peace a Chance*). It was a great party, though, with plenty of singing, dancing and high jinks before we had to drive back through the night to our rented house in St Anne's. In the future, though, due to the increased workload of both groups the only brief encounters we had with the Beatles would be over a cup of tea and a sandwich at Abbey Road Studios or a quick thumbs-up and odd word of greeting at the annual NME poll winners concert.

Although the style of music the Shadows played didn't directly influence the Merseybeat boom, undoubtedly a high percentage of the groups who rode to fame on the new music tide of 1963 had either started life as a Shadows-type line up or had been so impressed with the legendary guitar work of Hank Marvin that they'd spent hours, days and weeks learning the early Shadows tunes in front of their bedroom mirrors. In fact at one stage it was almost compulsory for the lead guitarist of an early 60s group to sport a pair of Hank-style black horn-rimmed glasses, whether he needed them or not!

Maybe the new beat groups that emerged around 1963 didn't copy the Shadows music, but they were impressed by their musicianship and more often than not their managers and agents were keen to mould them into the image and presentation purveyed by Cliff's lads. Even the Beatles were once taken to see the *other* fab four in action, as Hank remembers.

Before we knew them, Brian Epstein brought the Beatles to see us at Liverpool Empire. He was obviously trying to impress upon John, Paul, George and Ringo that *this* was the way they should present themselves, in neat looking suits and dickie bows! It didn't seem to matter what they wore, though, their success was so phenomenal.

While the Beatles, Gerry and the Pacemakers, Freddie and the Dreamers, Billy J. Kramer and the Dakotas and Jet and Tony were spending most of the summer touring, the Shadows were at least based in one town and could have some of the day to relax, which gave Brian a chance to get some practice in for his favourite sport.

Off duty moments that summer for me were spent on the local golf course knocking great lumps out of the fairway and trying to hack my ball out of assorted gorse bushes. I also got into having a bash at painting on a very professional-looking easel and canvas — turning out many 'Pablo Bennett' originals, much to the amusement of the other lads. They spent a lot of time tearing round in their cars and watching film shows at the house that Cliff was renting.

After a strenuous 42-night tour on top of radio and TV commitments Licorice was only too pleased to be in one place for a while.

It was great to be able to take your clothes out of a suitcase and *leave* them out, although there *are* eight costume changes during the show, so the lazy days were no luxury, dad, they were a flipping necessity. I spent some of the Blackpool season, though, in Brian's bad books.

Licorice was amazingly forgetful — he always forgot to give me telephone messages and things like that, but he really took the biscuit one day, when he was showing a cousin of his round the theatre. My little Starlight tape recorder that went everywhere with me had the misfortune to be sitting minding its own business in the dressing room, when Licorice blundered in and spotted it, explaining to his cousin that I used it for putting down new song ideas. He then decided to give his awestruck kinswoman a practical demonstration, wound the tape back to the beginning and said, 'Go on, talk into the microphone, make some noises and I'll play them back.' It was only when I went to listen to play some of the potential future Shadows material to Bruce and Hank the next day that I discovered that Licorice had been tampering with the machine. I switched on and there was nothing but Licorice encouraging his cousin to record her voice for posterity. Hank

140

and Bruce decided it would never make a hit! Licorice as usual denied having touched it, but I could never be cross with him as he always looked so awkward and embarrassed when he eventually confessed to something.

Atlantis soared up to Number 2 during that summer season, and in response to music paper columnist Derek Johnson posing the question 'Do strings hinder the Shadows?' Peter Elwood from Cheshire wrote in, pointing out that of their last seven singles, the two that had stayed in the chart longest were *Wonderful Land* and *Atlantis* and *both* had strings and orchestral backing.

If the music press had a thing about strings, Hank had one about wasps.

I hate 'em so much that I used to take my air rifle out into the garden when the wasps were lying on the apples I'd shoot them. One day in late summer though I got a shock as I was blasting away like a bespectacled William Tell, when a disembodied voice shouted, ''Ere, stop killing them birds!' Well, peeing on a monkey's one thing but I'd never use sparrows for target practice, so I yelled back, 'I'm not shooting birds — I'm shooting wasps.' I never did discover where the voice came from. I've actually learned to live with them now . . . in fact some of my best friends are wasps . . . I might even use some on our next bee-side! I suppose I was lucky that I was only bothered by wasps, Bruce was having greater problems.

My obsession with getting my guitar absolutely bang in tune really had its roots back at the time we started turning pro with Cliff. We had to tune up in the dressing room without amplifiers in those days, so the best way of doing it was to press our solid guitars up against a wall, as that gave it a little more resonance.

Even then I'd be tuning and re-tuning right up till the moment we were due on stage, but during the 1963 Blackpool summer season, it dawned on me and everyone else that I was getting worse. I'd turn up at the ABC Theatre at three o'clock every day just to make sure my guitar was in tune for the 6.15 performance, and eight times out of ten I was still out of tune, or imagined I was, by six! Occasionally the tension would be so great I'd jump into my E-type Jag and storm off to London, but sometimes I *was* able to discuss it rationally with the guys. I should really have gone to see a doctor. Everything had to be exactly right for me; I was, and still am, a perfectionist, and a stickler for time-keeping, so Hank's erratic attempts at promptness, and Licorice's devotion to *his* activities really got my nerve ends jangling that summer!

According to Brian the atmosphere was often very strained while Bruce was tuning his guitar.

It was an impossible situation, you couldn't clean your teeth or even clink a glass — his nerves were totally shattered by his mad fixation.

I didn't know whether his obsession was due to the fact that he wasn't a great solo player, and felt a little inhibited by his own technique, thereby imagining that his great power and contribution was to get things perfectly in tune. Being a drummer I wasn't too worried about it — besides, once we'd been on stage for a couple of numbers his guitar would have gone slightly out of tune anyway, but you could hardly detect it with everything else that was going on.

A few weeks later a surprised British public opened their papers over breakfast to discover that Bruce had left the Shadows. He was only twenty-one years of age, but doctors told him he'd have a nervous breakdown if he didn't leave the group.

I worried about every little thing. Whether my shoes were polished, whether my suit was properly pressed, if my amplifier was going to work OK when I was on stage, timekeeping and tuning — you name it, I worried about it.

Hank recovered from the shock departure sufficiently to talk to the press.

We're going to miss him very much as an integral part of the group, quite apart from our personal feeling. However, we hope his departure will not affect the group's popularity. It'll be a big responsibility for me to be solely in charge of the team but I can always phone the office for Bruce's advice.

The transformation from world-famous guitarist to a desk job looking after the affairs of the companies of Cliff and the Shadows was to take effect when the tour of Israel and France finished at the end of October. Cliff was equally cut up.

It's going to be a terrible wrench for all of us after five years of close harmony. But you can't argue with your health. The main consolation is that we shall still be in close contact.

Just three years after their first hit the Shadows were to lose their third member, and while it was being strongly hinted from various quarters that with only twenty-five per cent of the original line-up

142

remaining maybe it was time for a name change, another bombshell was dropped.

After the summer season, Licorice had found himself at a personal crossroads. He was already a Jehovah's Witness when he joined the group, and as Brian Bennett had also been of the same faith for a short while, when years before he'd attended meetings with his mother, it was easy for him to understand the strong feelings Licorice had about his beliefs.

> An increasing amount of his time was being spent preaching from door to door and attending meetings. It was gradually taking over his life and causing a few raised eyebrows within the group.
>
> I was really the middle man between Licorice and the other two, I felt that it was up to me to explain to him that he couldn't turn up late just because he was talking to someone about the Bible.
>
> I conceded that it was a great thing to do, to want to seek the truth, but on the other hand the job had to be done, so I told him that he'd have to do some soul-searching and come to a decision.

Licorice announced his departure from the Shadows in October, as *Shindig* was sitting comfortably in a Top 10 headed by Brian Poole and the Tremeloes' *Do You Love Me?*

It was a black autumn for the Shadows fans; Bruce was leaving, Licorice was leaving and after a great year for former members Jet and Tony, during which they notched three Top 10 hits as a duo, Jet was in hospital after a bad car crash.

Despite his impending departure, Bruce was as desperate as the others to find a replacement for Licorice. Hank had ideas too, as he told the press.

> We may give an audition to a promising boy called Paul McCartney in an unknown group called the Beatles. Come to think of it he won't do, he's from Liverpool. We want a lad from Newcastle-upon-Tyne — the more Geordies in the band the better!

While the Shadows were going through a sticky patch personnel-wise, at least the sleeve notes on their first American album which was released to that time brought a smile to their faces, as it described them as the 'originators of surf music', when the nearest they'd ever had to a surfboard was a washboard! Maybe the inclusion of *Atlantis* gave the Americans the idea of calling the album *Surfin' with the Shadows*.

With the problem of finding a new bass player pressing heavily upon them Brian remembers travelling up to watch the bassist playing in Tony Meehan's group.

Bruce and I had had a tip off that Tony's bass player, John Paul Jones, might be the right guy to replace Licorice, but to be honest we didn't really feel that he looked the part — in fact when we first saw him on stage with his long cigarette holder and very fair complexion he just didn't look right! John later joined Led Zeppelin — I mean who are we to stand in his way! Fortunately though, Bruce had another idea in the shape of a guy called John Rostill.

John fitted the bill completely, he was a great bass player, having previously been with the Interns, and he looked good, so the guy whose professional career had begun when he was paid fifteen shillings for appearing at a Tooting and Mitcham Football Club dance was co-opted into the Shadows to become their third bassist. The week Bruce was due to leave he started having second thoughts.

I had a chance to relax and unwind while we were in Israel and I was considerably less irritable since the doctor had given me some pills to calm me down.

Another good reason for staying was the deal I'd done with John Rostill to overcome my problems with the guitar — I paid him ten pounds a week to tune it for me before each performance!

As well as the personnel changes that the end of 1963 brought there was a residential all-change too. Hank and Billie bought a new house in Totteridge for £12,500 and Brian and Margaret Bennett moved into their old one. Bruce and Anne were still living in a cottage-style house in North Harrow which they had bought for £6,000 back in 1961. Writing hit songs and having hit records brought other benefits too, like holidays abroad in good hotels for a change! Hank really felt that things were changing for them.

Suddenly we didn't have to worry about how much money we spent, we could go into any restaurant and order anything we liked or walk into a men's outfitters and buy several suits at one time — we really felt we could do anything. Bruce and I both became 'two-car' men — Bruce had a three-litre Rover and E-type Jag, while I had a three-litre Rover which I bought for £1,600 and a Triumph TR4 which had set me back £1,000. We also learned to accept being well-known and recognised in public places, although it did have its uses — in restaurants for example, they really looked after you and you got good service everywhere. For Brian and myself buying new houses was a major step at the end of 1963, but it would be at least the spring before we could settle in, as there was another film to be made first.

John Rostill

11 | *The Canaries, Belgium, Germany, Austria, France, Great Yarmouth and All Stations to the London Palladium*

(Christmas 1963 — Christmas 1966)

In the winter of 1963, umbrellas and raincoats were the order of the day, but to dispel the English gloom a recipe for a film was found. Take one cold wet December day at Gatwick, add one gleaming jet full of Susan Hampshire, Melvin Hayes, Una Stubbs, Richard O'Sullivan, the Shadows and Cliff Richard. Spread another 129 people evenly between the plane and thirty-nine other vehicles, mix in fifty tons of equipment, including lights, film cameras, make-up, wigs, costumes, generators, typewriters, and whisk briskly to the Canary Islands off the north-west corner of Africa — and whaddya know you've got a show! Well a film, or two films to be exact, as *Wonderful Life's* slightly complicated story line was a film about a bunch of filmmakers making a film! The cast ended up being there for ten weeks, based at the Santa Catalina Hotel in Las Palmas, the capital of the largest of the seven Canary Islands, Gran Canaria, where most of the location work took place. The adverse weather conditions necessitated a longer stay than was intended, as Brian recalls.

> Most of the film was done on the sand dunes and if there was a rainstorm during the night the cameramen would discover that when they looked through their cameras the next morning the sand would be a different colour, which would spoil the continuity of the scene, so we'd all have to hang around in our costumes waiting for the sand to dry! Then as we were at last about to shoot someone would point up at the sky and say, 'Hang on, Guv, there's a cloud up there,' and you couldn't suddenly have clear blue sky in a sequence, then a flaming great cloud a few seconds after that and completely clear sky again moments later, so we'd all hang about again waiting for the cloud to pass — it was crazy. In one scene, Susan Hampshire is tied to the mast of a boat that's

146

Discussing what's wrong with Brian

Relaxing during a break in filming

heaving and pitching like mad, and I'm all kitted out as a pirate who is supposed to come along and slit her throat, but I was never cut out to be Blackbeard. I felt a lot more at home being a landlubber back in Las Palmas Green, so it's not surprising that I was wretchedly seasick.

It felt as though we re-did the take of that sequence a hundred times, but you can't turn to the director when the cameras are rolling and say, 'Can I throw up please?' so it was 'Action' — heave — 'Action' — heave. Sid Furie, the director, must have been as sick as I was. I remember there was one part of the film where Cliff and Richard O'Sullivan were to have a gun fight, for which they used a little village called Castelroma. The inhabitants had never seen anything like it before, and the whole population turned out, including hundreds of tiny Spanish children all watching wide-eyed as the cameras were set up. After a few run throughs, Sid Furie yelled 'Action' and Richard and Cliff started firing at each other like mad, sending the crowds screaming back to their houses, not realising that they were using blanks.

It was without doubt a rather confusing film. Hank always reckoned that there was a film in there somewhere trying to get out!

The plot was complicated. Basically in the film we are drifting on a raft (living out Kon-Tiki fantasies!) and end up in the Canaries (it was a low budgie film!) where we stumble across a film crew making *The Daughter of the Sheik* in which we become vaguely involved before deciding that we could do it better, so our gang set out to make a film within a film within a film! A little sanity was at hand though as our wives were over there with us — they weren't daft! My wife Billie was there, Margaret Bennett, and Una Stubbs' husband Peter Gilmore (later to star in *The Onedin Line*). Bruce's wife Anne and some of the others came over on the banana boat with Billie because she had claustrophobia and wouldn't fly. They left from the City of London docks and were having a reasonable voyage until they were hit by a force nine gale when they got out into open seas.

Bruce was amazed by some of the strange characters working on *Wonderful Life*.

There was Paco, our kamikaze driver who negotiated the mountain roads en route to the location like he was at Brands Hatch, and the assistant director Freddie Slark who had a peculiar way of referring to the stars of the show like Cliff and Susan Hampshire. He'd say, 'Right, let's have the "big money" in for the next shot.' Many of his odd phrases and mannerisms were eventually used in the film. The whole ten weeks was a mixture of fun and boredom, I think, for most of us, but to John Rostill it was a never-to-be-forgotten experience, as he hadn't yet played a note for the Shadows but found himself in the Canary Islands making a film. If we'd made films like *Wonderful Life* every year I don't think I'd have needed my holiday home in Portugal. Cliff bought one too, and Peter Gormley and Frank Ifield, in a little fishing village called Albufeira on the Atlantic coast, which was a great place to escape to when the pressures of tuning my guitar got too much.

Geronimo, the Shadows' thirteenth hit single, stayed in the charts the whole time they were in the Canaries and the follow-up, *Theme for Young Lovers,* entered the chart as they embarked on a British tour with Cliff, with John playing bass on stage with them for the first time, which greatly pleased Brian.

John was the best bass player we had. He was very steady which meant I didn't have to concentrate quite so much on keeping my timing rigid and I could experiment a bit. He was not only great to play with but he had a real good time as well.

Early in 1964, the NME published their complete analysis of the best selling charts for the previous year, which showed the total hit parade merits of every artist who appeared in the Top 30 during 1963. As was customary, thirty points were awarded for every number one position and so on down to one point for number thirty. The Top 10 artists were:

1.	Beatles	1,741
2.	Cliff Richard	1,323
3.	Shadows	899
4.	Gerry & the Pacemakers	894
5.	Frank Ifield	838
6.	Roy Orbison	772
7.	Billy J. Kramer	680
8.	Jet Harris & Tony Meehan	668
9.	Billy Fury	623
10.	Freddie & the Dreamers	584

Despite the onslaught of Merseybeat, the Shadows had improved upon the previous year's placing, moving up from Number 4 to Number 3, and fans of the group were delighted that between them the Shadows, Cliff and the Shadows and Jet Harris and Tony Meehan amassed an incredible total of 2,890 points. In the year's LP table based on the weekly album chart where ten points was awarded for a

Number 1 and so on down to one point for a Number 10, the Shadows also had fantastic success:

1.	*Please Please Me*	374
2.	*West Side Story*	302
3.	*Summer Holiday* (Cliff, Shadows)	252
4.	*The Shadows Greatest Hits*	180
5.	*Meet The Searchers*	146

Jet Harris was on a twenty-nine date round trip of Britain which overlapped the Cliff and the Shadows string of one-nighters, but by the end of both tours there were traumatic experiences in store not only for Jet but also for Hank.

I think Jet was hit very badly when his girlfriend Billie Davis announced to the press that their romance was over, and just two weeks after that a tragedy nearly struck the Marvin household. Our 18-month-old twin sons Peter and Paul were out playing in the back garden of our house in Totteridge when we suddenly realised that things were too quiet and went to see what all the silence was about! There was a gate that fenced off the goldfish pond from the rest of the garden but somehow they must have opened it and got through, because Billie found them floating unconscious on top of the pond! It was one of the most awful experiences of my life seeing those two tiny bodies face down in the water. We got them out but quick and Peter soon recovered, but I had to apply mouth to mouth resuscitation to Paul for quite some time, while the ambulance was on its way. They both went into hospital for treatment and observation and fortunately came home none the worse. Funnily enough, they both became really good swimmers.

Due to the fact that the incident involved a well-known personality, the story did a lot to increase people's awareness of the importance of the 'kiss of life' in a situation like Hank's. The press sensibly featured it heavily with bold, eye-catching handlines like 'Hank of the Shadows saves his twin son with the kiss of life'; 'Shadow Hank saves his baby's life' and 'Shadow Hank saves his twin sons Peter and Paul.'

A fortnight later, Hank, John, Bruce and Brian and Cliff were off again, this time a European tour, with *The Rise and Fall of Flingel Bunt* entering the chart the week they left for Belgium. The tour later took in Germany, Austria, France and a country surrounded by Norway, Lapland, Finland, Russia, Poland, Germany and Denmark. Sweden, like Great Britain, is a kingdom, which maybe gave it a working atmosphere similar to our own. Everyone who was involved in one particular Swedish gig remembered the occasion with amazing clarity.

Bruce recalled it was absolutely pouring down.

We'd been driving for ages, and the weather being so dreadful we were desperately trying to cheer ourselves up with optimistic remarks.

'It'll probably turn out to be one of our best performances.'

'We're bound to pull out all the stops to compensate for the weather.'

'It might clear up.'

Our happy banter soon petered out when Brian pointed out that it was in fact an open air gig. We were obviously in for a good soaking. Talk about 'the rockin' pneumonia and the boogie woogie flu'!

After a couple of hours, silence and deep gloom had descended upon us and we were motoring through desolate countryside in miserable conditions when I saw an old track to our right leading into a field. Half-joking Cliff said, 'If we go right here I'll go mad.'

Our driver Sid Maurice said, 'Prepare to go barmy, boys,' and swung the motor in through the gate and across a field. David Bryce and the crew were already there, as they'd been checking the venue out and arranging the equipment, and realised that the Shadows and Cliff would not be in the greatest of moods, in fact in all probability wouldn't want to play at all.

It would be a gross understatement to say that David wasn't looking forward one little bit to the lads arriving, but he had resolved to cheer them up as much as he could. In one of the three caravans being used as dressing-rooms he found the answer. Diving equipment! It was there primarily because the main power cable had to go under water, and obviously the equipment came in pretty useful, but D. Bryce had other ideas. Dave and two or three of the crew dressed themselves up in wet suits, flippers and rather fetching see-through head gear complete with snorkel, and stood by the entrance to the field, in the rain. It had an immediate impact on the occupants of the vehicle churning its way towards the stage in the middle of the waterlogged football pitch. Bruce thought it was hilarious.

We collapsed. The sight of four frogmen capering about in the torrential rain somewhere in the middle of Sweden appealed to our sense of the ridiculous. We literally fell about, but it had the desired effect — it immediately dispelled all the gloom and despondency and gave our spirits a real lift. Of course we did the gig, but the weather didn't let up — if anything it got worse. We got changed and sat in one of the caravans while the support act was on, wondering how he'd go down with the crowd. I must admit we exchanged worried glances when we heard the terrific applause he got. I mean, he was OK. Not that wonderful, but all right. But from the sound of the applause he'd have brought the house down if it hadn't been open air. He certainly brought the rain down. Anyway he came off, we got the 'go' signal and on we went. Two things struck us. The first was that the entire 4,500 crowd had large multi-coloured umbrellas. And the second was that they couldn't possibly have applauded the support act so enthusiastically as they only had one hand free — and single-handed applause is a little difficult!

The mystery was solved afterwards when he confessed that he'd brought his own applause tape in case his act didn't go down too well!

While we were away the album *Dance With the Shadows* escaped, which included our versions of standards like *Zambezi, Temptation, In the Mood* and *Chatanooga Choo Choo*.

By early June the tour was over for the Shadows, but two astronauts notched up forty-five world tours in Gemini Nine, and Surveyor One did a one night stand on the moon.

Back on earth there were more problems for Jet Harris as he was finally divorced by his wife Carol, and Cliff told the London *Evening News*, 'People think I must be a millionaire, but I'm not. Nowhere near it!' *Wonderful Life* must have helped swell the coffers a little, though, not just for Cliff and the Shadows but for the National Association of Youth Clubs which benefited from the première of the film, attended by all the cast, in the presence of Princess Alexandra and the Hon. Angus Ogilvy. The two Shadows instrumentals in the picture were *Walkin'* and *Theme for Young Lovers*.

Shortly afterwards, during the summer show in Yarmouth, the Shadows put together a twenty-five minute film called *Rhythm and Greens* with themselves as the stars and Cliff as an extra.

In one part they had me playing King Canute — I'm telling the waves to back up, but needless to say it was scripted so I got swallowed up by the sea. I couldn't help feeling that they were getting their own back on me for things they had to go through in previous films!

Many Shadows fans have never seen *Rhythm and Greens*, as it has only been distributed once as support film to Dirk Bogarde's *King*

Attending the premiere of *Wonderful Life* at the Empire
Theatre, Leicester Square

A scene from *Rhythm 'n' Greens* (a film)

and Country and is consequently a rare piece of footage, but, as Brian says, it was basically like *The Goon Show* meets *The Magical Mystery Tour,* although the fun-filled twenty-five minutes pre-dated the Beatles effort by three years.

One idea behind it was to portray a short but hilarious history of life on Britain's beaches. We started off as cavemen singing the title track and we briefly became Romans, pirates and legion-naires.

John and Bruce had an old-fashioned duel in which I somehow got shot, and not content with that I'm then shown playing cricket with a difference on the beach, where I'm tossed grenades and bat them out towards enemy ships. I'm sure John, Bruce and Hank were trying to tell me something, as in the next sketch I eat a grenade made of licorice and blow myself sky high! I know licorice can have a certain effect on you but I didn't think it was that bad. Robert Morley did a commentary for the picture, a guy called Christopher Miles wrote and directed the film, and as well as starring in it we wrote *The Drum Number, The Lute Number, Ranka Chanka, The Main Theme* and the title track *Rhythm and Greens* which became a hit in September and stayed in the charts until we started to tour Britain with Cliff in October.

Admittedly the charts were being swamped with Merseybeat in 1964 but one magazine early that summer published a very far-sighted and accurate article on the consistency of the Shadows, and their future path.

You can beat your drums about the Beatles' success but surely aren't the Shadows one of the best groups ever? Can you name any other instrumental discs in two or three minutes that have been chart hits in the last five years without naming a Shadows number?

The Shadows have not, surprisingly, turned to vocal numbers, but they're on safe ground sticking to their instrumental style, composing their own numbers, backing Cliff on his world tours and appearing in his films. The Shadows have the ideal existence. They don't have to worry too much about their future, for they are linked with Cliff and it's hardly likely that *he'll* ever be any smaller than the great success he is now, and of course they have their own act.

When the Merseybeat, the Liverpool sound and the R 'n' B panic is all over you can bet that the Shadows will still be making hits. The names may change now and again, but the style and the hits just keep on coming.

154

You're pretty, what's your name?

An early Roman record player

Me nervous?

'It's one for the money.'

An early recording session

Tea and sympathy with Peter Gormley

'The Police' — all we need now is a hit record

'Queen' — all we need now is a hit record

Shadows relaxing between tides

Brian showing Cliff his new dress

Rehearsing for a Danish tour

Rehearsing for a French tour

'Was it good for you, too?'

Brian with helicopter on head

Just prior to their third Royal Variety appearance, in November 1964, the Shadows gave the press a retrospective look at their *Rhythm and Greens* venture. Hank felt that it was good experience for them.

> It's done us the world of good as performers; our appetites have been whetted by our appearances in Cliff's films, and we were tickled pink at the prospect of making one on our own. Cliff appeared as King Canute in one scene, and got a ducking for his troubles as he met the same fate as the original. The film was originally scheduled to be called *A Load of Rubbish* so you can judge from that what it's going to be like.

Bruce echoed Hank's sentiments and explained:

> We can't just go on bashing out the same old numbers on our guitars year after year without any attempt at experimentation.

Viewers to the Royal Variety Show on BBC TV on Sunday 8th November were treated to the Shadows opening their set with *The Rise and Fall of Flingel Bunt* followed by Hank's solo of *Tonight* from *West Side Story,* then all four singing the folk song *Five Hundred Miles* which led on to Cliff's appearance. Among the other artists on the bill who queued up with the Shadows to be introduced to Her Majesty the Queen were the Bachelors, Cilla Black, Kathy Kirby, Brenda Lee, comic Bob Newhart, Lena Horne, *That Was The Week That Was* star Millicent Martin, and compere David Jacobs.

During the summer the Shadows had been writing furiously for their forthcoming pantomime with Cliff at the London Palladium, as well as doing the Great Yarmouth season and filming *Rhythm and Greens. Aladdin* opened at the Palladium on 22nd December, four weeks after the Royal Variety Show. Cliff played the lead role, and one of his friends in the pantomime was Wishee, better known as Bruce Welch.

> John got lumbered with the role of Poshee, Brian was Noshee, Hank was Washee, and I got stuck with Wishee. It was great working with the late Arthur Askey as he was a real pro and if anything went wrong would just bash on regardless, due to his amazing ability to ad lib. As Widow Twankee, Arthur shared top billing with Cliff and ourselves, but despite being cast in that role still managed to pepper his performance with some of his time-honoured catch phrases, like "'Allo playmates' and 'I thang you', the latter being traditionally spoken with his thumb and forefinger clamped firmly over his nose. He was great. Una Stubbs was the Emperor of China's daughter, Princess Balroubadour, and the famous Blackpool clown Charlie Caroli played Chief Inspector

A family shot

'One in Hole'

Brian and Hank relaxing during a duel

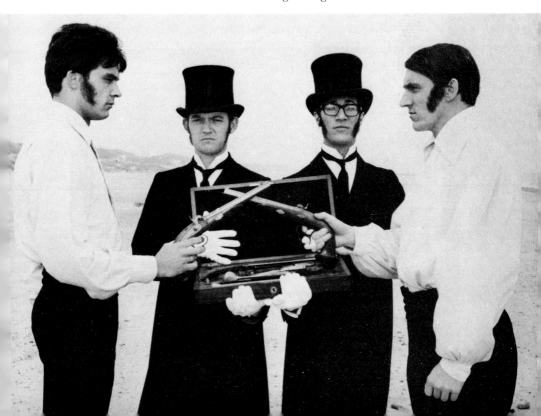

Bath Robe, aided, abetted and hindered by his two side kicks Little Jimmy, the gormless one who just stood there with his mouth open and never spoke, and Lord Henry Lytton (who swore to us that he'd actually been christened 'Lord' and that it helped him get great service in hotels).

Our producer Norrie Paramor did most of the orchestration and the orchestra was actually conducted by Billy Tennent.

Considering all that talent, seats were a bargain, ranging from seven and six to twenty-two and six! I remember there was an advertisement in the programme for *Aladdin* that offered a fortnight in Egypt at a luxury hotel for full board for a week for just sixty-nine guineas and on the back cover was an advertisement for Senior Service cigarettes at four shillings and tuppence for a packet of twenty, just over 20p in today's money! As well as backing Cliff on some of the numbers, John, Brian, Hank and I wrote all the musical score and we were featured on three instrumentals *My Oh My*, *Little Princess* and *Genie with the Light Brown Lamp* which stayed in the chart through December, January and most of February. In all, *Aladdin* ran for three and a half months which was rewarding but very gruelling.

A month before the pantomime the Shadows released their first vocal A side since *Saturday Dance*, a slow Jerry Lordan song with the title of *Mary Anne*, which stayed in the chart for ten weeks, reaching Number 17 and giving the group their first ever vocal hit.

Although the Shadows singles were still regularly making the chart, the placings *were* gradually becoming lower. They were no longer making the Top 10 but consistently hitting somewhere around the twenty mark, and as the Shadows flew off with Cliff for a tour of France, Spain and Switzerland their nineteenth hit single *Stingray*, backed with one of the many tongue in cheek titles *Alice in Sunderland*, just sneaked into the Top 20 at Number 19. None of the Shadows really rated *Stingray*, especially Bruce.

I didn't like it at all. It certainly wasn't one of our best. Although there's been a depression in record sales at the moment that wasn't the reason *Stingray* didn't do well, it was because it wasn't too good.

The organisation of the whistle-stop tour was, as always, the responsibility of David Bryce.

We took in three countries in ten days, playing places like Marseilles, Casablanca, Zurich and finally Geneva where we performed in a

164

In 'panto' with the late Arthur Askey

type of boxing ring — that's what they call learning the ropes! We had the end of the act worked out with military precision almost to the second. As the exit was so far away from the stage, and we were right in the middle of the audience, the only way we could get away without being mobbed was to be plunged into total darkness and make a dash for it. Near the end of the set, Cliff was singing about two feet away from hundreds of screaming girls and Bruce felt a little mischievous, knowing how Cliff liked really winding the audience up to fever pitch. Sidling over to Cliff halfway through the last number Bruce yelled in his ear, 'Let's have a riot then' and Cliff really turned it on. The girls were going mad, climbing on the seats and screaming their heads off. Suddenly the song finished. An ear shattering scream. There was total darkness, and we all made a run for the door. It would have been a great escape but we were only halfway to the exit when the full lighting came on, picking us out like startled rabbits. With a little help and a lot of luck we put our heads down kept on running and just made it, but what a scare.

Another unconventional escape was effected at Newcastle's City Hall. As the final chord died away we dashed off the back of the stage and down a passageway, pounded through the kitchens puffing like crazy, sprinted round a swimming pool and eventually went down a lift shaft to a side door. It was only a yard or two to the car but we could hear the deafening noise of a large crowd, who obviously hadn't left a convenient gangway for us to walk through. We made a run for it and nearly all made it. Bruce was missing. Suddenly there was a piercing scream from the centre of the crowd and a well-known rhythm guitarist wrenched himself free of the madding crowd with his face contorted in pain. We feared the worst, somebody, maybe Bruce, had either been knifed or had suffered some other dreadful injury. We were genuinely worried.

'What happened?' gasped Hank.

Bruce pouted and stood there like a scolded schoolboy mumbling, 'Somebody pulled my hair.'

An idea for a musical based on *Tom Brown's Schooldays* that Brian and Hank had been working on was temporarily shelved, and on their return from the July tour the Shadows' second vocal hit, *Don't Make My Baby Blue* went into the chart and climbed up to Number 10. It was to be their last Top 10 hit for over thirteen years.

Other frequent visitors to London's Abbey Road Studios where the Shadows made their records were, of course, the Beatles, and it was during their time there recording *Rubber Soul* that George Harrison had a quick natter with Hank.

> George was emphatic that the Shadows should do more vocal numbers, as he really liked our current single and thought we ought to concentrate a lot more on songs instead of just instrumentals. Paul McCartney had actually offered us an instrumental which he thought could be a hit for us. He wandered into Studio Three at Abbey Road and played it to me on the piano He had no words then and so just sang the tune. I thought it was a beautiful melody. He said he'd send a cassette but it never arrived. Later, when I heard their new *Revolver* LP, I realised why. He'd written words and it was now *Here, There and Everywhere.*

Following the release of *War Lord* in November 1965, the Shadows' music once more filled the stalls, boxes and circle of the famous London Palladium, as Frank Ifield starred in *Babes in the Wood,* but Bruce, Hank, Brian and John didn't appear, as a long run in one place was not only a big commitment, but Brian felt that he was cut out to be a musician rather than spending every Christmas playing Noshee or his *Babes in the Wood* equivalent.

> After three months I got fed up being pushed through a mangle by Arthur Askey, and asked myself what the hell I was doing capering around the London Palladium like a nancified Charlie Chan, when I really wanted to be a serious arranger, so I ducked out of the Christmas pantomime in 1965 — and the other guys obviously felt the same.

During 1964 and 1965 groups like the Beatles and the Rolling Stones had gone from strength to strength, to be joined by many new groups with a harder edge who blazed their way into the hearts and heads of teenagers all over Britain: groups with their roots in rhythm and blues, like the Animals, Manfred Mann, the Yardbirds and the Pretty Things, with a reputation for playing hard and smiling seldom which Hank had something to say about at the time.

> I deplore the passing of the smile on stage and the current trend for down-turned mouths and lantern jaws. How can you entertain other people if you don't look entertained yourself? I think groups of the calibre of the Barron Knights might well have an important function to play, the way they send up other artists on their records. If today's groups can't be laughed with then they must be laughed at. Laughter is the criterion!

And Bruce was equally outspoken.

167

We have a reputation for playing clear-cut sounds and unbent notes and we want to keep it that way because that's how we feel about music — we don't like it cluttered up. All this 'Yeah, yeah, yeah,' lark is only what we were doing four years ago in *The Young Ones* with *We Say Yeah*. Any change over the years has been subtle because we know that when we lose our identity the Shadows are finished. We write and compose from 10 am to 5 pm most days. The charts are nice but we don't need them like we used to . . .

Even Brian had something to say about the awareness of new wave of the beat groups seemingly obliterating the pre-Beatle era acts, with the exception of Cliff, from teenagers' minds.

When I pick up the sticks I like to be aware of tradition. There were a lot of great drummers before Dave Clark and Ringo Starr, like Gene Krupa, Louis Belson and Buddy Rich.

But a couple of months later Hank had nothing but praise for one of the new breed of guitarists, and gave the impression that he was suddenly keen to keep up with the new trends.

I watched Jeff Beck of the Yardbirds at *Ready Steady Go* and he gets a fabulous sound. I'm all for anything that creates new ideas for guitars. I've got a few fuzz boxes lying around — it's a great sound, but you must use the box sensibly otherwise the effect is lost. I first heard a foot-pedal being used by Big Jim Sullivan, and realised how fabulous it was. Push forward and you get maximum volume, push back and it's lessened. Turn to the left and it puts on full bass, turn to the right and it turns up treble. In my guitar collection I still have my old five-string banjo, as well as a four-string; I've got a battered old Zenith that I've had for donkey's years which I picked up for a fiver, a lute, a bazooka, a Ramirez flamenco guitar, a Gretsch Country Gentleman, a Gibson Jumbo, a six-string Fender bass, a Burns twelve-string electric, a Burns double-six, which is a twelve-string but with six bass strings and six guitar strings and two Burns-Marvin guitars, one in green and one in white. There are so many good players around, though, it gets me worried!

1965 had seen the release of two more albums, *The Sound of the Shadows* and *More Hits*, and their first LP of 1966 was *Shadows Music* which included a version of the Frank Sinatra classic *Fly Me to the Moon*, Liszt's *A Sigh (Un Sospero)* and a Brian Bennett composition *Benno-san* that yet again demonstrated the Shadows' love for titles that were plays on words — this particular one sounding like a Dr

Bennett's Medicine Show cure for all ills!

The Shadows' third vocal hit *I Met a Girl* reached Number 22 in April and the follow-up, *A Place in the Sun*, written by Jerry Lordan's wife Petrina, only made it to Number 24.

By Shadows standards positions like that weren't terribly healthy and it seemed as if warning bells were ringing in Hank's head as he was interviewed for *Beat Instrumental* magazine in September.

When Bruce and I first came to London we used to hang around the Freight Train coffee bar, playing the juke-box. The owner, Chas McDevitt, used to import obscure rhythm and blues records from the States and we'd just listen and copy them. We'd pick up phrases from Bo Diddley and the Drifters — it was fabulous music and we just couldn't get enough of it.

But the British guitarists then showed a lamentable lack of feeling. If they could play melody it was simply a series of single notes — no sound at all! Up in Newcastle we'd been following the way American stars like Scotty Moore and James Burton got the twangy bent notes and simply sat down and copied them.

The standards in 1958 were really poor, even among the better, more gutsy players, but now, younger players get to hear the sounds early and grow up with them. I'd say half the American records which make it nowadays are bad or poor like the archaic sounds on Tommy James and the Shondells' *Hanky Panky.*

I was even disappointed with the Beach Boys *Pet Sounds.* I asked myself where the Beach Boys themselves were, amongst all those weird sounds and that orchestration. Brian Wilson must have got carried away by his genius.

God Only Knows was marvellous though! I also thought the Walker Brothers *(Baby) You Don't Have To Tell Me* was a poor attempt, which didn't do as well as expected. That's because unlike the Stones or Beatles they don't have die-hard fans who'll buy every record they make. We thought our *A Place in the Sun* would have got higher than Number 24; in our opinion it was one of the best singles we've ever made and the fate of our previous single (our third vocal 45) wasn't much better. Although maybe we should do more and more vocal numbers — it's easier right now to get a vocal away as opposed to an instrumental.

There's a lot being said about Indian music in the pop scene, so I went to see Ravi Shankar playing his sitar in concert and I think it was the most moving performance, musically, that I've ever attended. His records are nothing compared with his live performance. Yet the nearest we've got to Indian music is something we've written for the new film with Cliff — *Finders Keepers.* But we'd never push the Indian stuff too far, the gimmick has already worn a bit thin so there's no point in hammering the subject.

Finders Keepers, which featured the Shadows more than any of Cliff's previous pictures, was set in Spain, at a time when the Americans have supposedly dropped, and lost, a mini-bomb on a Spanish village called San Carlos. The only people oblivious to the situation are a group called Cliff and the Shadows, whose car has broken down on a mountain on their way to an engagement in the town, and when they eventually arrive there it's completely deserted. The local USAF base has even forbidden the locals to fish. Cliff and the Shadows' new-found friend, played by Viviane Ventura, explains that it is very important for the locals to fish that night as it is a sacred festival, so the lads attempt to persuade the USAF commander to change his mind. Their first attempt at helping fails, despite their being smuggled into the Air Force base in laundry baskets hung on donkeys, but their second ruse works. Although they become heroes to the people of San Carlos they are not too popular with the camp commander, who ignores their claim to have located the bomb and locks them up.

They naturally escape and join the race back to the bomb along with a hotel keeper turned reluctant spy played by Robert Morley and a cook portrayed by Peggy Mount who also turns out to be a spy. *Finders Keepers* ends on a happy note, of course, with everybody blending into the finale at the Grand Fiesta.

It was during the filming of *Finders Keepers* that Hank first met Carole Naylor, who was one of the dancers in the film.

As well as dancing in the film I was also appearing in *Hello Dolly* in the evenings. The first place Hank ever took me to was a club called the Pickwick where the jazz trio the Peddlers often played. Romance must have been in the air at that time as John Rostill met a girl called Lyn who was dancing in the film as well and started taking her out. I think Bruce was more into football than anything else at the time.

I remember rushing straight from the set of *Finders Keepers* to watch various World Cup football matches at Wembley and White City — my all time favourite player was in the England squad at that time, the legendary Bobby Charlton — I even bought his book *Forward For England.* The entire team actually came to Pinewood Studios during the World Cup for lunch and to look around, which was a great thrill for me as I was a real devoted follower of the England team and was lucky enough to be able to go to the

World Cup Final at Wembley and witness Geoff Hurst scoring the hat-trick that clinched England's victory over Germany.

In spite of increasingly lower chart positions the *Record Mirror* poll published on 5th November 1966 proved the Shadows' supremacy as the world's top instrumental group, even though three of their last six single releases had been vocals.

They polled over three thousand votes more than their nearest rival, Herb Alpert, with Sounds Incorporated beaten into third place just ahead of Booker T and the MGs, Junior Walker and the All Stars, and the Ventures.

Top instrumental group or not, the Shadows persisted with vocals yet again on their new single which was one of Hank's compositions.

I was sitting at home watching a film one night when the melody came to me for *The Dreams I Dream.* I immediately started working out ideas on the piano and eventually recorded it myself putting down bass, drums, guitar and piano on a tape recorder in my front room. It wasn't terribly good quality, but it was great fun. The other guys were knocked out with it, so we recorded it.

Sometimes I get stuck with a song and have to put it to one side for a couple of weeks, then dig it out and have another crack at it, but with *The Dreams I Dream* the verses came in a couple of hours and the whole song took about half a day to write — although I ended up with several middle eights and had to eliminate all but one!

It was in September 1966 that the Shadows first met seventeen-year-old Olivia Newton John at a gig in Bournemouth and for Bruce it was love at first sight.

She was over here with her singing partner Pat Carroll from Australia, but I got her alone one day and asked her out. To which she replied, 'I don't mind going out with you but I'm not going alone.' So Pat had come with us!

I desperately wanted Olivia to audition for our third pantomine *Cinderella* which lined up at the Palladium at Christmas but she declined and flew back to Australia and her steady boyfriend in November. They were troubled times for me, my wife Anne had found out about Olivia, Olivia had gone back to her boyfriend, and there was a lot of squabbling going on within the group!

John Rostill, who more often than not was described by the press in the same three words, 'dark good looks', seemed happy enough though when he was voted 'Player of the Month' by *Beat Instrumental* in January 1967:

Really I owe all the fabulous things that have been happening to me to Lonnie Donegan — he was my idol and the star who got me interested in guitar playing. I used to copy his discs note for note, but I had to argue with my mother for six months before she bought me a guitar.

John, along with Hank, Bruce and Brian, wrote all the music for the 1966 pantomime, in which they performed alongside the Ugly Sisters, Hugh Lloyd and Terry Scott, with Pippa Steel playing Cinderella and Cliff as Buttons. Again the Shadows couldn't resist indulging their love of humorous titles and included a delightful title worthy of the Reverend Spooner himself, *The Flyder and the Spy*. Cinderella also heralded the return to the boards of the legendary Wishee, Washee, Poshee and Noshee, this time disguised as Baron Stoneybroke's men. They did two instrumental tracks and most of the time seemed to deviate from the script and appear as anything but the brokers men they were meant to be. In one scene, Hank and John even came on as scruffy schoolboys and proceeded to eat the contents of a goldfish bowl which admittedly did bear a slight resemblance to sliced carrots.

Also in December 1966 the Shadows and Cliff attended the première of Sylvia Anderson's technicolour puppet extravaganza *Thunderbirds Are Go* which starred Lady Penelope, the famous Tracy Family of International Rescue, Parker and remarkably lifelike puppets of Hank, Bruce, Brian, John and Cliff. They are the group at a glittering nightclub called the Swinging Star where they appear as 'Cliff Junior and the Shadows', singing and playing *Shooting Star*, written by Brian, John and Hank. Brian, John and Hank also wrote *Lady Penelope* for the film which together with two other tracks they performed on the soundtrack, *Zero X Theme* and the *Thunderbirds Theme* made up the four numbers for their EP, *Thunderbirds Are Go*.

1967 lay ahead with a blossoming romance for Bruce, and Cliff talking openly about quitting showbusiness, saying that he wanted to be 'an ordinary teacher in an ordinary secondary school'. The rumblings of discontent within the Shadows were growing louder, and their next release would be their last hit for eight years.

12 / Fading Shadows

(1967 — 1968)

By the end of 1966 the whispers of Cliff leaving the music business were growing louder, and of course the press turned to the Shadows to ask the obvious question, 'If your singer quits, what about your career?' Hank gave them their answer.

> What it will mean is that we'll have to come out and really work on our own. We've never worked exclusively with Cliff, but the image of him and us together as one unit has grown up, not unnaturally, in people's minds. I suppose it's been a bit too convenient to let Cliff be the leading light in the past, but don't forget we've had twenty-four hit singles and nine hit albums of our own, so even if he did give up singing we'd still go on as a group. Next year we'll be working almost exclusively without Cliff, because he's involved in a couple of films, and we'll be taking in tours of Australia, the Far East and Denmark as well as various residencies in England which include two runs at the Palladium. We've always had a loyal bunch of fans who've grown with us, so I don't think that John, Brian, Bruce or I have any fears for the future. Personally, despite all the talk, I don't think that Cliff will give up singing, I think that he will cut down on his showbusiness work to give himself more time for other things he wants to do. I also think he'll continue to make records and TV shows and do some appearances on stage, because I think he basically *needs* showbusiness, it's part of him. He needs an aura of adulation around him at times, and for that reason I don't really believe he'll give up singing.

A lady called Mary Clifford had previously organised a 'Stay in Show Biz Cliff' campaign and by the end of 1966 had collected 19,000 signatures. The petition was handed to Cliff at the Palladium.

Maybe the petition worked, or more likely Hank's assessment was correct, but in January 1967 Cliff quashed all the speculation about the possibly of him quitting showbusiness, which would undoubtedly

173

have affected the Shadows in one way or another although they were a separate entity. Speaking on a BBC Radio religious programme he said, 'I've found I can mix both my Christian life and my showbiz life as we are Biblically told, as a job that we're going to give to God.'

Licorice hadn't been able to handle both religion *and* music, Cliff had decided he *could,* and the same decision would soon face Hank.

Hank, Bruce, Brian and John's next recording was the theme from a new film, set in Morocco, starring Gene Barry, Leslie Phillips and Cyd Charisse. *Maroc 7* was released in April and although it stayed in the charts for two months, its highest placing was Number 24.

At the tail end of the *Cinderella* show at the Palladium, Bruce bumped into the Seekers' road manager who told him, 'A friend of yours is in town and would like to see you.' Bruce made it to the phone faster than you could say 'Kip Keino'. Olivia was back!

> I called her straight away, and we started seeing each other. Dwayne, my son, was six then so it wasn't an easy decision to make, but Anne and I eventually parted, and Olivia and I moved into a rented flat overlooking Lord's Cricket Ground in St John's Wood. We were up on the ninth floor, so there was a grandstand view for test matches, in fact some of our neighbours used to rent their balconies out!

However much in love Bruce and Olivia were, it did nothing to improve her cooking, as Shadows recording engineer Peter Vince discovered when he and his wife were invited round one night.

> We'd just finished a session one evening, when Bruce suggested going back to his place for something to eat. My wife and I were starving, so we took our rumbling tums across St John's Wood and up the lift to the ninth floor.
>
> Olivia duly brought out something to drink and a couple of dishes of those little cheese footballs. All set for a good evening, I thought, but about an hour later there appeared to be no aroma of food in the air, and I'd seen more footballs than an out-of-form goalkeeper.
>
> Despite a few hints and some well-timed coughs we were still wading through the spherical dairy produce after the second hour, and when Bruce and Olivia spent the third hour totally engrossed in each other on a mattress in the corner of the room, I felt it was time to go! We never did get the meal, and I wondered how Bruce didn't waste away with all that exercise and no food except cheese footballs!

174

On April 29th 1967 Hank and Bruce appeared on *Juke Box Jury* and the album *Jigsaw* was released in July, and included several versions of other people's hits, ranging from the Everlys' *Cathy's Clown* to the Easybeats' *Friday on my Mind* and *Semi-detached Suburban Mr James*, a hit for Manfred Mann the previous year. Even a composition by engineer Peter Vince was included, *Chelsea Boot*, which was despatched to the media as a seven inch sampler, with the title track on the flip-side, but was never actually released as a single. Peter was also to contribute a song to the next album from Hank, Bruce, Brian and John which was due for release at the end of the year.

It was a number I'd written called *Alentejo*, but in between doing sessions for that album and some things with Cliff, Bruce had started to work with Olivia in the studio, working with her both as a solo singer and on occasion backing vocals for the Shadows — she's even on the Shads' version of *The Day I Met Marie*. She had such long hair that it often hid her headphones, and I wrongly assumed this one particular day that she didn't have any on. Bruce had a habit of always clasping his hands over his crutch while he was working, so as he, Hank and John were adding some vocal backing, I pressed the intercom and said, 'For God's sake leave it alone, Bruce!' I couldn't understand why Bruce started glaring at me until Olivia turned round and I could see she was wearing headphones and obviously heard every word! Oops!

The labours of 1967 weren't all confined to within the four walls of Abbey Road. In August the Shadows won the Split Song Festival in Yugoslavia, singing *I Can't Forget*, which never saw the light of day as a single in Britain. Every 45 the group had released since 1959 had made the chart, until *Tomorrow's Cancelled*, which escaped in September and failed completely.

A solo single from Brian Bennett, *Canvas*, fared no better a month later, but the Shads were as much in demand as ever when it came to touring and residencies.

Even their experiences gained through nearly ten years in the business didn't help them in one particular northern residency, as Hank remembers the four of them losing out rather badly!

For one particular week's residency in Darwen in Lancashire we were lucky enough to secure the services of two excellent lighting engineers, who were not only good at their job but also very decorative! A pleasant change from working with three blokes all the time! I think it was their first and last time as spotlight operators, but Olivia and my Carole obviously enjoyed their temporary job for seven days. I seem to remember the place had been an old pub at one time, and the owner, who was a millionaire builder, had lashed out a lot of money to convert it into a pretty flash club called the Cranberry Fold Inn. Maybe he should have spent some of it on the several acres surrounding the building, as it was pretty inaccessible one way and another during winter, so he could really only earn out of it for a few months of the year. That didn't stop him giving the Shadows an expensive gold watch each at the end of the week, which of course was met with a deluge of the usual gags from the guys, evergreens like, 'Get them on tick did you?'; 'Second hand are they?' and 'Hour thanks for the watches.' The Marx Brothers ride again! The last laugh was on us though, as the elegant time-pieces turned out to be gold-plated and worth just twenty-seven pounds! The alternative he'd offered us as a bonus was a thousand pounds in cash!

During the summer the Shadows undertook some gigs in Australia and Spain, but broke their journey to play in Israel, which turned out to be a real headache for David Bryce.

We picked the worst possible time to land in Tel Aviv to play the Rammett Gan stadium — unbeknown to us the third Arab-Israeli war was brewing and the soldiers at the airport took our AC 30 amps to pieces (obviously checking to see how we got that unique Shadows sound!), tore the skins off the drums and even held them up to the light! Not a stain and shining white!

Pete Seeger, the American political folk singer, who not only popularised other people's songs but actually wrote classics like *If I Had a Hammer, Where Have All The Flowers Gone?* and *Little Boxes,* was also on the bill at Tel Aviv. He, along with every other artist on the bill which included Nana Mouskouri, had been less lucky than us during the rigorous searches through equipment by the military. In fact, we had the only amps that worked!

It wasn't the most comfortable feeling being in Israel at the time as there was an awful lot of tension. We flew out on 4th June, the day before war actually broke out, and as we touched down in Australia we learned that Israel had destroyed the Egyptian, Jordanian and Syrian Air Forces within hours and then knocked out the three armies over the next six days and ended up occupying all Sinai to the banks of the Suez Canal, the west bank of the Jordan and the Syrian hills above Galilee. It seemed strange that all this violence was taking place in an area that had such strong religious connections. We'd almost expected to bump into Biblical characters — not tanks.

Life - lines of the SHADOWS

	HANK	BRIAN	BRUCE	JOHN
Real name:	Hank Brian Marvin	Brian Bennett	Bruce Welch	John Henry Rostill
Birth date:	October 28, 1941	February 9, 1940	November 2, 1941	June 16, 1942
Birthplace:	Newcastle-on-Tyne	London	Bognor Regis	Birmingham
Height:	5 ft. 11 in.	5 ft. 9 in.	6 ft.	6 ft.
Weight:	142 lb.		192 lb.	
Colour of eyes:	Blue	Brown	Brown	Brown
Colour of hair:	Dark brown	Brown	Dark brown	Brown
Parents' names:	Margaret and Joe	Hilda and Lauri	Mrs. S. Welch	Henry and Elsie
Family:	One brother	—	—	Two sisters
Present home:	London	London	London	London
Instruments played:	Guitar, banjo, piano	Drums, violin, piano	Guitar	Bass, guitar
Education:	Rutherford College, Newcastle-on-Tyne	Winchmore Hill Secondary Modern	Rutherford College, Newcastle-on-Tyne	Rutlish Grammar School
Musical education:	Nil	Learnt to play the violin as a child. When time permits, takes lessons for drums	Nil	Self-taught at first, lessons later
Age on entering show business:	16 years	17 years	16 years	17 years
First public appearance:	Kalin Twins tour, October 5, 1958	With dance bands in London	Kalin Twins tour, October 5, 1958	On Everly Bros. Tour
Biggest disappointment in career:	"Saturday Dance" just missing charts.		Not being able to fly home to England when Cliff returned for NME Poll Concert	
Compositions:	"Foot Tapper," "Dancing Shoes," "Funny Feeling"	"Summer Holiday," "Stars Fell On Stockton," "Little B"	" Bachelor Boy," " Summer Holiday," "Dancing Shoes"	
Biggest influence on career:	"So many it is hard to choose any one "		Buddy Holly	
Hobbies:	Horseriding, archery, walking	Golf and listening to classical music	Driving, listening to records, Western films	Driving, music
Favourite colour:	Blue	Orange	Turquoise	Blue
Favourite singers:	Cliff Richard, Bobby Darin, Buddy Holly	Frank Sinatra, Ella Fitzgerald	Cliff Richard, Buddy Holly, Everly Brothers, Jerry Lee Lewis	Tony Bennett, Peggy Lee
Favourite food:	Indian curry	Anything	Indian curry	Steak, etc.
Favourite drink:	Lager	Lager	Tea	Tea
Favourite clothes:	Casual, smart suits	Suits	Casual	Suits, etc.
Favourite bands:	Ray Charles		Ray Charles	
Favourite instrumentalists:	Chet Atkins, Barney Kessel, Duane Eddy		Hank B Marvin	James Burton (guitar player with Rick Nelson)
Favourite composers:	Rodgers and Hammerstein		Buddy Holly Norman Petty	Goffin and King
Car:	Rover 3 litre	Ford Prefect	E-type Jaguar	
Likes:	Being lazy . . . doing one-night stands	Good music and friendly people	Travel . . . tea	Good music and sincerity
Dislikes:	Impoliteness . . . rainy weather	Snobs	Going to bed . . getting up	Women drivers
Tastes in music:	"Any type, providing it's well played"	Anything well played	Nearly everything	Good rock 'n' roll and piano jazz
Personal ambition:	To be top guitarist in Europe one day	To stay happy	To be happy	To travel
Professional ambition:	The Shadows to be top world instrumental group	To write a symphony	To be part of the biggest group in the world	To learn the bass really well
Other facts:		Backed Marty Wilde on most of his recordings. Recordings with the Krew Kats: " Trambone" / "Peak Hour" / "Samover" / "Jack's Good."		

During the plane journey from Israel to Australia, Hank wrote a song that would become a hit for Cliff four years later.

> I'd been browsing through some books at the airport and I picked up *Silent Spring* by Rachel Carson. I suppose my conservation consciousness was becoming more acute and I felt strongly about damaging pesticides being sprayed indiscriminately over the countryside, killing not just the harmful insects but creatures like bees and butterflies and others, essential to the world's natural balance. So I wrote this song *Silvery Rain* about my feelings on the subject (a number that Olivia was to record on her album *Physical* fifteen years later).

Hank had been busy writing generally. In fact a song he'd written during that tour — *The Day I Met Marie* — was selected as the August release for Cliff and scooted into the Top 10 within a couple of weeks.

Brian Bennett was busy too, releasing a solo LP *Change of Direction* in October, proving that he, like the others, would be capable of standing on his own two feet should the group ever fall apart.

> For *Change of Direction,* I basically put together a six-piece group to make the album, comprising John Rostill on bass, ex-Krew Kat Jim Sullivan on guitar and sitar, ex-Checkmate Alan Hawkshaw on piano and organ, Alan Skidmore on tenor and flute, Fred Crossman on French horn and me on drums.

Brian's predecessor in the Shadows, Tony Meehan, was also in the studio, producing a new single for his former partner Jet Harris who was making his first record since his car accident. Despite a valiant attempt at a return to the big time after his life had been in ruins, the song *My Lady,* written by Troggs leader Reg Presley, didn't help him regain his former stature.

The uphill struggle for Jet coincided with a struggle of a different kind for the Shadows, as the break-up was nearer than any of them imagined, and the final year would be a grim one for the group, wracked with arguments, tears, depression and only one release under the once proud name of the Shadows.

The album *From Hank, Bruce, Brian and John* was released in December '67, just prior to the group's appearing on television in a Christmas Day adaption of *Aladdin*.

As Big Ben chimed the old year out and the new year in, thousands of young revellers gathered in Trafalgar Square to sing carols and the Number 1 song of the moment, the Beatles' *Hello, Goodbye*. But for the group that was once as powerful as John, Paul, George and

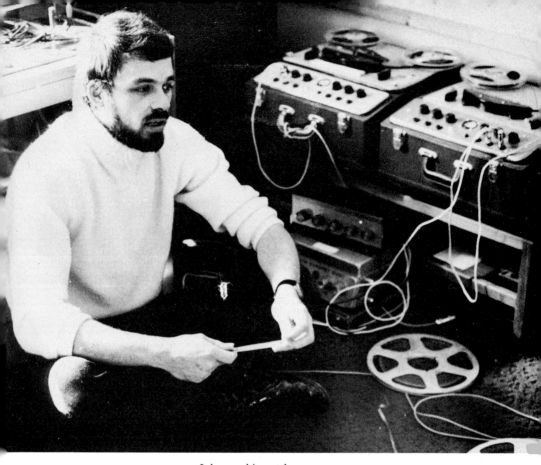

John working at home

Recording at Abbey Road with engineer Peter Vince

Ringo, it was 'goodbye' to ten years of success and 'hello' to a new era.

On New Year's Day 1968, the Shadows made their debut in their first West End Show without Cliff when they undertook three weeks of cabaret at the legendary *Talk of the Town,* becoming the first ever group to appear at a venue that was normally sacrosanct territory, playing host only to artists of the calibre of singers like Eartha Kitt and Sammy Davis Junior. Through two strokes of fate their run there produced first a former Shadows line-up, and then a quartet who'd never played together as a four-piece.

John Rostill had been getting increasingly depressed for no apparent reason, other than a broken love affair with his girlfriend Lyn, and suffered a minor nervous breakdown, leaving the guys potentially without a bass guitarist for the remaining two weeks of their residency, but Licorice Locking came to the rescue and stood in for him. So for the first time since the end of 1963 Hank, Bruce, Brian and Licorice were on stage as the four Shadows. Almost immediately the 1963 vintage line-up was terminated due to Brian being taken ill with appendicitis, leaving the Shads to call once more on an ex-member of the group. So the remaining dates were fulfilled by a Shadows line-up that only ever existed for just over a week, Hank, Bruce, Licorice and Tony Meehan!

During the Talk of the Town appearances, Hank's first solo single *London's Not Too Far* was released, but failed to make any dent in the chart.

I got quite a lot of radio plays on it, but for some reason it suffered the same fate as *Tomorrow's Cancelled* and Brian's *Canvas.* It didn't seem to affect our career at all, though — we were still in demand for appearances not only in Great Britain but Scandinavia, Germany, Belgium, France, the Far East, South Africa and Australia. In fact during the time I was keeping my fingers crossed for *London's Not Too Far,* we undertook some dates down under, although it was a tour of mixed fortunes.

In Adelaide a promoter called Jack Neary had booked us for an evening show at the really luxurious Hotel Australia. Tickets really cost an arm and a leg so Jack hit upon an idea of doing an extra afternoon concert for younger people who couldn't afford the price of evening tickets. David Bryce OK'd it, saying he didn't mind the extra organisation and we all thought it seemed like a good idea at the time. Then we saw the billing! 'A Tea Dance With The Shadows'!!!! What did they want, an hour long version of *What a Lovely Tune?* That was the nearest thing to a tea dance tune *we'd* ever recorded. Anyway, we peeped into the room and saw them literally laying out the tables and chairs, bone china cups and dinky milk jugs. Bruce took one look and said something like 'Oh no!' (with a capital 'F'), was more than a little rude to the manager of the hotel, and refused point blank to perform. A cast iron excuse was needed to extricate ourselves from the wretched tea dance, so we put our heads together. The promoter would never wear the reason that Bruce just didn't fancy playing, so we came up with an excuse that proved we had a lot of front — Brian's back! He'd been suffering for a while with his back, so we were able to get a doctor's note saying he was unfit to play. It was just like getting out of PE at school. To be honest we didn't realise initially that the tea dance was for the younger kids who hadn't got much money, but when we found out, we relented and did our stuff for them.

One of David Bryce's many headaches on tour was Bruce's ability to get very distressed if a theatre was only half full. For some reason on this particular tour of Australia there were a few spare seats dotted around the auditorium, which immediately came under the Welch eye as he peeped through the curtains. He was obviously upset, and the next day let it build up so much inside him that he walked out. With many commitments to fill, some quick thinking was called for.

As luck would have it we did know a local chap who played guitar — we'd met him in 1967 while he was playing guitar behind Cliff. Derby Wilson was a Sydney cab driver known as 'the humble cabbie' and we set to work to give him a crash course in 'Shadow-manship'. We taught him all the movements including the famous 'cross-over' step, showed him all the chords, went over the chords again, practised the steps again, rehearsed the steps with the music, coerced a tailor into knocking up some clothes in double quick time, bought him a new white shirt and a bow tie, and took him through a final run through! It wore us out, but not Derby, he was so thrilled at this big break he must have phoned his entire family, who all descended on the venue to see 'the humble cabbie' playing with the Shadows. Fifteen minutes before curtain up as Derby was standing in the wings like a greyhound in a trap, waiting for the electric hare, Bruce turned up. Poor Derby, the guy must have felt like the bottom had fallen out of his world, he just stood there and said, 'My mum was coming to watch me, too!'

After the disappointment of nearly being a Shadow, Derby returned once more to his 'humble cab'. And after *his* brief reappearance with the Shadows at the Talk of the Town, Tony Meehan had returned to record producing, working mainly with French singer Richard

Anthony and the Dutch group Wishful Thinking, and confessed that he hardly ever touched the drums any more, but was happier writing and arranging.

Following Licorice's brief return to the group he was keeping his hand in by playing double bass in a trad jazz group, the Thames City Jazzmen, doing odd residencies and one-off gigs.

Even Jet Harris had been in the news again. Although the major car crash which had virtually ended his career had made headline news quite a long while before, the final outcome of the inquiry had only just been decided upon. The bus driver in the accident had been found negligent, and the former Shadows bass player was awarded £11,500 damages!

In March 1968, five years to the week since *Summer Holiday* got to Number 1, the Shadows released *Dear Old Mrs Bell* the same day as Cilla Black's *Step Inside Love*, the Four Tops *If I Were a Carpenter*, Simon and Garfunkel's *Scarborough Fair* and the Beatles' *Lady Madonna*. One critic described the Shadows' new offering as 'a pretty little song about the isolated life of an old-age pensioner which has a pronounced nostalgic quality and an appealing lilt. The tune is hummable and melodic, and the lyric is highly sentimental — probably more acceptable to adults than to teenagers. I like the scoring with violins and cellos weaving a rich embroidery around the vocal. On the whole I can't help thinking that it's a bit too "twee" for the charts.' Despite *Dear Old Mrs Bell* being the Shadows' first single for six months, the public refused to buy enough copies for it to make the Top 50. *Disc* magazine summed up the general feeling towards the group, when they stated that 'The Shadows are *still* four of the dearest loved creatures in pop.'

During March and April the 'dearly loved creatures' toured the Far East, where the Japanese had already bought vast quantities of the album *The Shadows in Japan* the previous year, which included Geordie classics like *Omoide No Nagisa*, *Kimi To Itsumandemo* and *Gin-Iro-No Michi*. Despite a long flight Bruce clearly recalls the arrival.

When we touched down the first thing we were greeted with was the news that Cliff was at Number 1 in Britain with *Congratulations*. After a tiring flight it gave us such a lift that we immediately despatched a telegram. All the telegrams Cliff must have received about that particular chart-topper obviously read the same as ours 'Congratulations' — corny but we figured that we couldn't use any of his singles titles from the previous year — *All My Love* hardly fitted the bill; *I'll Come Running* was definitely inappropriate as

182

Blian, Bluce and fliends in Japan

'Guitar Tango'

we'd only just arrived; and *It's All Over* wouldn't exactly have gone down a bomb either!

Despite the success of the tour, the musical blend portrayed on stage certainly wasn't as harmonious on a personal level, but the internal bickering of the group was overshadowed during the tour by news of world events. Conversation in the hotel would invariably turn to the conflict in Vietnam or the problems in Rhodesia as well as two other blows to the world that occurred while the Shadows were in the Far East — the assassination of Martin Luther King in Memphis, and the death of the world's first spaceman Yuri Gagarin, ironically killed in an air crash.

The Far East tour over and back in Britain, the Shadows' Palladium season with Tom Jones in May was followed by the Bratislava Song Festival where the Shadows deputised for Cliff, before going off for a well deserved holiday.

On 17th August 1968, the *New Musical Express* carried a 'No smoke without fire' story, under the banner headline 'Shadows will not disband.'

The Shadows will *not* disband at the end of the year despite wildly exaggerated reports to the contrary. But there will be at least one personnel change with drummer Brian Bennett definitely quitting the group in December, and founder member Bruce Welch considering the possibility of leaving at the same time.

Their manager Peter Gormley commented:

Bruce had been talking about settling down for some time, and now that Brian is going and the group is having to be re-shaped, Bruce feels that this might be an opportune time for him to leave too. But nothing will be decided until the boys return from holiday at the end of August. If Bruce does leave, he will probably go into music publishing and management, but whatever happens the Shadows will continue — both Hank Marvin and John Rostill are quite determined about that.

On their return from holiday the Shadows set off for a short tour of Denmark before joining Cliff for a lengthy season at the Palladium. It was their second time at the theatre within six months, although it was Cliff's first appearance there since *Cinderella*, two years before.

In the autumn both Tom Jones and the Shadows along with Cliff, Vikki Carr and Georgia Brown, starred in a series of *Saturday Night Spectaculars* screened by London Weekend Television — the new TV company which assumed responsibility for weekend programmes as from 2nd August 1968.

184

THE KALIN TWINS
Exclusive Brunswick Recording Artists

The Kalin Twins — 'When, when you smile, when you smile at me . . .'

GPO ⬤ GREETINGS TELEGRAM

S173 GTG 2.42 LONDON T 21= GREETING=

HANK AND BRUCE STAGEDOOR LONDON PALLADIUM W1 =

ITS BEEN A GREAT TEN YEARS WHATEVER HAPPENED TO THE

KALIN TWINS = CLIFF +

Bruce and his wife Anne were finally divorced, and he became engaged to the girl who was named as 'the other woman', Olivia Newton John.

If Bruce seemed a little steadier and a little happier, Hank wasn't. John Rostill was giving him a hard time.

John was a moody person. When we were in Australia, we never saw John except for on stage, he just used to disappear every day. The joke between the rest of us was that we reckoned he sellotaped up all the windows of his hotel room and just sat in there with a carton of two hundred Rothmans! He'd adopt a very aggressive attitude, picking on things I did, splitting hairs, and generally being unco-operative for no particular reason. It's not enjoyable working with people when they're like that. I remember one day during the Palladium season with Tom Jones, John sat there with his face black as a thunder cloud and suddenly spat out, 'I despise you Hank! Everything that Bruce does you do.' I bit my tongue and asked him what he meant.

'Well, Bruce bought a Rolls Royce, so you have to buy a Rolls Royce, things like that.' As it happened, although John didn't know it, I really wanted a Jag, but there were problems with the insurance, so it was a very unfair criticism, but John seemed to think that if Bruce were to sneeze, I'd catch a cold!

The atmosphere in the group was definitely getting far worse, we were working a lot, too much probably, we were together virtually the whole time, doing live appearances, writing and recording. I think really we were getting increasingly disenchanted with the music, as we felt we weren't going anywhere. We'd been working *solidly* for ten years and we'd got to the stage where we were locked into an image. It was 'all the hits all the time' and little room for new expression. And talking of expression, and on a lighter note, we had encountered a wonderfully typical 'jobsworth' when we were working with Tom Jones earlier in the year.

As every singer and musician knows, the name is given to any bumptious commissionaire or the like who follows his orders to the last letter, without any room for flexibility or common sense and answers any reasonable request with the classic line, 'I'm sorry sir, it's more than my job's worth.' On one occasion at the Washington Hotel in Stockton-on-Tees, Tom had a young lady in his hotel room when there was a hammering on the door.

'Who is it?' yelled an obviously preoccupied voice from the land of song.

'It's the manager — 'ave you got a girl in there with you?'

'What if I have?'

186

'Against the rules sir — no girls allowed in the hotel bedrooms.'
The Welsh voice boomed back,
'Do you know who I am?'
'Well, sir, I . . .'
'I'm Tom Jones, the singer.'
'I don't care if you're Buck Jones the bloody cowboy, it's against
the rules!'

Among the many tributes to the tenth anniversary in show business
of Cliff and the Shadows in September 1968 was one from journalist
Andy Gray that seemed to sum up the group's success pretty
succinctly.

> The Shadows were voted the top instrumental group in the NME
> for eight years running! A remarkable achievement, and all the
> more so when it's recalled that they've always won by the largest
> number of votes each year — literally thousands ahead of their
> nearest rivals. Hank and Bruce are still only twenty-six, and
> although they are both very rich young men, they still get more
> satisfaction from their work than their money. Let's hope they
> continue for a long time to come, because, using the initials of
> their hit *FBI,* they are easily the 'Foremost British Instrumen-
> talists'.

Tributes paid also to the men behind Cliff and the Shadows —
agents Leslie Grade and Eddie Jarrett, manager Peter Gormley,
recording manager Norrie Paramor, touring managers Sid Maurice
and David Bryce and ex-publicists Les Perrin and Edna Bowers.

By mid October, according to the newspapers, uncertainty still
surrounded the future of the Shadows. Bruce Welch announced that
he would definitely leave the group on 14th December, in order to
manage the Shadows' music publishing interests, but confusion still
reigned over Brian Bennett's situation. Brian himself said, 'I too
have made up my mind to quit the Shadows on 14th December
immediately after the Palladium season with Cliff,' but in a conflicting
report a Shadows spokesman admitted that Brian had decided to
remain with the group! For one week of the Palladium run, Brian
was playing a dual role, as he was also backing Joe Brown, who was
appearing in cabaret at the Talk of the Town.

During the autumn of apparent indecision and uncertainty over
the future of the Shadows, the musical scene was making many twists
and turns away from the straightforward and 'conventional' music
and appearance of the British top instrumental unit. Jimmy Page
announced that on leaving the Yardbirds he was going to release an
album which he'd cut with his new group — Led Zeppelin — an

outfit which was to be the vanguard of a new musical era, and Jerome Ragni and James Rado's 'tribal-rock' musical *Hair* allegedly heralded the arrival of a new permissive society complete with a liberal sprinkling of four-letter words previously unuttered on West End stages. Even if gently at first, the establishment was being rocked, but the Shadows and Cliff, refusing to be swayed or influenced, stuck to their guns and in October released an album cosily called *Established 1958*! The title did imply that the act had a solid foundation even to the extent of it sounding like the suffix to a firm of family solicitors. The end however was nigh.

It nearly came at the Talk of the North in Eccles. John always got to the gigs an hour and a half before the others, basically because, after five years, he was still tuning Bruce's guitar for him.

I was still paying John to tune my guitar, and he'd also tune my spare guitar and his own bass. I trusted John totally, and never questioned his tuning the way I'd questioned my own.

Hank would always arrive second, and Brian and myself would turn up next, when all the instruments were in tune. The night we played at the Talk of the North we were staying at the Piccadilly Hotel in Manchester, and had changed into our tuxedos there, arriving at 11.15 virtually ready to be on stage by 11.30. John was alone in the dressing room, and his face, as it had increasingly been over that year, was black. He was fuming when he demanded to know where Hank was. Brian, Olivia and I hadn't seen him for hours, and had imagined he'd already be there. He turned up with five minutes to go, breezed in with a 'Hi fellas', picked up his guitar and said, 'Give us a "D", John.'

John told him that he was late and flatly refused to co-operate, and even Brian, who never caused any trouble or aggression and was always one for shrugging things off, muttered, 'You should really have been here, Hank.'

I had the Rolls running outside and as the fur flew in the dressing room I yelled, 'Fuck it, fuck the lot of you, I'm going home!' John just glowered and Hank burst into tears.

I just broke down. Bruce was about to run out on us, John had got it in for me and my fuse just went. I ran out of the building and gulped in a mouthful of cold Lancashire air. I went back ten minutes later having regained my composure a bit, to find that Olivia had persuaded Bruce not to go home, as we'd got a job to do and a contract to fulfil.

As far as I was concerned it was all over that night.

Much to the consternation of the manager of the place, Joe

Pullen, we eventually went on half an hour late, and the usual veneer of professionalism that you can summon up when things aren't all they should be was noticeably absent on stage that night!

Bruce's suggestion that they should do the Palladium season with Cliff and then call it a day seemed to meet with approval all round. So on 19th December 1968 the line-up of Hank Marvin, Bruce Welch, Brian Bennett and John Rostill, one of the world's most famous groups, played together for the very last time on the stage at the London Palladium behind the guy who they'd first met in a Soho tailor's in 1958 being measured for a lurid pink jacket.

As the final curtain came down the rest of the lads presented Bruce with a clock that told the time in different countries all over the world. A world which had been taken by storm over the last ten years by a group who bowed out on the stage of Britain's most famous theatre.

13 / Best Part of Breaking Up

(1969 — 1973)

So the beginning of 1969 saw Hank and Bruce and John and Brian going their own ways.

For Bruce it was a comparatively non-musical year mainly spent decorating and organising the house at Hadley Common he'd bought with Olivia.

I'd been working solidly since 1958 so I thought I deserved a break, although I was spending a certain amount of time in our 'Shadows Music' office at 17 Savile Row listening to new songs. I got very domesticated and bought Olivia a red setter which we called Geordie, and later a companion for him who got saddled with Murphy. The first part of the year was really spent around the house or in the office, but later on in the autumn Olivia and I got away up to Edinburgh for a while, and I was delighted to be able to show her a glimpse of Newcastle through the window as our train pulled into Central Station on the return journey. With the two setters locked firmly in the guards van, I'm eagerly recounting a potted history of my life on Tyneside when two brown hairy things with long ears hurtle past the window! I leapt up, flew out of the door and accosted the nearest porter.

'My dogs are loose, have you seen them?'

'Mmm, I think they went that way,' he said with a wide unhelpful sweep of his arm.

South! They'd headed south! They must be homing setters, I thought, as I tore off down the platform in just my shirt and trousers. It looked as if they'd gone down the track and over the Tyne railway bridge. I jumped on to the track and ran flat out, yelling, 'Murphy! Geordie!' as loud as I could.

In retrospect I realise that anyone running out of Newcastle Station shouting 'Geordie' would undoubtedly be set upon by the nearest team of platelayers and gangers, but I survived any potential problems in that department and hoofed the two hundred yards over the bridge and into Gateshead. Gasping for air and freezing cold I realised I'd lost them. There was nothing for it but to go back. I'd only gone the length of half a dozen wooden sleepers when a tell-tale rumble and a shrill hoot brought me news I didn't want to hear — my train was pulling out of the station and heading towards me.

Well, I thought as I pressed myself flat against the edge of the bridge, I've had lots of good times, things are obviously being balanced out now! No dogs, hardly any clothes, freezing cold, out of breath, my train moving off with Olivia on it, and no money — things couldn't get worse! Could they?

As the train rattled past me I looked up and saw Olivia, not even looking out of the window for me or showing the slightest concern, and worst of all she was patting Geordie and Murphy!

After a lot of grovelling to the station master I caught a slow train to Kings Cross which crawled in hours later. Needless to say I didn't exactly walk through the door, kiss Olivia on the cheek and enquire about her health!

In March 1969 Hank released a solo single *Goodnight Dick* but it failed to trouble the British Market Research Bureau.

As well as releasing that single I also suggested an album of film themes to Brian and John, but I think we'd just about finished one track, *Chitty, Chitty, Bang, Bang,* which we'd given a country and western flavour, when the project collapsed and we called it a day.

For money and money alone we did a few gigs as the Shadows with Brian's buddy Alan Hawkshaw on keyboards. Our first gig was at the Poco a Poco club in Stockport, and when we arrived there was a telegram for Alan. '. . . So you're trying to fill the footsteps of the giant — stop — Bruce Welch.'

There were no plans at all for reforming the group, we literally just did it for the pounds shillings and pence, and the Far East tour for the yen!

We actually recorded a live album at Sankei Hall in Tokyo which included a handful of our hits plus songs like *A Little Bitty Tear, Putting on the Style* and a live version of a track that we'd previously recorded without Bruce, *Slaughter on Tenth Avenue,* which came out as a Shadows single in October 1969. I'd released another solo single in July called *Sacha* which hovered just under the chart for a few weeks, but I was disappointed that it didn't get many radio plays. It seemed that so many producers at the time had a thing about instrumentals, but at least I had the satisfaction of knowing it was a good record, and it topped the charts in Australia for six weeks.

The week that *Slaughter on Tenth Avenue* was released Hank and Cliff were sitting comfortably in the Top 10 with one of Hank's songs *Throw Down a Line,* and Hank spoke at length to journalist Gordon Coxhill.

Cliff flipped over *Throw Down a Line* as soon as he heard it. I think he liked it partly because it gave him a chance to sing something with some guts again after a string of lighter singles, and partly because I wrote it. Not that he would record a song just because I wrote it, but I think he was pleased that the number came from within the family. The record seems to be selling very well and it would be very nice to have a Number 1 again as it's been two years since I was last in the charts, and I don't really have to tell you how good it feels.

What does annoy me is the attitude of a lot of the new talent. I agree that the music is the most important thing but everybody, no matter what their reputation, needs a definite stage act, a presence, a decent speaking voice. No audience likes to strain their ears listening out for the introduction, and nothing's worse than a group coming on stage and then spending ten minutes tuning up. I can imagine though how anybody must feel who's making their debut at a big concert, although I have learned to disregard my nerves now because I know they'll go away. I remember once looking at my guitar in my hand just before I went on stage and it was shaking all over the place, so much so that I had to hold it still with my other hand. As soon as I'm on stage, though, and we go into the first number, I'm all right — I'm told that my nerves don't show, but I can certainly feel them in my stomach.

Hank also chatted about some of his favourite groups at the time, which included Jethro Tull, Blind Faith and a group he actually went along to see, Deep Purple, in concert with the Royal Philharmonic Orchestra. He also talked about fellow guitar hero Eric Clapton.

Eric is a far better guitarist than me. I agree that in music it is difficult to say what is good, let alone what is best, but I sit at home and listen a lot to Clapton — he's such a magnificent technician. It's all a question of environment, as I was interested in the blues as a youngster but we went through the skiffle days, met Cliff, and got into the type of music we did. It has been a very time-consuming eleven years and sometimes you get so involved with your own scene there just isn't time to look around and see what everybody else is up to. One day I happened to hear the Cream and I couldn't believe it. I had to sit down and wonder what the

192

strange sounds were that Eric Clapton was getting out of his guitar. You see his musical life has been steeped in blues, and he hasn't had the outside influences to change his path. Could I play exactly the same way he does? I don't know, but there's not much point in doing so even if I could. I enjoy performing, but I don't like being away from home for too long at a time and I have to find time for my writing, which is very relaxing, besides providing me with a few bob — and I must find a way of improving my guitar playing.

When the bubble had burst at the end of 1968 no one was more relieved than Brian Bennett.

Both Margaret and I thought 'Thank goodness that's over!' Although we'd had so many good times together, there were so many tours that I found myself away from home most of the time and you couldn't really conduct a normal married life like that.

Having said that, immediately after the split, Cliff asked me to be his musical director, so I waded back into the deep end with him at the Talk of the Town.

In March I went to Washington with Tom Jones, which was like old times, playing with my old mate from the Krew Kats, Big Jim Sullivan. Tom's manager, Gordon Mills, asked if I would like to be their permanent drummer, which would mean following my week in Washington with six weeks in Vegas and extensive touring in the United States. I turned him down and jacked it in after seven days — I didn't want to get into long tours again, so I packed my bags and came home.

I did tour Japan later in the year with Cliff as his MD and was rather proud to see the words 'Brian Bennett Orchestra' on the posters!

I picked up six brass players, a big rhythm section and three Japanese girls who were great singers, in fact the whole lot of them were so keen that on the train between gigs the guards van would sound like a London club, with everyone bashing out songs! They really had enthusiasm and I *love* enthusiasm. Before one show, the radio was broadcasting non-stop typhoon warnings, so we were told not to venture out of the hotel, which was a great disappointment as the weather didn't look that bad. Then it came upon us like World War Three, and we were thirty storeys up! The building started swaying violently, all the trains were stopped, cars were hurled upside down, trees were uprooted and it rained cats and dogs for ages.

The next day we went by car to Osaka and there was just total devastation everywhere, it was dreadful.

Every spare minute I got on the tour, on trains, in cars and in hotels was spent studying. I'd enrolled in the Berkeley School of Music and was taking a postal course in arranging, which meant writing down all your exercises, sending them off, and four weeks later they'd come back marked. I only stuck it for six months, but it was lucky I got most of my work correct, or I'd have been writing out a hundred times, 'I must not get involved with Far Eastern tours, Cliff Richard or typhoons.'

Despite the break up, we did the Far East tour as the Shadows as a purely financial thing, but there was still a lot of friction between Hank and John. John was invariably in a really black mood, very depressed, and the slightest little thing would trigger him off. At one point in Japan we were stuck in some traffic and a guy in the car next to us wound down the window and asked if he could have our autographs. Hank, obliging as always, gave him the winning Marvin smile, and asked John if he could borrow his pen. In the confusion of all of us signing, and with the traffic starting to move again, the guy accidentally roared off with John's pen. John went bananas!

'Where's my pen?'

'Sorry, John, but that guy went off with it by mistake.'

'But I lent it to *you*.'

'Look, it was only a cheap Bic.'

'But it's gone now.'

'Look, I'll buy you a whole packet of Bics . . .'

'But it was your responsibility.'

'It's really not worth bothering about — I'll buy you another one as soon as we stop.'

'I don't want *another* one — I want mine . . .'

John went on and on about his pen for ages, and got increasingly petty about it. In Japan, he and Hank were like an estranged couple trying to make another go of things, but it was obviously never going to work.

In some ways I was a busy little 'B' in 1969, as I also formed the Oak Tree Music Publishing Company, with a chap called Mike Hawker who was a successful song writer having written such numbers as Dusty Springfield's hit *I Only Want to be With You,* which also became a hit for the Bay City Rollers and the Tourists. An amazing fact about that song was that all three versions got to Number 4 in the charts! Mike also wrote Helen Shapiro's 1961 chart topper *Walking Back to Happiness.*

1970 moved in. Mike and I found ourselves with a song, *Wind of*

194

Change, in the final six for Eurovision. In the end we came second to *Jack in the Box,* but were more than pleased with our first effort.

1970 for me was mainly a year of sessions and writing. On session days I'd leave home at seven in the morning to get to the studio for eight because although the recordings didn't start until ten, you could often sneak in a commercial or two during that time — we called it 'The Greedy Hour'.

Sessions were hard work. Ten till one, two till five and seven till ten. I used to be absolutely knackered when I crawled home at 11.30! The king of the jingles writers at that time was a guy called Johnny Johnson — he used to write most of the good ones. I played on loads of them, things like the Maxwell House coffee advert with Georgie Fame and the Typhoo tea commercials!

In February 1970, Cliff and Hank released *The Joy of Living* as a follow-up to their Top Tenner of the previous year *Throw Down a Line* but its chart ascent was prematurely arrested at Number 25. Hank released no solo singles during 1970 but *was* offered a job with a group who'd been chart regulars for three years — the Move.

Roy Wood and Bev Bevan called the office and asked me if I wanted to join. It was a pretty tempting offer, as they'd had five Top 5 hits on the trot including *Blackberry Way,* which had actually topped the chart, and a Top 20 hit with a thing called *Curly.* But even as *Brontosaurus* stomped into the Top 10 I had no real regrets about not accepting. We had a long chat about the pros and cons and possibilities, but the deciding factor was that I didn't want to go tearing off round the world again, much as I loved Roy's material.

It was a pity really, because I do lean more towards the performing side of music as opposed to session work, as I don't read music very well. Therefore I was very happy to appear in some TV specials with Cliff and Una Stubbs. Michael Hurll, who now does *Top of the Pops* amongst other programmes, was the producer, and his assistant was Phil Bishop, who also went on to produce *Top of the Pops.*

I remember one TV special with Cliff, shot in Scandinavia, where I was dressed up as an Olympic athlete complete with flaming torch! My part in this particular sketch was to jog up to strangers on the street and with completely straight face say, 'Excuse me, but could you direct me to the Olympic Stadium?' People's reactions were hilarious, but the look on *my* face beat them hands down as I sprinted in my best Lasse Viran manner up to the gentleman out doing his shopping. My casual remark of

'Olympic Stadium' went down a bomb and he greeted me like a long lost brother — it turned out that he'd won an Olympic medal, boxing for Finland!

It was great working with Cliff, he's always fun to work with, he really has got a great sense of humour, and it was a treat to work in that kind of atmosphere, after the bickering and pettiness that we'd experienced in the latter days of the Shadows!

On 30th May at a reception to celebrate his fiftieth single *Goodbye Sam, Hello Samantha,* Cliff revealed that his favourite single of the fifty released so far was Hank Marvin's *The Day I Met Marie,* which is still one of his favourite songs to this day. Brian Bennett also released a single during 1970, *Riding on the Gravy Train,* under the name of Thunder Company with pianist Cliff Hall who is now a permanent fixture on stage with the Shadows.

Twenty months after leaving the Shadows, Bruce Welch announced that he was returning to active playing again after being fairly quiet on the musical front, but during his lay off, he'd become increasingly worried about his weight.

I've always had a slight weight problem, so I'm forever trying new types of diets and ideas for losing a few pounds. Eager to have a go at anything, I spotted an ad in the paper that said 'Colonic Irrigation' and assuming that a good clean-out once a month would decrease my weight I trotted off to the address on the bottom! The clinic at Seymour Place was attended by three lovely white-coated nurses, who ordered me to strip off and lie on a table with my knees tucked up to my chin — it was like having a baby — or so I'm told! They then grabbed hold of this tube coming out of the wall and shoved it up my backside. You're then supposed to control your overwhelming desire to go to the loo for three minutes while the enema takes effect, which was absolute torture — I could only hold myself back for about thirty seconds!

Anyway, despite the severe discomfort, my visits continued for a while, until one particular appointment, when I was doing my thing with my legs up in the air and one particularly attractive nurse in her early twenties was sticking the tube up my bottom. The situation I was in, absolutely naked, and in the position of a turkey trussed for Christmas was pretty embarrassing anyway, but when she leaned over and said, 'I've got all your records you know, *Wonderful Land* is my favourite,' I could have died. I never went back!

While Bruce was being irrigated, new musical plans were being formulated.

196

My mind wasn't *just* full of nurses and clinics, I was getting restless, and started writing again. I chatted to Hank about doing something without actually using the name 'the Shadows' or just bashing out instrumentals the whole time. As we talked and kicked various ideas around — whether to perform as a duo or add a new voice — John Farrar's name cropped up. We'd met him in Australia while he'd been playing with a group called the Strangers, and had been very impressed by both his guitar playing and his singing, as he had an amazing falsetto. Olivia knew him from Melbourne, as he went out with her ex-singing partner Pat Carroll, so we rang him and asked him if he wanted to come to England. He arrived during August so the three of us took off to Portugal for a working holiday. Hank and myself had already written ten songs and finished a couple more which we wrote with John, *My Home Town* and *Faithful.* While arranging and routining, we found that in John we had new influences and dimensions — it was a real three-way thing as he was much more a musician than me and on a par with Hank. John had a tremendous talent for arranging vocal harmonies so we did a lot of West Coast harmonies stuff, along the lines of Crosby, Stills and Nash, with John organising who sang what.

He had great ears! (They were pink and shell-like!) Seriously though, John would pick great harmonies out and say to us, 'Right, Bruce, you sing that line, and Hank you do this line.'

We learned a lot from him. John and I were kindred spirits, because we both had real dedication and absolute determination to get things right. Although he was pretty quiet, he said what he wanted to say through his music. As I was getting increasingly involved with Hank and John, Olivia had spent most of the year with a group called Toomorrow, which was put together with the intention of being a Monkees-type thing, you know — the instant formula for success! The good-looking guy who fronted the group was Ben Thomas. The other two members of the group, Chris Slade and Vic Cooper, had both been members of Tom Jones' backing group, the Squires, an outfit whose ranks ex-Shadow John Rostill also passed through. Despite Olivia having to spend quite a bit of time in the States during the year, she was back in England for the first night of the group's film, simply called *Toomorrow,* at the London Pavillion in August, but it didn't set the celluloid circuit on fire, which must have pleased Susan George as Olivia just pipped her to the post for the part.

In October 1970 Bruce, John and Hank attended the opening of

George Martin's new recording studios, Air London, and released the album *Shades of Rock*, which included three Beatles' tracks, *Paperback Writer, Get Back* and *Something*, as well as the Rolling Stones' *Satisfaction*. The main trio on the album were Hank, Brian Bennett and Alan Hawkshaw, with assorted bass players, who included John Rostill, Herbie Flowers, Dave Richmond and Brian Hodges. Music reviewer Allen Evans said:

> Everything is moving on, and the Shadows, although we thought they had broken up, are back with a heavy beat, plenty of fuzz guitar, a wailing organ, and a machine-gun drum, as they rip through a series of rock classics.

Marvin, Welch and Farrar did their first television on Cliff's second series in January 1971 which went out early on Saturday evenings, released their first LP, *Marvin, Welch and Farrar*, and a single, *Faithful*, in February. For their tour of Germany, Belgium and Switzerland in March the group was augmented by Brian Bennett.

> They asked me to drum, and I said yes. It was reasonably harmonious from my point of view, I was enjoying playing the material, and got on very well with John Farrar who was and still is a great musician. I played drums on their next album *Second Opinion*. That LP and the next single *Marmaduke* were released in November.
>
> '71 was a busy year for me, I started writing with John Rostill and he put out a single *Funny Old World*. John and I were good mates, as bassist and drummer often are, so we wrote a lot together. He was the first of us to move out to Hertfordshire and get a home studio going, as Hank and I eventually did. John was a real electronics wizard, his demos were good enough to release as they were, but we still used Abbey Road to record.
>
> Also that year, Cliff was going to make a film called *Xanadu* (coincidentally Olivia was to make a film called *Xanadu* nine years later!), a picture about young people oppressed by society, with the script by Alan Plater, and I was invited to write the music.
>
> Most of the scenes were to be shot in Newcastle, so I went off there and we embarked on a series of meetings, script alterations and listening sessions. We had songs lined up like *Sing a Song of Freedom* that Guy Fletcher and Doug Flett had written, and some Marvin, Welch and Farrar songs too — *Thousand Conversations* was one of them.
>
> For four or five months I listened to and rejected stacks of potential songs.

Marvin, Welch and Farrar

Marvin, Welch, Farrar and friend

In one of the scenes, this young couple were chased into one side of the Jarrow tunnel by a brass band, only to be confronted by a massed bagpipe band who'd entered from the other side! I auditioned a colliery band, which I was going to conduct, but that didn't work out, as the script was being changed every day, and I eventually argued with the director and opted out. The last scene was due to be Cliff and his co-star disappearing off to Xanadu singing the finale *We're Gonna Find Xanadu*. They never found it, as the whole film fizzled out in the end!

After that, Peter Gormley asked me to do some producing for his company Festival so I found myself working with a group of five Welsh schoolgirls called Sweet Rain for whom I produced a new version of the old Patience and Prudence number from 1956, *Gonna Get Along Without Ya Now*.

I also worked with Dahlia Lavi and Barry Crocker who'd been in the film *The Adulation of Barry McKenzie* with Barry Humphries.

In 1972 I played with Wasp. Wasp was formed by Steve Gray, who's now with Sky, and comprised Clive Hicks on guitar, Duncan Lamont on sax, Dave Richmond on bass, Steve and me. Steve had met a chap called Robin Phillips who used to run the KPM library, which housed all types of music for different occasions, films, TV series, radio shows — you name it, they supplied it, but someone had to record it, and that's where we came in. We mainly recorded in Brussels, as the Musicians' Union had no agreement that allowed library music to be recorded in the country at that time. That was ten years ago, and I *still* work with Robin Phillips on writing music for TV and films.

Bruce had problems on the Continental tour, trying to convince promoters that they weren't to be called the Shadows.

We eventually got our own way and went out as Marvin, Welch and Farrar, and received pretty good reaction from the critics, including a great review in the magazine *Rolling Stone*. The cabaret boom was still on, so we did places like Batley Variety Club with our new act, which comprised all acoustic guitar/vocal numbers, most of them completely unknown, and invariably trooped off stage to the sound of our own footsteps!

The trouble was as soon as they saw Hank, they'd be yelling, 'Come on, mate — give us *Apache*,' and 'How about *FBI*, Hank?' It seemed impossible to shake off the Shadows tag.

By now Hank had married his girlfriend Carole, and the small ceremony at Barnet Registry Office at 9.00 am and champagne

John Farrar — smiling. Writer, producer extraordinaire and tax exile

breakfast that followed were attended only by the happy couple along with Bruce and Olivia.

In keeping with the majority of show business honeymoons the celebrations were cut short due to work commitments — in this particular instance a rehearsal at Bruce's house at Hadley Wood, a mere hour and a half after Hank and Carole tied the knot. Bruce and John Farrar had started producing Olivia's records which resulted in an immediate hit for her with her debut single *If Not For You,* which made the Top 10 in the spring of 1971. Six months later her single *Banks of The Ohio* also went into the Top 10 and stayed in the charts for seventeen weeks. Bruce admits that at the time Olivia didn't have the most powerful voice in the world, although she had a great ear for music, which combined with his constant striving for absolute perfection became a recipe for success. In December 1971 the whole 'family' toured the United Kingdom: Marvin, Welch and Farrar, along with Brian Bennett, Cliff and Olivia. 1971 had been a good year for the girl who had previously been known to the British public as 'the one who's on Cliff's TV series' — she'd had two Top 10 hits and had established herself firmly. The previous twelve months had also been good for Cliff with four hits, *Sunny Honey Girl, Silvery Rain, Flying Machine* and *Sing a Song of Freedom,* but record buyers hadn't dipped so deeply in their pockets for the offerings of Marvin, Welch and Farrar. Neither of their singles *Faithful* or *Marmaduke* nor their second LP *Second Opinion* made the charts. However the debut album did enter at Number 30 only for the record company to be taken by surprise and have no stock of records to meet the demand, thereby losing out on a potentially big album. Exactly a year after her first single Olivia's third hit *What Is Life* crashed into the best sellers and really put her on the map as a major artist. Two weeks later, at the end of March 1972, after a five year love affair, Olivia broke off her engagement to Bruce Welch. Bruce was shattered.

> I went haywire. I felt that I had nothing to live for. I left Hadley Wood and took a flat, where I hit the bottle, and one night swallowed enough sleeping pills to kill myself. For two days and nights I was in a coma in the Middlesex Hospital and nearly didn't make it. When I became aware that I was going to pull through, I realised I really had no one to turn to, I couldn't really talk to Cliff or Hank because in their eyes suicide is a crime or at least I felt that. I really had no one to lean on, my ex-wife Anne and my son Dwayne were living in Majorca, I had no parents to support me . . . and of course no wife or girlfriend. When I finally pulled through and it was time to leave hospital, I was helped by

202

my own personal Florence Nightingale, a lady called Berta, the wife of a friend, who sat and talked, and listened, and talked, and listened ad infinitum. She was great, a real tower of strength to me when I needed help. Peter Gormley was also fantastic to me during that dreadful period, but despite having a couple of good friends like Berta and Peter I was still hitting the brandy bottle every day and as it's a depressant vast quantities of the stuff certainly weren't helping me to help myself. I seemed to be recording mainly for the Courvoisier label. My saviour as far as alcohol was concerned was a gentleman called Dr Rose who succeeded in weaning me off the hard stuff . . . I've stayed firm friends with him ever since. Without a doubt, 1972 was the worst year of my life.

In September, Marvin and Farrar toured the Far East with Cliff and Olivia, taking John Rostill and Brian Bennett; Brian recalls:

I'd been doing lots of session drumming throughout the year, for all sorts of people, even the great Ella Fitzgerald, when Hank and John asked me to join them on the September tour.

We had a lot of fun on that trip. I remember Olivia insisted on authentic Japanese suites in the hotels — and she always got them! She was a fun person to be with. We all played cards a lot, and charades, and we drank a lot of that lovely hot Japanese saki. We didn't realise how potent it was, and one night sat there drinking for hours. It was only when Cliff got up to walk out and fell flat on his back that we knew it was powerful stuff!

The following morning I was sitting in the Tokyo Hilton Coffee Shop (which had the delightful name of 'The Origami' and had paper birds all over the place) tucking into a big breakfast, when two apparitions materialised with a greenish tinge on their faces — Cliff and Hank didn't look at all well! Another morning when we were having breakfast, there were some really rude Americans on the next table who had been yelling and shouting at the poor waiters throughout the meal.

'Hey you, another coffee!'

'Quick, more toast!'

'Hey you waiter, come here . . .!'

John Rostill especially was getting increasingly angry with their overbearing attitude and sat there threatening to go and smash the worst of the bunch in the face. We were all so incensed by their bullying tactics that we were giving John plenty of encouragement, but in the end he backed down saying, 'I really want to go and hit him but he's bigger than me so I won't — that's diplomacy!'

The Far East tour was certainly different to one I'd been on a few months before when Alan Hawkshaw and I worked with Ray Davies and his Button-Down Brass! That was a Mediterranean cruise, one hour a night, no pay, but you could take your family and have a completely free holiday!

While Brian had been working his hind legs off, Hank and Carole had become increasingly involved in studying the Bible.

In 1967 a young Christian woman called Anne had been calling on all the people in our neighbourhood, and after several unsuccessful attempts to find Carole at home, left a letter inviting her to find out from the Bible what God's purpose for mankind was. Our curiosity was aroused because although Carole and I were not religious, we, like many others, often wondered if there was any real meaning and purpose in life. Following Carole's reply to her letter, the young woman Anne and her husband John discussed many scriptural topics with us over the next few months. We were fascinated to learn simple Bible truths such as that God has a personal name and that name is Jehovah. Anne and John then moved to Northern Ireland where they worked as full-time volunteer evangelisors and we carried on our discussions with other Jehovah's Witnesses.

Still interested in finding out more from the Bible, but not yet really committed, in 1971 we moved to a small farm we had bought in South East Devon. It lay in a beautiful unspoilt valley with not a pylon in sight. Even the poles that carried the electricity and telephone lines stood unnoticed in the borders of the thick woods that covered part of the land. The woods also concealed badgers and wild deer and although we occasionally thrilled to see anything up to seven deer at a time cautiously crossing our fields, we never once saw a badger, only the signs that they were there. One afternoon when Bruce and Olivia were staying with us, I proudly took Olivia, who loves animals, to see the badgers' sett, leading the way boldly through the thick undergrowth. I arrived at the sett a few yards ahead of her and promptly broke wind. 'Look Livvy, this is where the badgers live,' I said divertingly, hoping she wouldn't notice a smell that would have peeled the bark off a tree. She gasped for air. 'Is that how badgers smell? It's awful.' Not wishing to malign Mr Badger and his family, I sheepishly owned up, at which point we both collapsed with helpless laughter.

During the three years we lived in Devon, Carole and I continued

204

The musical director of the Brian Bennett Orchestra with Olivia and Cliff

to associate with the local congregation of JWs in Honiton and had gradually made necessary changes in our lives in order to conform to Christian principles. For example, it took quite a while for me both to eliminate swearing from my vocabulary and to avoid telling and listening to obscene jokes. I realise this doesn't bother most people, but a Christian is one who, like Christ, does the will of God and in the Bible in Ephesians 5, verses 3-5, it shows that to engage in such things is unbecoming for a follower of Christ.

One facet of our worship of Jehovah is to share in telling others of his purpose to restore this earth to a peaceful paradise through the means of Christ's Kingdom. Jesus set the pattern for this in his ministry and of course told Christians to pray for it in the model prayer usually known as the 'Lord's Prayer' or 'Our Father'. Our places of worship are called 'Kingdom Halls', where we have five meetings a week. Everyone is welcome, of course, and the emphasis is on learning scriptural principles and applying them in our lives. The 'Kingdom Halls' are also, from time to time, used for funeral services and weddings, which reminds me of the day Carole and I got married. We had obtained a special licence in order to avoid publicity and with Bruce acting as chauffeur and get-me-there-on-time best man, and he and Olivia as witnesses, we got married at nine o'clock in the morning. The lady registrar was delightful, every line was spoken in a soft romantic tone of voice and Carole, overcome with emotion, started having difficulty repeating her vows. The registrar encouraged her sweetly, while Bruce kept looking pointedly at his watch, because we were rehearsing at ten o'clock. Afterwards we went back to Bruce's house, which was being redecorated, and amazed the painters by drinking champagne at twenty to ten in the morning. Since then we have been blessed with two beautiful children, Tahlia, who is ten, and Ben, seven. When our little girl was only four months old in April 1973, Carole and I were baptised and as Tahlia has grown physically, so we have grown in knowledge of Bible truth and the application of it in our lives.

So fifteen years on from the halycon days of the 2 Is coffee bar, Hank had become one of the Jehovah's Witnesses, Bruce was picking up the pieces of his shattered life, John Rostill was suffering increasingly from depression and Brian Bennett was heavily involved in session work and composing music for television. In October of that year, the Shadows — Hank, Bruce, Brian and John Farrar — reformed and released a single *Turn Around and Touch Me*. It was the first time

Bruce had worked for a year and a half.

I'd stopped drinking brandy completely by then which made me feel a whole lot better in myself, and my love-life seemed as though it was taking a turn for the better, when Olivia moved back in with me in April. One year after we'd parted, we tried to make a go of it and really worked hard at a reconciliation, but it didn't work out. In June 1973 Olivia and I parted for good. Working with the Shadows again got me off my backside and gave me something to be part of, and apart from that I'd always been and still am, immensely proud of the Shadows. I started writing songs with John Rostill which we often used to demo in the studio at his house. He was knocking out some very good songs around that time, including *Let Me Be There* and *If You Love Me Let Me Know*, which we took down on a Revox tape recorder and I took them to Peter Gormley's old house on the Thames at Sunbury. Peter liked them, which resulted in Olivia releasing *Let Me Be There*, but it failed miserably in this country, only selling about eight thousand copies. One of the songs I wrote with John was *Please Mister Please* which was inspired by the breakup of my relationship with Livvy. We expected great things of the song and thought it stood an excellent chance. John had been in the States playing with Tom Jones until the summer, so maybe he'd absorbed the type of music that was right for America, because events were soon to take a strange turn — but it was too late for John.

During November the two of us had been writing at his eight-track first-floor studio in his house in Radlett, which we called 'Radlett Notown' as a sendup of Tamla Motown. On the night of the 25th we'd arranged a session for the following day. He seemed cheerful enough as he guided me out of the drive and I yelled, 'See you tomorrow — late morning.' I never saw him alive again. I turned up at about 11.30 and went into the kitchen for a cup of tea with Margaret, John's wife. We sat and chatted for ten minutes or so and I began to wonder where John was.

'Oh, he's been up in the studio for hours.'

So we sat for a bit longer and chatted and laughed, completely unaware of the tragedy we'd both face during the next half hour. I finished my tea and went upstairs to the studio.

'John, I'm here.'

No reply, I tried the door, but something appeared to be jamming it on the other side. I banged on the door.

'Come on John, open up, it's Bruce.'

Nothing. I dashed back downstairs to Margaret, 'He won't answer, there's something peculiar going on.' Margaret told me there was a ladder in the garage so I rushed out and got it, shoved it up against the first floor windowsill and climbed up. Cupping my hands over my eyes, I peered into the studio. The door wasn't jammed, it was blocked by John's piano and John himself was lying at a strange angle with his bass in his hand. As the windows were locked, I couldn't get in, so raced back down the ladder and into the house where with the help of their little boy's nanny, I forced the door open. John was sitting there, with his hands still on the strings of his guitar — he looked as though he was still playing. But he wasn't. He was dead.

I went numb. I couldn't believe it. Margaret was inconsolable.

The events that followed seemed unreal. The coroner came and pronounced that John had been dead for five or six hours. The tragedy was compounded by the fact that he never lived to see the success of his songs *Let Me Be There* and *If You Love Me Let Me Know,* both of which became million-selling hits for Olivia in the States. Not being able to do any wrong in America with songs that were unsuccessful in Britain, Olivia had yet another million seller with *Please Mister Please,* so although the Shadows as such have never broken on the other side of the Atlantic, our songs couldn't have been more successful. It was such a pity that John wasn't able to reap the benefits of his talent.

John's death hit Brian very badly too:

It gave me a severe jolt when John died. He often used to write to me from Las Vegas while he was out there with Tom Jones, but when he came back he seemed depressed and disillusioned. Only a couple of evenings before he died, he'd been chatting with Alan Hawkshaw and me about his future plans and was discussing the possibility of going back with Tom, and he was very morose and seemed pessimistic about the future.

The Shadows' own future was soon to take a strange turn, although a return to the chart seemed a million miles away in 1974.

14 / The Reform Bill

(1974 — 1982)

Rocking with Curly Leads was released in December 1973 and met with fierce competition in the chart from such strong albums as McCartney's *Band on the Run*, Lennon's *Mind Games*, Elton's *Yellow Brick Road*, no less than three David Bowie albums, Yes, Pink Floyd and the Who's *Quadrophenia*.

Despite the inclusion of a couple of Who tracks (*Pinball Wizard, See Me, Feel Me*) *Curly Leads* didn't achieve the recognition it deserved.

In an attempt to relax, lose weight and generally get himself together, Bruce spent most of March 1974 at Forest Mere Health Farm in Hampshire — those few weeks changed his life.

Lynne was actually married when I bumped into her at the health farm, but I knew immediately that she was the lady for me. It was just one of those instant things. I'd been through such a bad time over the previous couple of years it was great to realise that there was someone in the world who was really meant for me. She was thirty at the time and had a little boy Jason who was three, so I knew it wouldn't be a flash-in-the-pan romance as we were both pretty mature people. Lynne really helped me retain my self-respect and although I try to be as much of a disciplinarian at home as I am in the Shadows, she doesn't let me get away with it! My nickname for Lynne has always been 'Kipper' for reasons which I'm not going to reveal, but when *Miss You Nights* came out a couple of years later in 1976 every copy had the words 'For Kipper' scratched on to the vinyl at the end of the groove!

1974 was a busy year for Brian Bennett.

John Foster, the guy who initially discovered Cliff, started managing me and I got more and more involved with different musicians which really helped me broaden my musical outlook. In '74 I met Deke Arlon who was managing a singer/songwriter called Ian Page, and along with guitarist Colin Green, I agreed to play on

Ian's album. Nothing new in playing on someone's record, but we recorded it at James Garcia's studio in Colorado and stayed in a super log cabin right next to a trout stream. The thought of travelling across the States by rail wasn't immediately appealing, but when the guard came into our cabins with massive torpedo-style joints we travelled 'high' class as well as first class — it was the first time I'd flown by train! In my book, Los Angeles at that time was the music centre of the world, there was so much talent and enthusiasm in the city, as well as the record company guys having a much more positive attitude than their English counterparts.

As well as arranging the States trip, Deke also asked me one day if I would arrange a track called *Doll Man* for him.

'Sure,' I said and got my pen out to write down the line up.

'You'll need a lot of paper,' he said, 'It's for the London Symphony Orchestra!'

Arranging for the LSO was a real feather in my cap, but the day I did it was pretty hectic, as we did the track on the same day as the British Open Golf Tournament at Lytham St Annes, and John Foster and myself had a four-hour car dash to get there. The main reason was to have my picture taken with the winner (Gary Player) to promote my tune *Chaseside Shoot Up*, the BBC 2 golf theme. I also arranged the theme for the TV programme *Robin's Nest* mainly due to the old ties with Richard O'Sullivan via things like *Summer Holiday.*

In August I joined Georgie Fame and the Blue Flames who by then were a twelve-piece outfit. We opened in Penzance on 15th August and embarked on a fairly lengthy tour which often included nights at London's Bag o' Nails club where several show-biz people turned up to see us — even Paul McCartney came one night, with Linda. Georgie went down in a big way that evening — his Hammond organ had a shiny wooden seat and at one point as he was really getting into a number he slid right off, and crashed down on to the nearest table which was full of champagne bottles and glasses! On the adjoining table Paul and Linda seemed fairly unconcerned with Georgie's antics!

I did Reading Festival with the Blue Flames, which I was a little worried about, but it turned out really well, and all the other acts on the bill stood at the side of the stage and cheered us. I remember Mitch Mitchell even joining us for a week for some reason — the band were real loons — our coach driver actually ended up in hospital with nervous exhaustion! Alan Skidmore (one of the world's greatest jazz players) was on sax and when we were in Dunfermline he launched into a twelve minute sax solo while the

210

rest of us went and sat in the audience! That was quite a weird night as we ended up surrounded by really heavy Scots blokes yelling, 'We want *Bonnie and Clyde* and *Yeah Yeah.* We didn't pay guid money jus' to hear you play this rubbish!'

'74 for me also meant a couple of albums with Frank Pourcel and sessions for Labi Siffre and John Farrar, who was undoubtedly the most professional musician I've ever worked with.

Back in 1973, Cliff and Shadows' promoter, Eddie Jarrett, had asked a guy called Brian Goode to put together a band to back one of the artists, Labi Siffre, who'd had three Top 30 hits during '71 and '72. He was going to be guesting on an Olivia Newton John show from Manchester. It was through Labi that Brian met Cliff's manager Peter Gormley, who'd also been looking after the Shadows, but with less and less to do in that direction had been devoting more of his time to Cliff and Olivia. It was through this meeting that came the work out at the house at Upper Harley Street, the base for Peter and Norrie Paramor, but it wasn't until 1975 that Brian was going to become an integral part of the Shadows story.

Artists themselves sometimes find publicity hard to come by, but it's very rarely that newspapers devote space to the men behind the scenes! In December 1974 the press devoted a full half page to promoter Eddie Jarrett, who'd been handling all the tours for Cliff and the Shadows virtually from the outset. Extracts from the article, by Guy Adams, sum up and coincide with the artists' impression of his character.

> Eddie Jarrett secretly cried to himself when he had to start working down a Welsh pit three days after his fourteenth birthday — it still brings a lump to Eddie's throat as he remembers those days and look down on London from his luxury eighth floor flat in the West End . . . Exhausting round-the-world trips have taken him to more than fifty countries . . . He is recognised as the 'Mr Nice Guy' of the often nasty show-business agency world.

Eddie also promoted the Seekers for many years and Athol Guy from the group probably sums up Eddie best:

> It was through the faith, efforts, guidance, promotion and financial backing of Eddie Jarrett that the Seekers arrived as a force on the entertainment scene, not only in England, but the rest of the world. We are indebted far beyond any meagre percentage that he took from our earnings. In fact there were times when his percentage of our earnings was far less than he expended from his own pocket in our promotions!

Peter R. Vince, our recording
engineer of long standing
(formerly of Harrow,
Middlesex)

Alan Hawkshaw

The Grade Organisation's
disco dancing team 1960:
left to right, Bernard Lee,
Sid Maurice, David Bryce,
Peter Prichard,
Peter Lavoie

Ian Samwell

Jack Good and
John Foster

Peter Gormley (the Godfather) relaxing
between shaves

Eddie Jarrett our agent, who believed
in us from the start

Brian Goode relaxing between invoices

David Bryce relaxing between haircuts

A wonderful testimonial, which Hank, Brian and Bruce heartily endorse.

27th October 1974 turned out to be a pretty important day for the Shadows, as Hank recalls.

> We played together as the Shadows at a charity concert at the Palladium in aid of the widow of BBC producer Colin Charman, and our appearance sparked off an idea in the mind of one man in the audience — BBC boss Bill Cotton. That germ of a thought came to fruition, as we were asked to be the Eurovision artists that year, which would mean playing six final songs on television and going to Stockholm to appear for Great Britain with the winning song. We didn't really exist as a group, but we got together and did some concerts at Croydon, Eastbourne and Bournemouth to get the feeling of playing as a unit again. Initially though there was no one to look after us as Peter Gormley was spending an increasing amount of time on Cliff and Olivia's careers, but he did suggest that Brian Goode from our Harley Street headquarters kept an eye on us, as general co-ordinator.

> With Peter spending more and more time in America, due to Olivia's success there, I found myself looking after the Shadows, our first project together for me being Eurovision. It was only when the songs were whittled down to the final six that Bruce and Hank found out that one of the songs *This House Runs on Sunshine* was by Mike Redway and . . . Brian Bennett! It probably smacked of nepotism to an outsider, but the whole voting system is totally above board — the demos that are listened to by the panel all have blank labels and TV Centre is guarded like Colditz while the voting is in progress! I don't think Hank thought much of the song, and Bruce wasn't too impressed either.

> No, to be honest it wasn't a world-beater but we thought it was the most amazing coincidence that Brian was performing on Eurovision *and* his song made the final half dozen. The eventual winner was a number written by Paul Curtis called *Let Me Be the One.* The atmosphere for the contest itself was electric: not only were the Stockholm audience great, but knowing that we were going out to three hundred million people around the world was an incredible feeling. We had a minor upset in that Brian, in accordance with the contest rules, wasn't allowed to use his new pink Premier drum kit that had been specially designed for

214

him and had to use a black Ludwig. I don't think the sponsors at Premier were terribly pleased! Despite our optimism running high, we ended up in second place behind Dutch group Teach-in with their song *Ding-a-Dong* but at least had the satisfaction of getting one place higher than them in the British chart — they got to 13 — we made 12! We were back in the best sellers for the first time in eight years.

As well as the Shadows bouncing back into the singles chart, March also saw the release of the album *Specs Appeal* which included all six Eurovision titles and helped to create a new demand for the Shadows in the wake of Eurovision. Instead of being general overseer it looked as though Brian Goode would have his hands full.

Suddenly my phones were buzzing and everyone wanted the Shadows again, but it was never meant to be a long term reunion, so we played the Paris Olympia and took Abbey Road producer Tony Clarke and RAK mobile studio over to capture what we all thought was going to be the group's very last performance. The guys had no real live legacy except for the early stuff with Cliff, and we decided that Paris would be an ideal place, as the Shadows had always been even bigger than Cliff in France.

A lot of the Shadows' 60s hits were on that live album as well as some contrasting tracks, from *Sleepwalk* off their first LP to a rock 'n' roll medley comprising *Lucille*, *Rip It Up*, and *Blue Suede Shoes*. Theoretically that was the end. Actually it really was the end for Brian Bennett, he arrived at the hotel in a real state.

I'd been in Brussels to do some orchestral music with a sixty-piece orchestra, and on the last night we all had a few wines with our meal after working. Keen to relax even more, two French horn players brought a few bottles of 'vin blanc' et 'vin rouge' with them — which naturally I had to try! After the lengthy session, I had to get a train straight to Paris to join Hank and Bruce, and already fairly well lit, I had the misfortune to find myself sharing my compartment with a whisky rep!! At the start of the journey he had a suitcase full of samples in the form of miniatures — by the time we got to Paris I think our *medical* samples were the same proof as his product! I crashed into my hotel bedroom at five in the morning and collapsed under a heap of drums and manuscripts which is where Hank and Bruce found me, dead to the world, late the following morning! Paris didn't look so gay that morning even through a pair of dark shades!

Run Billy Run was released in June as the follow-up to *Let Me Be the One* but failed to chart despite the Shadows' new lease of life. Later in 1975 John Farrar moved to America as Olivia Newton John's producer and Bruce started working with Cliff, which came rather out of the blue.

Peter Gormley had the feeling that Cliff's records were getting a little bland for the singles market and virtually said, 'Whoever comes up with the right songs gets the chance to produce Cliff.' He hadn't had a Top 10 record since early '73, had had one hit in '74 and hadn't charted at all during 1975 — pretty amazing, as until then he'd not missed a single year in the charts since 1958.

I found a great song in the States called *Honky Tonk Angel* which Marvin, Welch and Farrar produced, and it looked all set to be a hit, until a newspaper printed an article saying how amazed they were that Cliff should record a song about a 'lady of the night'. This set him thinking, and resulted in a telephone call to the American Embassy where a spokesman confirmed that a 'Honky Tonk Angel' was indeed 'a woman of ill-repute'. After that, Cliff resolutely refused to promote it! Fortunately there were no problems with the other songs I'd found — in fact they turned out to be classics! I was so happy at locating *Miss You Nights, Devil Woman* and *I Can't Ask for Anymore than You* that we decided to do a whole album. That was how *I'm Nearly Famous* was born and started the resurgence of Cliff's career. In producing the album I also put the group together, which included the backing singers that Cliff still uses to this day, Tony Rivers, Stu Calver and John Perry. Tony, of course, had led his own group, the Beachboy-style Castaways, for many years before joining Harmony Grass while John Perry had been with the Beatle-backed group Grapefruit. *Devil Woman* went to the Top 5 in the States, and really helped put Cliff on the map there and *I'm Nearly Famous* had such a fantastic world-wide reaction and was such a dramatic shot in the arm for his career that his records were taken seriously for the first time in a long while. Our association continued with *Every Face Tells a Story,* the *Green Light* album and, most recently, *We Don't Talk Any More,* which was Cliff's biggest selling single ever.

In May, another shot at the singles chart missed as the new Shadows single *It'll Be Me Babe* failed to get off the ground. In June, Brian Bennett put his money where his mouth was and made a single *Thunderbolt* before drumming in the Knokke Song Festival with a group that Hank was producing. Brian had also started producing for and writing with actor Dennis Waterman which resulted in the album *Downwind of Angels,* on which he used the Belmont choir from his son Warren's school.

216

I was so impressed with the choir that I wrote a complete suite for them to perform based on *The Hobbit* by J.R.R. Tolkein. I called it, not surprisingly, *The Suite from the Hobbit!* When they had actually sung it on stage I stood in front of Warren and his school friends. When I took a bow at the end I was so proud that I really had to fight back the tears! I think around this time I was starting to get this image of myself as a writer of serious works — I even grew a beard to complete the picture! That was when I formed a new publishing company, Honeyhill Music Ltd, so called because my wife Margaret liked the sound of the name! I worked on a potential musical called *Life Cycle* that I thought would be good for Cliff, but nothing came of it.

In August Brian and his family, Margaret, Warren and daughter Sarah moved from Finchley to Mill Hill where he installed a four-track studio in the house in the Ridgeway. His neighbour turned out to be Graham Dene who was hosting Capital Radio's Breakfast Show.

I thought it was an amazing coincidence when Brian moved in across the road, as some very close friends of mine had lived next to Hank at one time and as a great Shadows fan I used to get terribly jealous when they told me tales of people like Cliff calling round, and the show-business gatherings there! Brian Bennett and I only used to socialise occasionally, as we kept entirely different hours — I was up at 4.30 every morning, and him being a bit of a night bird his bedroom light would often be going out just as mine went on! We had a sort of unwritten pact, that if he promised not to play his drums too loudly at night, I wouldn't rev my car up too much as I pulled off down the Ridgeway at 5.15. I remember Dennis Waterman being round there quite a bit as he was working with Brian at the time, and as Dennis and I both played for the same football team, we'd often jokingly try to persuade Brian to come and join us for a game — I think his usual excuse was that his back was playing up, and our gag about the defenders in our eleven having the same problem was quite deservedly met by a pair of raised eyebrows. I adore music anyway and am quite openly a harmony freak — I'm a sucker for Beach Boys stuff and things like that, so I loved going over to listen to Brian's songs, apart from any other reason — he was such a nice bloke, which was great to discover especially having been a Shadows fan since the day I rushed out and bought *Wonderful Land!*

In August 1976 Brian Bennett accompanied Cliff to Russia as his MD.

Brian also drummed for me of course, Cliff Hall was on keyboards, Graham Jarvis on drums, Dave Richmond on bass and Tony Rivers and the gang vocalising. We did a week in Leningrad (if you called it St Petersburg they kept you there!) and a week in Moscow.

I must admit when we got to Leningrad and I was shown my hotel room I was a little surprised. I'd not been expecting anything terribly flash but it was pretty basic to say the least, for the first major non-Iron Curtain artist to appear over there. I'd been sitting there contemplating my dismal surroundings for a while, when our keyboard wizard Cliff Hall came bouncing in.

'Hey my room's fantastic — I've got the Yuri Gagarin suite, it's really luxurious, you have gold candelabra, and a four poster bed!'

I thought I'd drawn the short straw until it transpired that the Russians had booked us in under our first names, Mr Brian, Mr Cliff, and so on, and with there being two Mr Cliffs, he'd got *my* room! The whole trip was a very interesting adventure. I think Mr Brian especially enjoyed it.

Yes, I was very moved by a lot of things I saw over there, for a start I went to the Hermitage Museum which had some incredible paintings of old Russian customs and cultures before the revolution — their faces looked very weird, and their features were unrecognisable as belonging to a particular race. There was another museum where I went every morning where there were a lot of revolution paintings and that wonderful masterpiece 'The Wheatfield' which used to blow me away every time I looked at it. The Tsar's summer palace was so breathtaking that I was moved to write about it, there were so many odd and beautiful things there, like the stones by the fountain — if you stepped on the wrong one you'd trigger off the giant spout of water and end up getting soaked!

At one point, we met up with a Russian diplomat and his lovely wife who were entertaining us to a lovely dinner complete with real Georgian wine when there was a power cut, and she ended reciting some very moving Russian poetry. When she'd finished, Dave Richmond stood up and recited Dylan Thomas poems, by candlelight, and we all literally wept with patriotic emotion through being so far from home. There was a lot of depression around, though: every shop had queues of people outside — you had to

218

queue to choose your article, queue again to get your receipt and a third time to collect your purchase! The longest queue of all was for Lenin's tomb which was literally miles long — I had my hands in my pockets when I went in, because I was so cold, but a couple of guards rushed over and whipped my hands *out* of my pockets! We had a sort of Clouseau-type KGB character who followed us everywhere in his very obvious-looking trilby and great coat. He was a great source of amusement to us, and became a big joke among the group! Maybe we should've played the Russian version of *FBI — KGB!* — I mean the routine we used to do for it was almost a Cossack dance anyway! The KGB were always present at the show, and whenever there was a standing ovation they'd rush up to the audience clicking their fingers shouting something that sounded like, 'Niet! Niet!' I'm pretty sure it meant something stronger than 'Night! Night!' One night after the show one stern looking Russian guard whispered, 'Great show' out of the side of his mouth and then went off to rebuke the audience for enjoying it! Pretty weird! They were no less odd in our hotel either. On every single floor, there's a standard fat Russian lady who checks your passport and papers every time you come in or out, and one day for no apparent reason she came screaming up to me and tried to half kill me by thrashing at me with a large broom! I felt I struck back with a blow for freedom though, by sneakily concealing a samovar, which is an urn for boiling water, out of the country in my bass drum. Being in Russia in 1976 seemed a far cry from the very early sixties when as a 'Krew-Kat' I actually recorded a number called *Samovar.*

Later in 1976 the Shadows album *Rarities* was released having been put together by Shadows afficionado John Friesen.

John Friesen is now the official mail correspondent for the Shadows, not only handling fan letters from all over the world but also stocking most of their records in his music shop in Middlesex.

I've always been a great Shadows fan, and spend a lot of time working on their behalf which actually gives me a lot of personal pleasure. I compiled the *Rarities* album and *20 Golden Greats* at the same time, but never actually got credited for the latter, as EMI changed *one* track on my suggested listing. For *Rarities* I gave EMI's sales manager Paul Watts a track listing for a cheap price album which I knew contained numbers that would appeal to Shadows fans who had all the obvious stuff. One of the suggested tracks was the instrumental version of *Friends* which had previously only been available on the EP *Themes from Aladdin,* but good old

EMI had initially gone ahead using the vocal version from the soundtrack before I pointed out the mistake! We also had problems just using the name 'The Shadows' on the LP, as there were some of Hank's solo numbers on there as well and we could have ended up getting clobbered under the 'Sale of Goods Act' so that too was amended. The English sleeve was pretty appalling, but the Australian cover was a great shot of the Shadows doing Eurovision. Surprisingly, seven years on, *Rarities* is still available, somehow having consistently escaped the deleter's inevitable guillotine. The album was successful, but it was swamped saleswise by the release in January 1977 of *20 Golden Greats* which tipped the album chart and went on to sell over a million copies.

It also overshadowed an album called *Rock Dreams* that Brian Bennett made at the end of 1976.

Cliff sang on some of my *Rock Dreams* and so did Dennis Waterman for whom I produced a second album, *Waterman*. In 1977, with the success of *Golden Greats*, Hank, Bruce and myself along with Peter Gormley and Brian Goode decided that we should concentrate on being the Shadows again, as there was without a doubt a large market for the type of music with which we'd always been associated. At the beginning of 1977 we started recording *Tasty* which was really a demo album, as we did it too quickly, as well as having been away from each other too long. We included several original numbers done in the old familiar twangy style, as well as covers of *Honky Tonk Woman, Goodbye Yellow Brick Road* and the old Ventures hit *Walk Don't Run.* Despite the inclusion of *Bermuda Triangle* the record didn't disappear without trace! Around the time of *Tasty* I also wrote an opera for Mill Hill School entitled *The Ballad of Salaman Pavey* based on a famous Elizabethan chorister who died of consumption at the age of thirteen.

Mainly due to *20 Golden Greats,* 1977 became a busy year for the Shadows as Bruce recalls.

I worked hard on that album, re-processing it in 'Mock Stereo' to make it more compatible for modern equipment. Although it turned out well, and the tracks were all popular numbers, one couldn't underestimate the power of EMI's TV marketing campaign. Their commercial development department had already successfully marketed the Beach Boys and Glen Campbell's respective *20 Golden Greats* so all the channels for a potential monster album had already been created. Whatever the reasons, we charted a mere forty-eight hours after being released — which was some going!

220

A present from a fan

We also did a tour in May which we called '20 Golden Dates' and received ten minute standing ovations every night — it was like early 60s revisited! I think 1977 was the year that the Shadows became businessmen first and foremost, although Hank *did* win an award in August!

Yes, another coveted trophy for the Marvin mantelpiece was thrust into my nimble fingers as I collected the CBS Arbiter award for services to British Music, along with Joe Brown and Bert Weedon. Actually Bert is featured every night we're on stage, you know — I take on his 'play in a day' guitar tutor! Talking of great players, at the end of the year, my album *The Hank Marvin Guitar Syndicate* was released featuring several other guitarists including Kevin Peek, Colin Green and Vick Flick.

In February 1978 the Shadows played a two week 'Twentieth Anniversary Thank You Very Much' at the Palladium with Cliff which was attended by many stars of showbusiness including Des O'Connor.

I went along, not only as a great fan of Cliff and the Shadows, but also as Hank Marvin was working on an album with me.

Journalist Allan Jones writing in the *Melody Maker* on 11th March gave the concert the slightly sarcastic type of review, which the public had almost come to expect from several of the music papers in the latter half of the 70s.

Cliff was flanked by Hank Marvin who looks more than ever like Marge Proops and Bruce Welch dressed in the most ill-fitting trousers I've ever seen. The Shadows played *Atlantis, Apache, Nivram, Walk Don't Run* and a Brian Bennett drum solo. Now Brian knows that the important thing about a drum solo is to keep the customer occupied — no one sleeps when this boy's behind the traps . . . Bruce got rather tired and kept complaining about being unable to breathe in his tight-fitting velvet jerkin.

It seemed that suddenly from 1976 onwards it became fashionable for the music press to knock anybody who was over the age of nineteen of who'd had a hit record.

In May Brian Bennett's concept album *Voyage,* on which he'd worked with Alan Jones and Frances Monkman was released.

'78 was an up and down year for me; I was pleased with the album and happy with the Palladium show but got severely brought down while I was in the States with Margaret my wife. The previous time I'd been there it had been in Santa Monica for the whole month of August with good friends like John Farrar and Olivia, but this time it was New York, we got caught in a violent blizzard, became hopelessly lost in the not-too-healthy district of Harlem and ended up having our hotel suite burgled. Apart from that things were great!

Margaret was really upset as she'd had all her jewellery stolen and as it had come from all over the world, had an awful lot of sentimental value. We called the police, but they were incredibly unhelpful, all we got was one curt line, 'It's all melted down by now, lady, whaddya want *us* to do?' Unbelievable! Have a nice day!

A highlight of '78 turned out to be some library session music I wrote, some of which became the incidental music for the popular TV series *Dallas,* and some was used for *Knotts Landing.* In July my son Warren started a school group, for which I often acted as an unpaid roadie — talk about coming a full circle, there I was humping drum kits around again!

For the autumn tour in 1978 the Shadows line-up was augmented by Alan Jones on bass, who'd also played with them on '20 Golden Dates', and keyboards player Cliff Hall.

Francis Monkman had briefly been the Shadows keyboards man on '20 Golden Dates', but as is his way, he soon got itchy feet and was off to do something new. I'd known Brian Bennett for ages, we'd often played on sessions together and kept in touch over the years so he recommended me to Hank and Bruce. It was Hank who actually phoned me to ask me to join, and as I was missing touring, I agreed. I never thought I *would* miss it to be honest, after working with Cliff Richard for over six years, and touring round the world to far-flung places like Japan, Europe and Russia. I'd imagined that I'd be content doing session work, but the call of the wild lured me back! Before playing with Cliff I played on all sorts of sessions for different producers. In fact there was a little gang of us who played on so many different artists' records that we'd turn up in the studio asking, 'Who are we meant to be today?' I played on most of the Bay City Rollers records for example, the bass on their records was either Les Hurdle or Frank MacDonald; Clem Cattini or Harold Fisher would usually be in the drum seat and more often than not Joe Moretti would play lead guitar — I think we had about a dozen hits as the Bay City Rollers!

There really was no thrill though like playing live with the Shadows, I honestly can't remember us playing to a bad audience

— we always got a fantastic reception, and I liked the fact that their programme was very mixed. They'd not only play the nostalgic stuff like *FBI, Wonderful Land* and *Apache,* but would feature Alan Jones and myself quite heavily.

After a brief spell in the printers' trade Alan Jones started playing bass with assorted Mecca groups and stood himself in good stead for the future by learning to read music, and getting involved in session work.

I took over the bass guitar for Tom Jones' Squires, when John Rostill left, and I spent three and a half years with Tom before getting back into sessions. I've played with stacks of different artists: George Harrison, Lulu, B.A. Robertson, Elvis Presley, Olivia Newton John, Gilbert O'Sullivan and Tom Jones, to name but a few. During the early part of 1977 Brian Bennett called me to ask if I'd like to do the '20 Golden Dates' tour with the Shadows, and as I'd previously worked with Hank and Brian, and with Bruce on Olivia's sessions, it seemed the right thing to do.

By the autumn of 1978, the Shadows had been three and a half years without a hit single, but things were to take a sudden turn in that direction, and nobody was more pleased than Shadows manager Brian Goode.

During September I was approached by a buyer for the record merchandisers who supply Woolworths, a chap called David Buckley. David had been to see the Shadows on tour, and had recognised what he thought was a tune with a lot of commercial appeal that the guys were featuring on stage — *Don't Cry For Me, Argentina!* The Tim Rice/Andrew Lloyd Webber song had been taken to the top of the chart only the previous year by Julie Covington, and a slightly different version of it had made the Top 3 a mere couple of months before for David Essex, so I doubted the wisdom of releasing an instrumental version so soon. Any misgivings I had were quashed, though, when David Buckley promised, 'You get the Shadows to record it, and I'll take 100,000 copies.' You don't turn down an offer like that, so the Shadows went into the studio and laid it down. We took it to EMI but our version hadn't really worked, as it hadn't captured that excitement that you only get from a live performance.

So I was stuck with a barely adequate take of *Argentina,* a record merchandiser screaming for enough copies for it to zoom into the chart, Hank on holiday in Barbados and Bruce away in Miami! I called up Brian Bennett and suggested we take the tape into

Since the mid 1970s Alan and Cliff have been permanent members of the Shadows line-up, appearing with the group on concert tours all over the world

Abbey Road and see what we could do with it. Despite his reluctance because of the absence of Hank and Bruce he saw the wisdom of trying to salvage a potential hit record, so we set about patching it up, and mixed in some applause from the Palladium tapes taken off the Cliff and the Shadows twentieth anniversary show. It worked! We ended up with a totally different sounding version which captured that 'live' feel. EMI flipped and released it. Strangely, it was not a hit by Christmas, and we thought that maybe David Buckley's ears weren't as commercially receptive as we thought, but by the first chart of the New Year it was showing in the lower regions. Two weeks later it was in the Top 40 — and it eventually peaked at Number 5 and ended up spending three and a half months on the chart. So twenty years to the month after first joining Cliff on a permanent basis the Shadows were back in the charts with their twenty-seventh hit single! As Alan Jones wasn't available for their two *Top of the Pops* appearances for *Argentina* they were joined on bass by a guy they'd known for twenty years from his days of playing Checkmates along with Alan Hawkshaw, Emile Ford's brother, George.

In January 1979 Brian Bennett set off for the Midem Festival in high spirits.

Midem is the venue of a yearly festival when publishers from all over the world get together to pick up and do deals on copyrights of songs and song catalogues. It's also a good excuse to bump into lots of old friends and live a relaxing few days. This particular year, I travelled down in Alan Hawkshaw's new Mercedes. We stopped off in Paris to go and see Cliff Richard as he was recording there, and then drove south until we got to Avignon at about nine in the evening, planning to stay there for the night and then on down to Midem the next day. We didn't make it the next day . . . or the next! In fact it took the police a couple of days to find the car and when they did all the tyres had been nicked! The worst thing was that all our clothes and cassettes that had been in the car were strewn and scattered along a five mile stretch of road. My cassettes, of course, were my lifeblood at the time, and without them I could do no business at all in Midem! We didn't get a lot of sense from the French Police. In fact the guy who interrogated us at their local HQ was just like Peter Sellers' Inspector Clouseau, and when his opening question was, 'What ees yourrr morther's medden name?' Alan and I temporarily forgot about our problems and fell about. So instead of doing some song trading we were stuck 'Sur le pont d'Avignon' for a couple of days with Clouseau.

226

Kenny Everett out to lunch!

Bruce, Lynne, Carole and Hank

The projected follow-up to *Argentina* was one of Hank's favourite oldies, *God Only Knows*.

I'd always liked the number, so we decided to release it, but while plans on that front were being formulated another suggestion arose. The theme music to the new film *The Deer Hunter*, was suggested to us by EMI. It was a Stanley Myers composition called *Cavatina* which John Williams had recorded some years previously. Brian Bennett had often suggested we recorded it, but we passed on it every time. Now the time was right. We went into the studio and completed it in one take, and who came in to hear the playback? John Williams.

At the end of April 1979 *Deer Hunter* entered the chart and eventually made it two Top 10 records in a row — a feat the Shadows hadn't achieved since 1963. Like *Argentina*, it stayed on the chart for three and a half months.

On 1st August 1979 Bruce took the plunge and married Lynne at Marylebone Registry Office.

The best man was a guy called Alan Lawson, my best friend outside the music business. The reception was at the Carlton Tower Hotel — there were hundreds of people there, including Hank and Brian, and it cost an arm and a leg. We went for our honeymoon to the George Cinq Hotel in Paris, and then on to my villa in Portugal.

1979 meant another British tour in the autumn and an album *String of Hits* which was scheduled for heavy TV advertising as Bruce well remembers.

Just as the TV album campaign was due to start, ITV went on strike. It lasted for ages and ages which just goes to prove that the best laid plans don't come to fruition! We were staggered that despite the problem of a lack of exposure in that direction we'd sold over 300,000 copies by Christmas! Early in '80 the ad went out at last, which resulted in us more than doubling our sales, so we ended up selling something like 700,000 copies of *String of Hits* which took us to the top of the LP chart. One of the most popuular numbers we featured on the tour and on the album was *Riders in the Sky* which had been a Top 10 hit for the American group the Ramrods back in 1961, so we re-recorded it, released it just after Christmas, and eventually got to Number 12, staying in the chart for three months.

In 1980 the contract between the Shadows and EMI expired after a

ehearsing for a tour of the
olydor offices

Just back from a world tour

partnership which had started at the end of 1958. Contracts invariably come to the end of a term of agreement, and more often than not a re-signing session takes place, as it had between the Shadows and the record company in the past. But Hank, Bruce and Brian were no longer the bright-eyed naive musicians that were happy as long as they were playing their instruments and had a few pounds in their pockets. During the latter half of the 60s they'd become businessmen, and having served EMI well over the years, set down their not unreasonable terms for a re-negotiation, aided by Brian Goode.

> Quite simply, Bruce, Hank and Brian Bennett wanted to retain the rights to their own recordings and lease them to EMI, just as many groups and producers were doing. They obviously thought that if unproven and up and coming acts could do it, the Shadows probably had an even bigger lever, judging by their success over the previous two decades. But despite four to five months of negotiation the record company wouldn't agree to what we thought was a very fair request, so we had talks with Polydor. We rapidly reached an agreement with them, whereby they offered us several hundred thousand pounds for a three year contract, with the Shadows providing three albums during that period.
>
> So after over twenty years of being an EMI group the Shadows formed Roll Over Records Ltd, and signed to Polydor.

In March 1980 the Shadows toured Europe, with George Ford on bass and Cliff Hall on keyboards, and their first album for Polydor, the aptly titled *Change of Address*, was released in September. To counteract this, EMI had already issued *Another String of Hot Hits* at the end of July, but as it was both albums sat comfortably side by side in the Top 20 for several weeks. Singles from the albums were released almost simultaneously. From *Another String* an instrumental version of Blondie's 1979 chart topper *Heart of Glass* failed to make the best sellers and *Equinoxe (Part 5)* from *Change of Address* only got as high as Number 50.

The album *Change of Address* went gold during the Shadows' forty-five date autumn tour, which took in eleven countries and resulted in them being presented with gold discs at the Mogador theatre in Paris.

In 1981 Brian Bennett produced a new album.

> I went into the studio with Cliff Hall and recorded what I felt was a beautiful LP entitled *Shadows in Ivory*, which was basically just Cliff and a piano playing numbers like *Kon-Tiki* and *Argentina*. Strangely enough not a single record company wanted to know — I couldn't get arrested with it!

Early in 1981 the Shadows raced around Holland, Germany and Spain promoting *Change of Address* before returning to England to record a new single — *The Third Man*. Initially known as *The Harry Lime Theme*, the Shadows coupled it with their self-penned *Fourth Man* — but timed things rather badly as they were all away on holiday when Brian Goode got a call for them to appear on *Top of the Pops*.

> I think *The Third Man* would have got a lot higher than Number 44 if the lads had been around, but they were having a tough time of it out in Barbados!

In July, with another tour coming up Brian Bennett took himself off to a health farm.

> I went to Champneys to get my body together for the tour, which meant a diet of grapes and jugs of hot water — not terribly pleasant, but while I was there I was determined to relax and watch a lot of telly. On 29th July I sat back to enjoy the Royal Wedding on ITV and was absolutely stunned when I heard the theme tune they'd chosen for their coverage — it was one of my tunes called *Sound of Success*. I felt so patriotic and proud, they could have taken my grapes away and I wouldn't have noticed! During the tour in September I really felt we were playing better than ever, we were all relaxed, had a lot of laughs and reminisced about the old days of tearing up and down the country in draughty vans. My mode of transport on the tour was about as far removed from our early method as you could get — it was a fabulously fitted-out bus, with TV, keyboards and amps set up and every modern convenience — it really was the height of luxury to be going down the M5 with your feet up watching *Where Eagles Dare*. It was on that tour that I first met Sue Barker. I'd been to watch a tennis tournament while we were in Brighton, and when I got back to the hotel I bumped into Sue. She was great, and got me a couple of tickets for the final, so I called up Alan Hawkshaw who is a great tennis fan and he came running down to go with me.
>
> Sue came to the show that evening, and to the Dominion Theatre concert two weeks later, and I believe that was the first time she met Cliff.

The tour certainly helped to put the new Shadows album *Hits Right Up Your Street* into the chart, where it stayed for the rest of the year and into '82.

1982 saw the release of the value-for-money double album *Life in the Jungle* and *Live at Abbey Road*, the latter being in front of a live audience of fans from all over Europe that had been organised by John Friesen.

1982 was the year that Hank spent most of his spare time on the tennis court in his garden, and was rarely spotted out of a track suit. He also had a solo hit record with *Don't Talk,* a song originally intended for Cliff.

1982 meant more library music for Brian Bennett, more hanging from doors in an attempt to sort his bad back out, and an increasing involvement with his son Warren's group Glass Ties for whom he produced an excellent single *Tight* which was released on EMI.

1982 was a business year for Bruce Welch — finding new songs and new groups, in particular three guys from Plymouth called Mercedes. It was also a year of trying out a number of allegedly well proven diets — he was spotted wading through a bag of grapes at more than one variety club function. He also continued to phone his Aunt Sadie every day. He absolutely adores her — she's now in her seventies and lives in a bungalow he bought her in Whickham.

For their manager Brian Goode 1982 meant cracking the whip to make sure the autobiography was ready for 1983, quite rightly assuming that any meetings between Messrs Marvin, Bennett and Read in particular would turn into an all day tennis match. Despite the fact that he deliberately hid our shorts on various occasions, you're now actually holding the finished article in your hand — although it was so evenly matched that it could still have been deuce — and then you'd have had to buy another book instead.

232

In May 1983, the Shadows were presented with the Ivor Novello Award
to mark their contribution to British music over the last 25 years.
These awards are the official 'Oscars' of the British Music Industry and they
are presented annually by the British Academy of Song Writers,
Composers, and Authors.

Some Tributes to the Shadows

Pete Townshend:

In all the years I have been a Shadows fan I have never once seen them play live. I have watched them on television, heard them on record and on the radio. They remain, to this day, a myth to me. Meeting Hank Marvin in John Stephen's clothes shop in Carnaby Street soon after the Who's first record was released, I was impressed by his caution when he praised it, saying, 'Good record, lad'. He spoke in a tone that implied it was good, not great, that the future might hold all kinds of shocks for me. I don't suppose he knew, any more than I did, that the Who would last nearly as long as, but not outlive, his own band. Whether we have ever made a record as good as *Can't Explain*, the song he praised, is doubtful, pop tends to produce early highs and later lows.

The last time I met him, apart from a fleeting chat at an award ceremony, we played together on Paul McCartney's *Rockestra* sessions. He was cool and professional, I was cool and drunk. It sobered me to hear him say, as he quit the session at six, that he was going to a Bible class, a class he himself was conducting. A few days later Bruce Welch and myself sat in the Abbey Road bar getting fairly well doused, it struck me that the Shadows have seen a lot of extremes, been through far more than we shall ever know.

*　　*　　*

By the time I was fifteen John Entwistle, Who bassist, and myself, had played together on and off in various bands for three years. We had started playing Trad. Jazz, but the emergence of the Shadows had turned our heads. It wasn't so much Rock and Roll that interested me personally, but Electric Guitar; the sound of it, the potential of it, and the feeling in the late fifties that it was the instrument of the musical renegade; that it would never become respectable.

I remember an evening in 1959/60. I was slightly wet, walking home in the rain from a rehearsal with the Confederates. The band was led by Pete Wilson, an acne plagued boy, tall and highly strung, not a great talent at guitar but charming and energetic; we rehearsed at his home in East Acton every week. I was carrying my guitar, and maybe an amplifier — the walk was about four miles and I would usually be tired by this time. On this

234

occasion I was ebullient and inspired. In my head, for the whole walk, rang the sound of a song I had heard on the radio for a few weeks, which Pete Wilson had played at the practice — it was *Apache* by the Shadows. At that time, on that evening, I had no idea what the title was, or even very much about the band that had recorded it. A strange fact, because for years I had been playing rhythm guitar in Pete Wilson's band, and Pete Wilson was Hank Marvin's greatest living fan. His dream was to own a Fender Stratocaster, a pink one, like Hank's, and to front a group playing Shadows material. It was a narrow brief, but it was music and I enjoyed playing with him especially as my friend John Entwistle was on bass. The song I heard seemed to embody everything that was prerequisite in a pop song. The fact that I could actually remember every single note of the melody, the shape, and the haunting quality of the song after only a few listens speaks volumes for its perfection in that medium. But what was keeping me so high on my toes on this long, damp, walk home, was the *sound* that rang in my head. The Shadows version of *Apache* had such a perfect sound. I don't know who produced or engineered it, perhaps you'll find that out somewhere else in this book, but they took the Shadows sound and simply presented it; studio tricks were at a minimum, but it was superbly airy and nicely balanced.

The minor chords were so cleanly expressed on the rhythm guitar, it seemed to me that no other instrument could express the voicings of a series of moody chords better than a guitar; I still feel that today, even the piano has less grace simply stating a chord sequence. Bruce Welch showed how beautifully this could be done again later on *Man of Mystery*.

Pete Wilson used to carry his adoration of Hank's playing to the extent of copying even fluffed notes and flicked passing notes. Our drummer Mick Brown, a comedian of high calibre, stated that the Shadows drummer Tony Meehan played fills that no other human being on earth could be capable of. Jet Harris, blonde and steel eyed, struck me cold with his good looks and threateningly solid bass playing; I was glad it was John's job to copy his parts, not my own.

As I arrived home, to a room without a record player at that time, me and my guitar started to face the future with a new feeling. I felt incredibly young, even at fifteen; immature I probably was, but I mean young at heart. The Shadows' existence elevated me, intimidated me, but somehow, being able to hear their sound in my head so completely, made me feel that I could aspire to create music of my own, and to move on. Three or four years later, again with Pete Wilson's help, I did create my own music when we recorded my first song, *It Was You*, at Barry Gray's home studio. Barry was a friend of Pete's father. We went to help Pete live out his fantasy of sounding like Hank on record. By this time he had his beloved Stratocaster, the most important detail about them being not the sound or the shape, both beyond reproach, but the fact that the screws in the scratchplate were American type Philips screws. These screws are common in Europe now, but in the early sixties they were an American trademark, a mystery, a wonder. Absurd? Of course not. So many young musicians dream about owning a particular musical instrument, or article of clothing, sported by their heroes. Today it is spikey hair dos and a Computer synthesiser, then it was a Fender guitar with cross head screws.

To Pete Wilson, a Fender Stratocaster was enough, but he was quick to see that John Entwistle and I had a real chance of really making it and graciously let us take over his recording time to work out our own songs. Pete was a gent all right, but he also liked Cliff. I really was not quite so sure. Today I think every record Cliff makes is wonderful. Then, I think I secretly liked him but would never have admitted it. Pompous little git I was.

But watching one of Cliff's horrible films the other day on TV I started to think about how important it was that the Shadows were playing instrumental music. There was a rage for it for a few years in the sixties prior to the Beatles' emergence. I suppose it was because so many of the male figureheads of Pop, the singers, were so manipulated by the industry, viz: Cliff on a pile of sand dunes suggesting to Susan Hampshire, (swoon) that they could *sing* the dialogue to a film scene they were having difficulty with. 'Hank! Bruce!' he shouts, 'Come and play for us'. Hank and Bruce sidle on and start to strum silent guitars while a full orchestra plays for Cliff to croon to. That kind of incident set me against Cliff and singers like him for many years. Why, oh why didn't the film makers realise that every kid *knew* it was phony phony phony? That it was the *music* we related to not the pop-pap? So the audience divided, the little girls giggled at Cliff in the movies and the boys hung on to the idea that the Shadows were real people with real charisma and talent. I believe that in Britain this is where the emergence of the 'Male-Man' happened in Pop. Later it went a bit awry when the Stones appeared and were simultaneously macho and effeminate, but by then the ground was well laid.

Singers seemed to have to sing 'down' to the female teenaged audience, it might not have been necessary at all, but someone, somewhere obviously felt it was. Instrumental bands didn't have to do this. Their material could be dramatic, filmic, or even genuinely impressionistic. To me, the Shadows explored all these avenues, but they were never butch in the way, say, Johnny Kidd and the Pirates were, and their loyalty to Cliff was also important to their male fans. It certainly helped Cliff's credibility to young male pop fans: if he was good enough for the Shads he must be okay. Time has proved that was true and still is. Cliff has survived and become an artist who cuts across all boundaries making great pop records.

*   *   *

I have never grown out of my love of the Shadows sound. Bruch Welch has become an excellent record producer and still plays economically and beautifully; Hank is still a great stylist and technician with a great gift for expression on the electric guitar. The early Shadows image, the four unique young men, committed, ambitious and professional, disintegrated when the early line up fell apart. Tony Meehan became an entrepreneur and producer, Jet Harris got stung, but threatens to re-emerge any moment now

236

I hear, but their powerful stance lives on in my mind. A greater image than the Beatles to my mind because the Shadows were a working band, not Pop stars. That always appealed to me as one who had been brought up in an atmosphere of working musicians by my father and his post war band the Squadronaires.

I know my story must be roughly the same as dozens of other musicians who took up the guitar post-skiffle in the late fifties. Some of them might have seen the Shadows play live, even met them, I am glad I didn't. The Shadows will always be a living myth to me — a legend — even though I can now prop up the bar with any one of them and talk music, family, religion. They are frozen in my mind as one of the greatest passions of my life, one I have not, after thirty years, come close to outliving.

Shakin' Stevens:

Cliff and the Drifters debut LP was the first I ever bought, and I realised when I heard tracks like *Driftin'* and *Jet Black* that the Drifters were far more than just a backing group as they proved with singles like *Apache* and *F.B.I.* That album really inspired me — the way the guitars came across certainly sparked off my interest in music. It broke my heart when a few years later someone pinched that LP from me!

Tim Rice:

Having been a dyed-in-the-wool Shadows fan since the early days, I was ecstatic to hear the news one day, that the guys were going to release *Don't Cry For Me Argentina.*

I could hardly wait to hear Bruce's tender treatment of my poignant lyrics blending sweetly with Hank's soaring harmonies.

My hasty enthusiasm was temporarily dampened when I realised that it was an instrumental treatment but it proved to be yet another Shads classic.

237

I feel I've been incredibly lucky to see the group as (a) A fan (b) As part of the same team when I worked as an assistant for Norrie and (c) As a writer.

Eric Clapton:

My original interests and intentions in guitar playing were primarily centred on quality of tone, for instance: the way the instrument could be made to echo or simulate the human voice. At the time when I was still thrashing around on the acoustic guitar trying to sound like Leadbelly or Jesse Fuller, there was someone who had already achieved this particular goal. That was Hank B. Marvin of the Shadows. He had found, and settled on, a clean, pure sound which disallowed any kind of hamfisted playing. Only the lightest touch was permitted. The result was a marvellous mixture of clear, sweet melody over a strong rock beat (and what a great drum sound). On top of all this, he looked like Buddy Holly and played a real Stratocaster! Unbeatable. . . .

My own playing has gone through many changes and a great deal of ups and downs over the years, and therefore it never ceased to amaze me that Hank managed to arrive exactly where he wanted, and then stayed there.

As for the Shadows, all in all they always seemed to me to be the ideal rock band. Able to play a complete set of instruments on their own and then back up Cliff without turning a hair. They have lasted for three decades, their music lasts forever. Hats off to Hank and the boys . . .

Steve Gray of Sky:

For many years I wanted to be a Shadow. Not one of the Triumvirate; the Big Three, of course; that would have been impossible: but they would use keyboard players on tour and string arrangers in the studio, and it was to this condition of 'Temporary Auxiliary Shadow' that I aspired.

I wasn't always a fan. In the sixties I had the educated young musician's arrogant snobbery towards what to me seemed music so outrageously simple that anyone could do it (though I could always recognise a Shads record when I heard one)! It was only when I got into making records myself as a session musician that I realised, from the inside so to speak, exactly what the Shads had done, and those simple-minded singles revealed themselves for what they are: classic monuments of instrumental pop music.

I finally achieved my ambition: one day in 1979 Brian Bennett rang up and asked if I would like to do the string arrangements on the Shadows new album; a few months later followed one of the nicest kicks I've had in this business when I opened *Music Week* and saw *String of Hits* at Number 1 on the charts.

So, twenty-five years you've been at it, and it doesn't surprise me in the slightest; and I'm sure the next twenty-five will be a doddle, too. And if you're going on the road anytime, and Sky's not busy, and you want a piano player, cheap . . .

Steve

Bert Weedon:

Ask any follower of pop music to name the most popular British instrumental group of the last two decades, and the answer is pretty certain to be — the Shadows. Ask what the secret is behind their success, and the answer is not so easy. Their popularity and success has been staggering, so just what is the touch of magic that the Shadows have? As a fellow musician who has known them and admired their success for over twenty years I have tried to put my finger on their special recipe for being the most successful instrumental group we have known.

Way back in the late fifties, Duane Eddy and myself were getting hit records as solo guitar players, then suddenly a quartet of young musicians exploded on to the record scene with tremendous success. They were of course the first British group with a guitar sound to hit the public's ear, for those days were dominated by solo instrumentalists — that is until the 'Shads' came on to the scene. Many groups subsequently tried to emulate their success, but always the Shadows stayed at the front. What was their secret — was it the special 'Fender' sound that Hank got, was it the dance step they moved to when playing on stage, was it the sex appeal of Jet Harris, the boyish charm of Tony Meehan, the good looks of Bruce Welch, or the special charisma of all four — who knows? Their music at that time was technically unsophisticated, but their records had an indefinable magic about them, and they notched up hit after hit — since those early days they have of course developed as composers and musicians, and are recognised as the inventive and fine performers they are today. It could be said that they started out as four boys who basked in the glow of Cliff Richard's success, but they immediately proved to the world that they were stars in their own right. Their recording manager, my good friend Norrie Paramor, cleverly picked hit after hit for them to record, and their appearance on stage and in films was all conquering, and always they produced that special sound that forever will be identified as the 'Shads'.

I think their secret is that although over the years their line up has changed several times, Hank and Bruce have always been there — two musicians who started out as young fellows so many years ago, and stayed together through every step of the journey to stardom. I feel that the real secret lies with these two men who have worked so hard and contributed so

239

much to popular music. I was very honoured when they wrote a number for me to record called *Mr Guitar*, and I would like to return the compliment to those two guitar picking mates of mine — Hank and Bruce . . . may they always be remembered as the real secret behind the success of Britain's favourite instrumental group, the Shadows. Long may they keep playing, singing and giving us so much pleasure.

Bert Weedon

Roger Taylor of Queen:

Around the year 1960 there existed in Britain a curious epidemic of about 39,000 instrumental beat groups. With a peculiar regularity they would tend to consist of four youths in identical shiny suits — one would play drums, the other three would wield salmon-pink Fender (or cheaper lookalike) guitars in choreographed poses, whilst executing a curious synchronised 'dance-walk'.

The lead guitarist would often wear horn-rimmed spectacles and the electric bass player would tend to be a swept back bleached blond. The bass player would usually get the girls.

All these groups would play almost exclusively covers of Shadows tunes. In many cases they would actually imagine themselves to *be* Hank, Bruce, Jet or Tony. These groups were the 'Shadows clones'.

I know — I was that group!

At this period the Shadows were the very anglicised version of what was originally American rock or 'beat' music. Their influence at the time in the UK (and notably France) cannot be underestimated. They had a new sound, they had that cool twang — they had style! Personally I lived and breathed them for years until newer, rawer things naturally came along.

For this influence and pleasure I thank them from the bottom of my tennis racquet and bedroom mirror.

Roger Taylor

Brian May of Queen:

On being asked to write a few words about the Shadows, a great torrent of memories washed over me. When I was a kid, there was no rock music as such. When Cliff Richard and 'The Drifters' made their first recordings, they brought the stirrings of the new American rock 'n' roll to England. Only a few months later, the Shadows' records had created a completely new style and standard which literally thousands of budding guitarists all over the country attempted to emulate.

240

Instrumental music was now, for years, *the* thing, right up to the time when the Beatles re-introduced the primarily vocal approach. For me, the Shadows were the heaviest, most metallic thing around. Hearing *Man Of Mystery, The Stranger, Apache,* etc. . . . I, in common with thousands of others, started to learn the single note lead style of Hank Marvin. None of us ever quite managed it. No one ever quite got that *sound.* Was it special pick-ups, we wondered? Was it the echo chamber? Was it special strings? I found I could get close to that wonderful creamy buzzing top end on the bass strings (on *Shadoogie,* for instance) by using brand new strings and an adapted flint-holder for a pick; I can remember trying to play whole lines on one new string! But that sound was elusive.

Bruce Welch created a style of rhythm playing too, and his (usually acoustic) sound on the records was a perfect foil. Then you realised what an immaculate rhythm section Tony Meehan and Jet Harris made, and what a miracle that combination of musicians really was. The final ingredient was undoubtedly *taste* — that was what raised the Shadows above all those imitators. Hank never played a phrase which he could only just stretch to — every note was given its true voice — not just played but played *right,* for its full length and with intended tone, and not left until it was fully formed. The music was never flashy for the sake of it — always tastefully powerful, light and shade, technical perfection.

I can remember some creep of a record reviewer saying (I think it was about *Kon-Tiki*), 'Isn't the Shadows' sound getting monotonous?' The next week *Wonderful Land* burst out with its revolutionary use of strings. I gleefully imagined the reviewer sitting chewing his fingernails in embarrass-ment for the next six weeks while *Wonderful Land* was Number 1 on the charts.

I remember taping and learning to play *Foot Tapper* before it was in the shops, and astonishing my friends who were still struggling with *Dance On.* I remember Ventures songs and Spotnicks tunes which were tests of speed, but the Shadows made the stuff that people wanted to hear. Taste! Class! Sound! Listen to *Atlantis* — there's a brief plinking introduction to each verse and then — *blang* . . . . . the first note of each verse says it all — the *sound* was enough. And *is* enough. Long live the Shadows!

Brian Bentley

A Record of Success

MOST HITS

Double-sided hits, double singles,
EPs and LPs only count as one hit
each time. Re-issues and re-entries
do not count as new hits, but re-
recordings or re-mixes of the same
song by the same act do count as
two hits. A record is a hit if it
makes the chart, even if only for 1
week at Number 75.

MOST TOP TEN HITS

The same rules apply as for the
Most Hits list, except that a disc

242

must have made the Top 10 for at least one week to qualify

55 ELVIS PRESLEY
47 CLIFF RICHARD
25 BEATLES
21 ROLLING STONES
19 ABBA
17 LONNIE DONEGAN
   HOLLIES
   FRANKIE LAINE (+ *1 with Jimmy Boyd, 1 with Doris Day*)
16 SHADOWS (+ *25 with Cliff Richard*)
15 STATUS QUO
   ROD STEWART (+ *3 with Faces, 1 with Python Lee Jackson*)

MOST NUMBER 1 HITS

17 BEATLES
   ELVIS PRESLEY
10 CLIFF RICHARD
 9 ABBA
 8 ROLLING STONES
 6 SLADE
 5 BLONDIE
   SHADOWS (+ *7 with Cliff Richard*)
   ROD STEWART
 4 BEE GEES
   EVERLY BROTHERS
   FRANK IFIELD
   JAM
   FRANKIE LAINE
   GUY MITCHELL
   POLICE
   T REX

MOST WEEKS ON CHART

This list is compiled from the first British singles chart on 14th November 1952 up to and including the chart for 25th December 1982

Weeks
1098 ELVIS PRESLEY
 861 CLIFF RICHARD (+ *7 with Olivia Newton-John*)
 402 BEATLES (+ *1 with Tony Sheridan*)
 391 FRANK SINATRA (+ *18 with Nancy Sinatra, 9 with Sammy Davis Jr*)
 361 SHADOWS (+ *404 backing Cliff Richard*)
 328 EVERLY BROTHERS
 322 JIM REEVES
 321 LONNIE DONEGAN
 312 SHIRLEY BASSEY
 309 ROY ORBISON

It is extremely difficult to list in correct order the individuals who have spent most weeks on the charts under all guises, groups and other pseudonyms. However, ignoring session musicians and uncredited contributions, a Top 10 of individuals who have spent most weeks in the charts whether alone, in duos or in groups, looks like this:

Weeks
1098 ELVIS PRESLEY
 868 CLIFF RICHARD
 786 HANK B. MARVIN
 765 BRUCE WELCH
 668 PAUL McCARTNEY
 565 JOHN LENNON
 514 DIANA ROSS
 457 RINGO STARR
 456 GEORGE HARRISON
 418 FRANK SINATRA

Diana Ross has very conveniently chalked up 257 weeks on her own and also 257 weeks in other combinations of groups and duos.

In addition, up to the end of 1982, the Shadows have spent 342 weeks in the albums charts. They've had 16 hit albums, 9 Top 10 albums and 4 Number 1 albums.

This information is compiled from *The Guinness Book of Hit Singles Volume IV* and *The Guinness Book of Hit Albums*

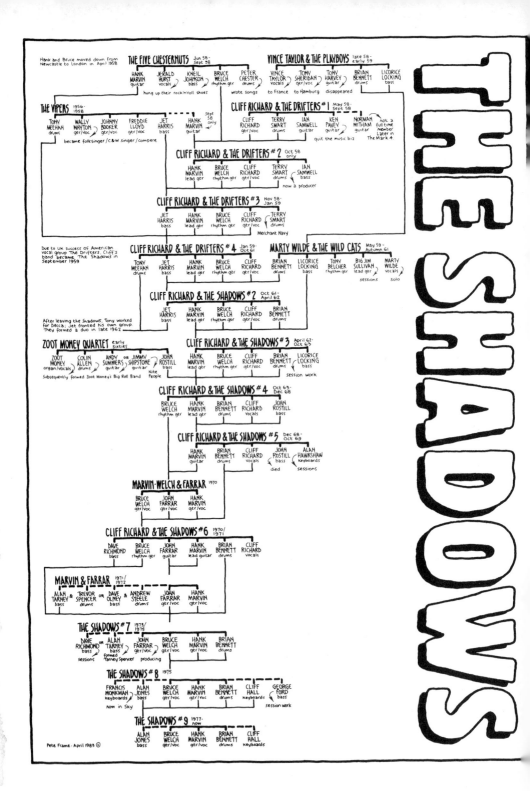

The Shadows Discography

	Cat. No.	Date rel	Date in chart	Highest position	Weeks in Chart
The Drifters					
Feelin' Fine/Don't Be A Fool With Love	DB4263	Jan 59	—	—	—
Jet Black/Driftin'	DB4325	July 59	—	—	—
The Shadows					
Saturday Dance/Lonesome Fella	DB4387	Dec 59	—	—	—
Apache/Quartermaster's Stores	DB4484	July 60	July 60	1	21
Man of Mystery/The Stranger	DB4530	Nov 60	Nov 60	5	15
FBI/Midnight	DB4580	Feb 61	Feb 61	6	19
The Frightened City/Back Home	DB4637	April 61	May 61	3	20
Kon-Tiki/36-24-36	DB4698	Sept 61	Sept 61	1	12
The Savage/Peace Pipe	DB4726	Nov 61	Nov 61	10	8
Wonderful Land/Stars Fell on Stockton	DB4790	Feb 62	March 62	1	19
Guitar Tango/What a Lovely Tune	DB4870	July 62	Aug 62	4	15
Dance On/All Day	DB4948	Dec 62	Dec 62	1	15
Foot Tapper/The Breeze and I	DB4984	March 63	March 63	1	16
Atlantis/I Want You To Want Me	DB7047	May 63	June 63	2	17
Shindig/It's Been a Blue Day	DB7106	Sept 63	Sept 63	6	12
Geronimo/Shazam	DB7163	Nov 63	Dec 63	11	12
Theme For Young Lovers/This Hammer	DB7231	Feb 64	March 64	12	10
The Rise and Fall of Flingle Bunt/It's a Man's World	DB7261	May 64	May 64	5	14
Rhythm and Greens/The Miracle	DB7342	Aug 64	Sept 64	22	7
Genie with the Light Brown Lamp/Little Princess	DB7416	Nov 64	Dec 64	17	10
Mary-Anne/Chu-Chi	DB7476	Feb 65	Feb 65	17	10
Stingray/Alice in Sunderland	DB7588	May 65	June 65	19	7
Don't Make My Baby Blue/Grandfather's Clock	DB7650	July 65	Aug 65	10	10
Warlord/I Wish I Could Shimmy Like My Sister Arthur	DB7769	Nov 65	Nov 65	18	9
I Met a Girl/Late Night Set	DB7853	March 66	March 66	22	5
A Place in the Sun/Will You Be There	DB7952	July 66	July 66	24	6
The Dreams I Dream/Scotch on the Socks	DB8034	Nov 66	Nov 66	42	6
Maroc 7/Bombay Duck	DB8170	April 67	April 67	24	8
Tomorrow's Cancelled/Somewhere	DB8264	Sept 67	—	—	—
Dear Old Mrs Bell/Trying to Forget the One You Love	DB8372	March 68	—	—	—
Slaughter on Tenth Avenue/Midnight Cowboy	DB8628	Oct 69	—	—	—
Turn Around and Touch Me/Jungle Jam	EMI2081	Nov 73	—	—	—

Let Me Be the One/Stand Up Like a Man	EMI2269	Mar 75	Mar 75	12	9
Apache/Wonderful Land/ FBI re-release	DB8958	75	—	—	—
Run Billy Run/Honourable Puff Puff	EMI2310	June 75	—	—	—
It'll Be Me, Babe/Like Strangers	EMI2461	June 76	—	—	—
Apache/Wonderful Land/ FBI re-release	EMI2573	77	—	—	—
Another Night/Cricket Bat Boogie	EMI2660	July 77	—	—	—
Love de Luxe/Sweet Saturday Night	EMI2838	Aug 78	—	—	—
Don't Cry for Me, Argentina/ Montezuma's Revenge	EMI2890	Nov 78	Dec 78	5	14
Theme from The Deer Hunter/Bermuda Triangle	EMI2939	April 79	April 79	9	14
Rodrigo's Guitar Concerto/ Song for Duke	EMI5004	Oct 79	—	—	—
Riders in the Sky/Rusk	EMI5027	Jan 80	Jan 80	12	12
Heart of Glass/Return to the Alamo	EMI5083	July 80	—	—	—
Equinoxe (Part V)/Fender Bender	POSP 1048	Aug 80	Aug 80	50	3
Mozart Forty/Midnight Creepin'	POSP 187	Oct 80	—	—	—
The Third Man (The Harry Lime Theme)/The Fourth Man	POSP 255	April 81	April 81	44	4
Telstar/Summer Love '59	POSP 316	Sept 81	—	—	—
Medley: Imagine/Woman/ Hats Off to Wally	POSP 376	Nov 81	—	—	—
Theme from Missing/The Shady Lady	POSP 485	July 82	—	—	—

ALBUMS AND CATALOGUE NUMBER

The Shadows   SCX 3414
Out of the Shadows   SCX 3449
Dance with the Shadows   SCX 3511
Sound of the Shadows   SCX 3554
Shadows Greatest Hits   SCX 1522
Shadow Music   SCX 6041
More Hits — The Shadows   SCX 3578
Jigsaw   SCX 6148
From Hank, Bruce, Brian and John   SCX 6199
Established 1958 (with Cliff)   SCX 6282
Hank Marvin (solo LP)   SCX 6352
Shades of Rock   SCX 6420
Marvin Welch and Farrar   SRZA 8502
Second Opinion (Marvin Welch and Farrar)   SRZA 8504
Marvin and Farrar   EMA 755
Rockin' with Curly Leads   EMA 762
Specs Appeal   EMA 3066
Live at the Paris Olympia   EMC 3095
Twenty Golden Greats   EMTV 3
Rarities   NUT 2
Tasty   EMC 3195

Thank You Very Much (4 tracks by the Shads, the rest by Cliff)   EMTV 15
String of Hits   EMC 3310
Another String of Hot Hits   EMC 3339
Hank Marvin Guitar Syndicate (solo LP)   EMC 3215
Change of Address   2442179
Hits Right Up Your Street   POLD 5046
Hank Marvin Word and Music (solo LP)   POLD 5054
The Shadows Live at Abbey Road/Life in the Jungle (double package LP)   SHADS 1
Hank Marvin All Alone with Friends (solo LP)   POLD 5104

COMPILATION LPs:

The Shadows: Walkin'   MFP 1388
The Shadows: Somethin' Else   SRS 5012
The Shadows: Mustang   MFP 5266
The Shadows at the Movies   MFP 50347
Rock on with the Shadows   MFP 50468
The Shadows Live (double LP)   MFP 1018
The Shadows Collection (6 LP boxed set)   World Record Club